The Red Scare in the
Midwest, 1945-1955
A State and Local Study

Studies in
American History and Culture, No. 36

Robert Berkhofer, Series Editor

Director of American Culture Programs
and Richard Hudson Research Professor of History
The University of Michigan

Other Titles in This Series

The Red Scare in the Midwest, 1945-1955
A State and Local Study

by
James Truett Selcraig

UMI RESEARCH PRESS
Ann Arbor, Michigan

Copyright © 1982
James Truett Selcraig
All rights reserved

Produced and distributed by
UMI Research Press
an imprint of
University Microfilms International
Ann Arbor, Michigan 48106

Library of Congress Cataloging in Publication Data

Selcraig, James Truett.
  The red scare in the Midwest, 1945-1955.

  (Studies in American history and culture ; no. 36)
  Revision of thesis (Ph.D.)—University of Illinois at
Urbana-Champaign, 1981.
  Bibliography: p.
  Includes index.
  1. Anti-communist movements—Middle West—History—
20th century. 2. Middle West—Politics and government.
I. Title. II. Series.

F354.S44 1982   977'.033   82-17545
ISBN 0-8357-1380-6   AACR2

Contents

Definitions and Abbreviations

This area of study demands continual definitions. I have used "leftist" to designate Communists and their supporters or sympathizers. I have not always made a significant effort to determine if a sympathizer was actually a Communist party member since in many cases the difference was immaterial in the case's development. A "liberal" will be an anti-Communist reformer. "Loyalty oaths" refer to non-Communist or nonsubversive oaths rather than to positive oaths of allegiance. The following abbreviations of organizations have been frequently used.

AAUP—American Association of University Professors
ACLU—American Civil Liberties Union
AFL—American Federation of Labor
CIO—Congress of Industrial Organizations
CP—Communist Party, U.S.A.
FBI—Federal Bureau of Investigation
HUAC—actually, House of Representatives, Committee on Un-American Activities
NAACP—National Association for the Advancement of Colored People
SISS—actually, Senate, Committee on the Judiciary, Subcommittee to Investigate the Administration of the Internal Security Act

Acknowledgments

My research was helped immeasurably by the Interlibrary Loan Department of the Library at the University of Illinois. Archivists at the University of Illinois, Wayne State University, and Olivet College were particularly friendly and cooperative.

At Baylor University, I had the good fortune to be taught by several outstanding history professors: Robert Reid, James Vardaman, Stanley Campbell, and Wallace Daniel. At the University of Illinois, I would like to thank Dr. Thomas Krueger, my advisor, and Dr. Joseph Love for their help prior to and during the researching of this study. Linda Duchamp and Les Foltos, two graduate students, gave me their friendship and critical encouragement.

Finally, I am grateful to my parents, Rev. and Mrs. J. F. Selcraig, for sparking and encouraging my interest in history.

Introduction

The year 1945 marked the end of World War II. V-E and V-J days were moments of happiness, relief, and fulfillment. Americans had no doubts about the just nature of their cause or about their continued glory. The postwar decade, in contrast, was a time filled with international and domestic tensions. Historians looking back at these events must struggle against seeing the Cold War or the Second Red Scare as inevitable. They were not.

The Cold War does not have an exact starting date. Even when the U.S. and the Soviet Union were allies, suspicion and secrecy existed. When the war ended, the victors tried to settle the fate of central Europe. Out of their different visions came international tensions: the Greek Civil War, the Truman Doctrine, the Berlin airlift, the Czech coup, among others. At the same time, the Communist forces in China were rallying against Chiang Kai-shek, who although corrupt and inept was pictured by the American press as honest and democratic. Mao's victory in the fall of 1949 seemed to confirm the global nature of the conflict between communism and democracy, between totalitarianism and freedom, between evil and good. The Korean War finalized the dichotomy, and changed the Cold War into a hot one.

If Americans conceived of the Cold War as global, then the Communists in the U.S. were just as suspect as Soviet soldiers. The Second Red Scare was certainly fueled by the Cold War, but it was not caused by these international tensions in any direct way. The Scare does not have an exact starting date either. Indeed, it has precedents in the 1930s and before.

Conservatives had long seen American Communists as a disciplined group controlled by the Soviet Union and dedicated to the violent overthrow of the government. The right-wing viewed leftists and liberals as overt Communist sympathizers, dupes, or weak conformists who could not defeat the totalitarian danger. These attitudes intensified after Franklin D. Roosevelt launched the New Deal, a program viewed as the beginnings of a social and political revolution.

Although these conservatives were unable to defeat FDR, they succeeded in raising the loyalty issue in the late 1930s. In 1938, the crusaders established a House committee to investigate un-American activities. In 1939, the Hatch Act prohibited Communists as governmental employees. In 1940, the Smith Act banned the advocacy of violent antigovernmental action. Similar actions occurred on the state level. California created its own investigative committee; Wisconsin banned the Communist party from the ballot; and New York established a legislative investigative commission.[1]

The Second World War interrupted these domestic concerns; it did not end them. The Communist Party, U.S.A., changed its tune, disbanding the party and supporting the patriotic drive. American wartime unity reigned so supreme that even the general view of the Soviet Union began to change toward a more positive image. If conservatives were reluctant to criticize the war effort and the alliance, they did not hold back their fire from their domestic enemies. Some ex-Communists continued their critical commentary on their formerly held dogma and its supporters. The American Legion supported proposals to outlaw the CP, and the Catholic Church remained critical of the atheistic nature of communism. Republicans attacked particular incidents, such as Roosevelt's pardon of Earl Browder, and generally charged that Communists had infiltrated the government and the Democratic party. The *Chicago Tribune*, the voice of Midwestern conservatism, asserted in 1944 that the New Dealers were "supporting the Communists and building them up for the day when they plan to bring the Red terror sweeping down upon America."[2] These conservative forces did not mold public opinion during the war, but there can be no doubt about the constancy of the anti-Communist movement.

In the postwar decade, these forces united to form the Second Red Scare. Conservatives formalized the House Un-American Activities Committee. Its investigation of Communists in Hollywood and elsewhere forced suspects to either name individuals as Communists or to take the Fifth Amendment in order to protect themselves. Those who had been named and those who did not talk were blacklisted. HUAC also heard Whitaker Chambers accuse Alger Hiss of being a Communist, a charge which because of Hiss' association with the New Deal seemed to indict that liberal program. The Justice Department successfully prosecuted Hiss for perjury, several Communist leaders for violating the Smith Act, and the Rosenbergs for treason. President Truman inaugurated a loyalty check of governmental employees, and the attorney general issued a list of subversive organizations. Congress passed the Internal Security Act over Truman's veto, and later enacted the Communist Control Act. Between 1950 and 1954, the Scare came to be symbolized by Senator Joseph McCarthy. His accusations, threats, and blustering were directed against anyone who opposed him.[3] These dry facts may not give the flavor of the times: the recklessness of the accusers, the tragedy of the accused, the principled opposition of a few, the compromises and silences of those caught in the middle.

Fig. 1.   Cartoon from the *Chicago Tribune*, March 28, 1948.
          ©1982 *Chicago Tribune*. Used with permission.

Fig. 2. Cartoon from the *Chicago Tribune*, September 14, 1952.
©1982 *Chicago Tribune*. Used with permission.

Yet this short summary of events on the national level must suffice as background in this work. Rather than examining these well-known events again, this is an analysis of the Scare on the state and local levels. It picks five Midwestern states—Wisconsin, Illinois, Indiana, Ohio, and Michigan. The current historical literature has a serious problem in the lack of state and local studies. In the early 1950s, a few states were examined, but these studies provided neither an analysis of the entire era nor an interpretative structure.[4] Recently, a few dissertations on individual cities and states have been completed, but these differ in approach to such a degree that they cannot be easily compared.[5] This study of the Midwest uses the broad approach in order to examine and compare the Scare in different locales.

Despite the lack of much historical analysis on the state and local level, two historians have boldly theorized on the relationship of the national level to the state and local level. In separate studies, Robert Griffith and Robert Goldstein have asserted that the activities of the federal government formed the Red Scare at the state and local level. According to Griffith,

> the rise of anti-Communism as an issue in national politics was accompanied by the growth of a derivative anti-Communist politics at the state and local level. . . . State legislatures responded almost slavishly to the force of federal law and precedent and to the anxieties aroused by national leaders . . . The politics of anti-Communism originated at the national level and then spread to the states.[6]

Goldstein asserts just as forcefully that "the federal government set a pattern, and the states and localities followed."[7] Along the same line but without addressing this specific question, Athan Theoharis has argued that President Truman legitimized the Scare.[8] The Griffith-Goldstein theory does not stress the influence of general national developments, such as the Cold War and long-standing antiradicalism. Their narrower theory suggests a simple, monocausal relationship with governmental leaders and federal antisubversive activities being totally determinative in forming the Scare. This study of the Midwest challenges the Griffith-Goldstein theory. The Red Scare was not caused so simply, but by a series of developments, both intensifying and calming, occurring at the federal, state, and local levels.

Basically, the Scare was formed by the conservative movement, which in turn drew strength from the rise of the loyalty issue. Although this movement lacked a unified organization and a single leader, it had a common persuasion.[9] Conservatives viewed internal communism as broad and dangerous, and they willingly exploited the loyalty issue to attain political power. McCarthyism, which formed one segment of this movement, has been accurately interpreted as a partisan vehicle used by Republicans in their drive for power.[10] This movement should be distinguished from right-wing "hate" groups with their open racism and anti-Semitism, but it nevertheless exaggerated the Communist threat, often used apocalyptic rhetoric, and occasionally saw vast conspiracies.

Reacting to this crusade was the liberal movement. It had never supported Communist positions, but it became more openly anti-Communist during this period.[11] It purified liberal organizations, and often endorsed legislative restrictions aimed at communists. Yet it never fully accepted the conservative crusade. Liberals differentiated between leftists and Communists, and were less inclined to inflict "extreme and gratuitous humiliations"[12] on radicals.

These two movements occurred within the traditional boundaries of American politics, and they occurred on all governmental levels. Their interaction was complex, not simple; it was fluid, not uni-directional. This interaction is the key to the Scare.

The Red Scare's existence on national, state, and local levels leads to an examination of its pervasiveness. Although the Scare occurred in every area of the country and in every type of organization, incidents nevertheless tended to occur where the target was most visible. Thus more controversies occurred in urban areas, particularly in the North, East, and West Coast, where the Communists had their greatest strength. In other areas, incidents arose but were relatively brief and sporadic.

The pervasiveness issue must also examine the effect of the incidents, or the degree of repression. Repression cannot be quantified, and as UN Ambassador Jeanne Kirkpatrick has learned, any attempt to distinguish between repressive forms and activities can be explosive. Yet definitions and interpretations are the historian's task. Thus, repression shall be defined as the restriction of nonviolent political expression. This study of the Midwest points out that incidents varied in duration and effect. "Nuisance incidents" affected individuals, but they were rarely effective in imposing restrictions or in energizing the community. "Significant controversies," on the other hand, involved many people—symbolically often the community, state, or nation—and had overt results.[13] Many Red Scare incidents occurred on the state and local levels, but beneath this similarity, variation marked the specific pattern: the timing, the degree of consensus, and the effect. Red Scare incidents did not develop uniformly in every city and state. The Scare's pervasiveness and repression were limited by the character of the two movements. They had disputes over what constituted proper loyalty actions; they lacked a formal organizational structure; and they operated within traditional channels which means the amorphous, nonideological character of American political parties. As a result, although the Scare characterized the postwar decade, it had a diffused rather than uniform effect.

This study, which basically is concerned with institutional responses to the Red Scare, is divided into three sections: state politics, the local level, and universities. Each section examines the interaction of national and local factors, the issue of pervasiveness, and the degree of repression. The response of these various institutions reveals both similarities and differences. The first section (Chaps. 1 and 2) on state politics finds a common thread of anti-Communist legislative proposals but also some variation in when, how, and what types of laws were enacted and enforced. For example, the conservative movement in Michigan achieved more legislative successes than in Illinois. The second section (Chaps. 3, 4, and 5) on the local level examines city elections and government, schools and libraries, and voluntary organizations. Again, local factors caused similar controversies to develop in different ways so that, for example, the loyalty issue was used successfully in a mayoral campaign in Detroit but not in Cincinnati. The final section (Chaps. 6 and 7) on universities considers both students and faculty members. Universities, having both some degree of automony and dependence on outside influences, are valuable institutions to study. In controversies concerning leftist students and professors, colleges occasionally used different procedures and arrived at different results. Not every "unfriendly" professor was fired, and most leftist students remained on campus. The differences between these incidents can be overemphasized of course, and this work does not dispute the general understanding of the Scare as it operated in the nation's capital. Yet, the state and local levels reveal complexity: the basic issue of loyalty versus nonconformity arising in different forms and often developing in different ways.

This study does not try to examine the state and local level throughout the country, but focuses on the Midwest. Observers have often noted that the area is distinguished by its "averageness, its typicalness."[14] Scholars have also agreed that this area can be considered a distinct unit.[15] In the postwar decade, the Midwest was the home not only of Senator McCarthy but also his supporters. In one list, these five states accounted for six of the eighteen McCarthyite senators and nine of the nineteen representatives.[16] Yet the Midwest also had a growing liberal voice, characterized by Adlai Stevenson and Walter Reuther.

By not focusing on just one city or state, this work will be comparative. It is an analysis of incidents rather than a unified narrative of one organization, one event, or one person. Indeed, the three sections can be read as separate case studies. The details of the many controversies, each with their own cast of characters, do present an obstacle to readers, but I hope that they will appreciate the comparative approach. Other scholars should adopt this method. We need to examine more fully the relationship between the federal, state, and local levels. We need to compare the First Red Scare and the Second. We need to move away from Truman and McCarthy.

Like all studies, this one has its limits. It does not pretend to be a complete history of the Midwest during this period. It does not even include all Red Scare incidents. Since it is a state and local study, it omits purely federal antisubversive efforts, such as the loyalty program and the Smith Act prosecutions.[17] Perhaps the work is limited most by the lack of conservative-oriented scholarship on the Red Scare.[18] The current literature is dominated by liberal and radical historians, who have articulated their respective theses well. This study follows neither position exactly, but borrows from both. Perhaps its greatest difference, however, lies not in analysis but in tone. In describing the Scare, I have not used a moral tone. Some people will not like this, but I prefer a more distant stance.

1

State Politics: Michigan and Wisconsin

The Second Red Scare in the Midwest should be viewed in relation to the political shock given by the Depression and the Roosevelt revolution. The New Deal might not have created a new order, but it directly threatened the old order—or so they believed. Before 1930, the Midwest was a bastion of Republicanism and business boosterism. Then the flood. In Michigan, the Democrats in 1924 had no representatives in the state legislature; in 1932, they had a majority. Conservatives, stunned by this development, were further outraged by the emergence of the CIO, the enactment of the Wagner Act, and the sit-down strikes. From Detroit and Flint to Gary and Milwaukee, the Midwest was ablaze with activism, occasionally with radical overtones.

The counterattack was not long in coming, and was more successful on the state and local level than on the national level. Conservatives could not defeat FDR, but they could regain control of state politics. The pattern of the Illinois House is typical. In 1932, it had a 80-73 Democratic edge; this went to 84-69 and then 85-66 in the landslide of 1936. Two years later, the Republicans regained their majority position, and they maintained it for the next ten years. The conservatives were further helped by the war, which ended unemployment, strikes, and the reform movement.

Out of this counterattack came the Communist issue. Before 1945, each state in the Midwest had enacted legislation to ensure loyalty and security. Despite this protection, the states again confronted the issue in the postwar decade. In the Second Red Scare, these states show a complex pattern of similarities and differences. If the analysis is limited to the enactment of antisubversive laws, then four of the five states acted uniformly. Yet this conclusion of basic uniformity must be changed after examining other aspects: the degree of opposition, the timing or pattern of the specific incident, and the type of laws passed. Certainly, the legislatures did not react "slavishly to the force of federal law and precedent," as Griffith would have us believe.[1]

The amount of opposition in the five states varied significantly, and constitutes the best measure of the states' responses to the Scare.[2] Michigan exhibited the greatest approval for the loyalty crusade, with Indiana, Ohio, and Illinois in the middle, and Wisconsin showing the greatest opposition. The Michigan governors and legislature endorsed antisubversive proposals with overwhelming support. Indiana gave similar support to two measures, but defeated other proposals, such as the creation of an un-American activities committee. Ohio had a relatively effective opposition in the early years of the postwar decade, but it lost much of its strength by 1951. Illinois featured a strong opposition of a partisan nature, especially after 1949. These critics defeated some proposals, amended others, and sustained two vetoes. Wisconsin showed the greatest resistance to the loyalty crusade by refusing to enact any loyalty legislation in these years. The strength of the opposition is perhaps best shown by listing the bills that either met defeat or were successfully vetoed:

Michigan	none that were not subsequently passed
Indiana	legislative investigative commission
Ohio	loyalty oath for public employees
Illinois	registration, outlawing CP, special assistant attorney general
Wisconsin	outlawing subversion, legislative commission, loyalty oath, barring Communists and users of the Fifth Amendment as public employees, registration

The states also exhibited different patterns in the timing and type of laws that they passed (see table 1). Illinois and Michigan approved their first laws in 1947, while Ohio waited until 1949 and Indiana until 1951. Michigan enacted the only registration law; Indiana required the only loyalty oath for lobbyists; and Ohio established the only special assistant attorney general. Even when the states passed a similar proposal, such as an investigative commission, they did it at different times, and, more importantly, the commissions operated in different ways.

This stress on differences should not be overemphasized, however. Obviously none of these events occurred in a vacuum. The Red Scare can be considered as a unified whole because of its relationship to the Cold War and because of the conservative movement, which existed on all governmental levels. The midwestern state legislatures did not act solely because of local factors. Rather, the pattern of the Scare at the state level resulted from a combination of federal influences and local factors. This chapter will examine the two states which show the greatest and least reflection of national patterns, Michigan and Wisconsin, respectively. The next chapter will analyze the other three states which fall between the extremes.

Table 1

Loyalty and Security Laws, 1947-1955

	U.S.	Michigan	Indiana	Ohio	Illinois	Wisconsin
1947	HUAC (legislative committee)	-legislative committee -registration of foreign agents			-legislative committee -denied use of unversity to subversives	
1949	HUAC registration*	-red squad in state police* -outlaw subversion*		-loyalty oath for unemployment compensation recipients	-temporary legislative committee	
1951	HUAC	-outlaw wills to subversives -registration** -bar subversives from ballot and public employment** -require testimony from public employees*	-outlaw CP subversion -bar subversives from public employment	-legislative committee		
1953	HUAC outlaw CP#			-legislative committee -bar CPs from public employment -require testimony from public employees -outlaw subversion -confiscate funds of subversives -special Atty. Gen.		
1955	HUAC		-loyalty oath for lobbyists		-loyalty oath for public employees	

*1950 session; **1952 session; #1954 session.

Michigan

The Red Scare in Michigan followed the national pattern in many respects. Republicans led the loyalty crusade, and they established a legislative investigative comission, enacted new antisubversive laws, and claimed victims through each method. Democrats, under the leadership of G. Mennen Williams, initially tried to limit the Scare, but soon joined the Republican efforts. The outbreak of the Korean War strongly influenced these liberals. The summer of 1950 found no significant opposition; the legislature passed bills by overwhelming margins. The Scare began to decline only when the courts ruled some of the antisubversive laws unconstitutional.

Local factors nevertheless were significant in the Scare's development. In 1947–1949, two attorneys general slowed its growth by refusing to enforce a registration law. The legislature refused to create a permanent HUAC-type committee because of the excesses of a particular state senator. Local factors, on the other hand, could aid the conservative movement. The loyalty crusaders had more opportunities to enact their proposals because the legislature, unique among the midwestern states, held sessions every year. The representatives were meeting in their off-year session when the Korean War broke out and when HUAC visited Detroit.

The Scare did not have an even, steady rise in Michigan. The pattern can be divided into four phases. For a few months in early 1947, the Republican governor and a state senator wildly exploited the issue. Their excessive partisanship, in conjunction with the attorney general's ruling against a registration law, caused a slow decline in the Communist issue during the next three years. This second phase ended in the spring of 1950. In this third phase, the Scare reached its peak. Initially, conservative legislators battled the liberal governor, G. Mennen Williams. The governor dropped his opposition to new loyalty legislation after the outbreak of the Korean War and as the fall elections approached. In other words, a strong bipartisan consensus emerged at this time. The legislature outlawed subversion and the CP; established a "red squad" in the state police; required subversives to register; barred subversive organizations from the ballot; and required public employees to testify before legislative investigating committees. After the summer of 1952, the Communist issue slowly declined but only because the courts began to rule some of these laws unconstitutional.

The first phase of the Red Scare in Michigan featured the activities of two prominent Republicans, Governor Kim Sigler and State Senator Matthew Callahan. Their efforts in early 1947 brought the issue into prominence on the state level. Sigler accused individuals of Communist associations, and Callahan investigated Wayne University. They achieved some successes, but their excesses ultimately caused a backlash.

In January 1947, the Scare erupted over a seemingly minor incident, the activities of the American Youth for Democracy (AYD) on the Michigan State College campus. The AYD, a leftist student group, allowed Communists as members, and had been denied university recognition on that basis. When the banned group distributed leaflets on campus, the college's president ordered an investigation.[3] This action in the state capital's twin city prompted Sigler and Callahan to take action.

Newly inaugurated, Governor Sigler exploited this opportunity to show his leadership. He directed the University of Michigan and Wayne University to examine their campus AYD chapters. A few days later, the governor turned his attention to state employees and ordered the state civil service director to probe their loyalty. Sigler also instructed the attorney general to investigate a union organizer of state employees, Foss Baker of the United Public Workers (UPW-CIO). According to the governor, Baker was a "Communist" who was "spreading his Communist propaganda" among state workers. Baker denied the charges. He accused Sigler of raising the subversive issue only to avoid other issues, such as wage increases and the creation of a Fair Employment Practices Commission. Several UPW locals defended Baker, but others disaffiliated, and the union soon removed Baker from his position. The governor's actions helped to convince many citizens of the immediate danger posed by subversives. One supporter wrote to Sigler that his actions had "put Michigan in the vanguard of investigating subversive activities. . . . [This] will make you a national hero and you might become President of the United States in 1948." Other citizens identified suspected subversives to the governor, and he forwarded these names to the state police.[4]

Buoyed by such support, the governor continued his campaign, and agreed to testify before HUAC. The state police commissioner recommended in a private letter to the governor that he attack Fascists as well as Communists and that he use the term "Red Fascists" to describe Communists. "Intellectuals" would thus be less likely to criticize his upcoming testimony, the commissioner concluded. Sigler however did not heed this advice. The governor testified that the state had 15,000 Communists and thousands of sympathizers. He identified several subversives, including UPW organizer Foss Baker, CIO officials R. J. Thomas and George Addes, and Democratic State Senator Stanley Nowak. Not only were these accusations strained or false, but Sigler's identification of twenty-two Communist fronts also lacked solid evidence. According to Sigler, the Fellowship of Reconciliation (FOR), a pacifist group, was a Communist front because it had scheduled Trotskyites as speakers, and the Civil Rights Federation was suspect because it had been organized by the Socialist Workers party.[5]

Many quickly protested Sigler's testimony, and this marked the decline of his effectiveness. Not only did many of those identified as Communists deny the charges, but liberals such as Walter Reuther condemned the testimony as an attack on labor and liberalism. The Fellowship of Reconciliation even won a retraction from the governor.[6]

While the governor waved his antisubversive flag, State Senator Matthew F. Callahan led the 1947 legislature into the arena. Callahan, a Republican from Detroit, fueled the controversy surrounding the American Youth for Democracy (AYD). Although the national AYD had been accused of being a Communist front organization, the president of Wayne University, David Dodds Henry, denied that the campus AYD chapter was subversive. Outraged, Senator Callahan sponsored a resolution to create a senate commission to investigate subversive activities at Wayne. Callahan promised that the probe would not be "a witch hunt or an investigation with brass band accompaniment." The senate amended the resolution to include an examination of all state universities, and on February 13, 1947, it established the four-man group, popularly known as the Callahan Commission.[7]

The Callahan Commission focused almost entirely on Wayne University, and contrary to the chairman's promise, did create a major confrontation with little proof of the AYD's radical nature. In the commission's hearings, President Henry continued to deny that Communists dominated the AYD chapter, and the Detroit Board of Education, the governing body of the university, supported his position. Senator Callahan believed otherwise. He announced his opposition to the university's appropriation unless it banned the AYD. On April 2, the senate's Republican caucus confirmed Callahan's proposal. This directly challenged the financial security of the university since the Republicans outnumbered the Democrats twenty-eight to four in the senate. A few days later, President Henry received a letter from the Department of Justice, which did not confirm but which noted J. Edgar Hoover's charge that the national AYD was a Communist front. President Henry strongly recommended that the Wayne AYD drop its national affiliation. When the chapter refused, he banned it.[8]

Senator Callahan quickly achieved three more successes.[9] A few days after President Henry's action against the AYD, University of Michigan officials withdrew recognition from its AYD chapter. Second, the senator, who believed that more antisubversive work needed to be done, proposed an extension of the investigative commission. The senate quickly approved the measure, officially naming the group as the Committee on Un-American Activities. Callahan's third success proved more controversial. His proposed bill required any person or organization affiliated with a "foreign agency" to register with the attorney general. Although the senator aimed the bill at the CP, opposition arose from the Michigan Council of Churches, American Jewish Council, Association of Catholic Trade Unions, CIO, National Lawyers Guild, and the CP. They argued that the vague definition of "foreign agency" could apply to the Boy Scouts, Catholic Church, or Red Cross. Moreover, the attorney general under this bill could abuse the investigative powers and harass critics of state government. The registration proposal, commonly known as the Callahan bill, received support from veterans groups and a few individual labor leaders hostile to the CP. The critics succeeded in deleting specific references to labor unions, but the senate passed the bill 27-4 and the house approved it 70-3. The small opposition tended to be liberal Democrats.[10]

After this legislative victory, the Scare did not continue to rise, but entered into a new declining phase which lasted until the spring of 1950. Just as Governor Sigler had burst so brightly onto the scene only to fade quickly after his rash testimony before HUAC, so Senator Callahan's glories began to dissipate. The Callahan Act soon ran into legal difficulties. According to Attorney General Eugene F. Black, he could not enforce the law because the legislature had not appropriated any funds for his office to determine if an organization constituted a "foreign agency." Even if funds had been made available, he would not enforce it because it interfered with the prerogative of the federal government in foreign policy and affairs. In other words, the attorney general declared the law unconstitutional. Despite this ruling, opponents of the law organized a petition drive to repeal the law by placing it on the ballot as a referendum.[11]

In the 1948 legislature, conservatives tried to resurrect the antisubversive movement, but their efforts proved unsuccessful. Attorney General Black and State Police Commissioner Donald S. Leonard drafted a bill to repeal the registration law and to create a "red squad" in the state police. The house deleted the repeal of the Callahan Act, hoping to avoid a direct insult to the senator, and passed the bill with only one dissenting vote. In the senate, the chairman of the Judiciary Committee did not believe that a new law was necessary to establish a "red squad." He correctly pointed out that the state police already had the power to investigate criminal activities and subversion. His opposition stymied the proposal and, as a result, the 1948 legislature enacted no new loyalty legislation.[12]

The Callahan Act thus remained on the books, but also remained controversial and unenforced. Liberal and leftist critics succeeded in having a referendum on the law in November 1948. They gathered significant support, but lost: 890,435 to sustain; 585,469 to repeal. A few months later, the law faltered again when the new attorney general, Stephen J. Roth, refused to enforce it because of its unconstitutional provisions. When the 1949 house directed him to test the law in court, Roth declined. He could not initiate any prosecution without evidence of an organization's relationship to a foreign agency, and he could not discover such evidence without funds. The law was never tested in court and never enforced.[13]

At this time, the legislature also seemed reluctant to push the antisubversive crusade into the field of education. During the 1948 session, a Republican representative proposed an amendment to the school appropriation bill requiring a loyalty oath from all teachers. The house immediately passed it on a voice vote, but the measure bogged down in the senate. Critics pointed out that the special session could only consider topics approved by the governor. Since the loyalty issue had not been included in his message, it could not be examined. The senate defeated the amendment.[14]

The last public appearance of the Callahan Commission also met with little approval. The commission, which generally had been inactive since the AYD controversies in early 1947, questioned a Michigan State College student, James Zarichny, in the spring of 1948. When Zarichny invoked the Fifth Amendment about his alleged Communist affiliation, the commission cited him for contempt. The senate reluctantly convicted him after much debate, but gave him a suspended sentence so that the student served no time in confinement. The commission's reputation was not enhanced by its harassment of Zarichny, a rather insignificant figure. Its final report, consisting merely of a brief summary of Communist activity in the state and nation, contained no revelations or proposals for additional legislation. The legislature did not reestablish the commission in any subsequent session.[15]

The slow decline of the Communist issue continued in the 1949 legislative session. The only loyalty measure, which proposed barring "past or present" Communists as teachers, died in committee.[16] The controversy over the Callahan Act and the inactivity of the Callahan Commission made the legislators hesitant to enact further legislation. The surprising 1948 gubernatorial victory of liberal Democrat G. Mennen Williams over Kim Sigler also temporarily took the wind out of the Republicans' sails. In other words, the slow decline of the Scare was caused primarily by local factors.

This temporary decline ended in the summer of 1950. Governor G. Mennen Williams had already tried to block Detroit from instituting a local loyalty measure in 1949, and he now tried to stop the conservative state legislators. The partisan struggle ended when the Korean War began in July 1950. The Michigan legislature soon had an overwhelming bipartisan coalition favoring antisubversive restrictions. This third phase marked the peak of the Scare, and lasted for two years.

In the spring of 1950, Governor Williams initially did not plan to open the special legislative session to antisubversive bills. This changed due to a local conference sponsored by the state American Legion. Meeting in the state capital on April 15 and 16, the Wolverine All-American Conference heard conservative anti-Communists, such as Benjamin Gitlow, J. B. Matthews, and Paul Broyles, warn of the imminent danger of the Communists and their allies in the country. The conference recommended that the state legislature outlaw the CP. Four days later, Governor Williams declared that the CP constituted "a fifth column of anti-democratic forces."

Warning against acting rashly, he noted that attempts to restrict Communist activities might not work. If the party was banned, it could change its name. If restrictions were placed on minority parties, this would hurt some legitimate groups. If laws restricted Communist beliefs, the result would be a "thought police." The solution, according to the governor, would be the creation of a "blue-ribbon panel" of legal experts to study existing statutes and to propose new, workable restrictions. The Republican-dominated senate, sensing an election-year issue, rejected Williams' recommendation for funding the panel. Instead, it created its own Senate Loyalty Commission (SLC) to probe disloyalty among state employees. The SLC's chairman, Colin L. Smith (R, Big Rapids), had been a member of the Callahan Commission of 1947–1948, and a similar performance seemed to be in the offing.[17]

The governor and the Republican legislators continued their bickering. The SLC under Senator Smith heard various witnesses favor the creation of a permanent loyalty board for state employees. None of these witnesses could identify any specific suspects, but a civil service official suspected several state workers because they still belonged to the United Public Workers (UPW). Not only had Governor Sigler attacked the union three years earlier for being Communist-dominated, but the CIO had recently expelled it for similar reasons. According to Senator Smith, such leftists might not be CP members, but they certainly held Communist beliefs. "They walk like a duck and quack like a duck," Smith concluded. The outbreak of the Korean War intensified Smith's concern. He recommended the creation of a subversive investigative unit in the state police, which could use informants and undercover work to ferret out the disloyal. "There will probably be some long-haired lawyers who will want to question the constitutionality of such a law, but . . . the present situation [in Korea and in the U.S.] is so serious that I believe that the American people are willing to stretch a point." Senator Smith urged the governor to allow the legislature to consider antisubversive proposals. "The question has moved from one of loyalty to that of security," the Senator concluded.[18]

The Korean War also influenced Governor Williams. On July 29, 1950, he agreed to allow the legislature to consider loyalty and security bills. Yet he continued his harsh criticism of Senator Smith's proposal for a "red squad" in the state police. Smith's bill lacked any definition of subversion, depended on spies and informants, and gave too much power to the state police commissioner. The governor asserted that such an investigative squad would be a "secret police system . . . and a 'gestapo.'" The state police should get increased funds to establish a "Security Squad," Williams recommended, but this unit would be limited to investigating sabotage and other overt acts. To counteract Smith's "hurried" effort, Williams established his "blue-ribbon" panel of legal experts on a volunteer basis.[19]

The SLC and Senator Smith, outraged by the governor's criticisms, naturally counterattacked.

We are at war . . . We must defeat the Communists . . . [and] the Communist fronts in ι United States . . . Unless we get hard—unless we quit playing pat-a-cake with the Communists within this Nation and State, America will fall to the menace . . . What's wrong with us?

Answering the last question, the SLC asserted that "Communists use the so-called liberals in their enterprise." While the Korean War raged and Congress considered the Internal Security Act, the legislature reconvened in mid-August. Senator Smith quickly submitted a constitutional amendment outlawing subversion. Only the CP and the Civil Rights Congress opposed the measure, although the governor urged delay until the legislators received the report of the "blue-ribbon" panel. Both chambers ignored the suggestion, and quickly passed the bill on the same day: 27-0 in the senate and 73-4 in the house. An overwhelming bipartisan coalition had emerged.[20]

After a short recess, the legislature quickly passed three more loyalty bills with almost no debate. By now the governor and the legislators were on the same team. The first measure was based on the recommendation of the "blue-ribbon" panel. It outlawed "subversive activities leading to the over-throw of the government." Both houses passed the bill unanimously. The second loyalty proposal amended the criminal syndicalism law to include acts of violence committed in support of "industrial or political reform." Prolabor representatives attempted to delete the reference to industrial reform activities, but they failed 42-27. Only one nay was heard in the house on the final vote, and none was heard in the senate. The final loyalty bill, based on Senator Smith's proposal, formally established an investigative unit, a "red squad," in the state police. In support of the bill, the state police commissioner argued for the necessity of secret files and undercover agents. "It is the duty of all Americans to report persons and conditions they think are dangerous to the American way of life. We have to fight fire with fire." A few critics, echoing the governor's earlier objections, warned that the bill gave too much power to the state police commissioner. The senate neverthe-less passed it without opposition, and the house approved it 56-9. Governor Williams signed all three bills.[21]

The reintensification of the Red Scare in the summer of 1950—the disappearance of any strong opposition—had several causes. The Republi-can conservatives thought that the job had not been finished in 1947. They also wanted a campaign issue in order to recapture the governor's chair. The Korean War increased fears of Communist activities dramatically. The governor's actions were also crucial. He could have refused to open up the loyalty issue, but he tried to contain the Scare by establishing a "blue-ribbon" panel. This only gave the conservatives the opening that they desired. The upcoming primary and general elections influenced his, as well as other moderate legislators', decision to prove vocally their Americanism. In other words, the reintensification occurred through an interaction of national and local factors.

The fall campaign of 1950, occurring in the weeks immediately after the legislature's adjournment, featured the Communist issue in three different ways. First, the constitutional amendment outlawing subversion had to be ratified by the voters. Opposition came from the ACLU, Detroit Bar Association, National Lawyers Guild, Americans for Democratic Action, Detroit Citizens League, and prominent citizens, such as the dean of the University of Michigan Law School. They argued that the amendment was unnecessary and potentially abusive. In this time of anxiety, their criticisms attracted significant support, but the antisubversive measure passed 628,936 to 403,255 votes.[22]

In the fall campaign, the loyalty issue also entered the Democratic primary in the Sixteenth Congressional District. The incumbent had died, and several contenders, including Stanley Nowak, had a chance to win. Some of the candidates—and Governor Williams—accused Nowak of Communist-front activities and party disloyalty. Nowak had long been an ardent leftist, and with a Progressive party endorsement, had challenged the Democratic congressman in 1948. The governor urged Nowak's defeat, and the voters agreed.[23]

Finally, the gubernatorial campaign featured the Communist issue. Williams' support of the antisubversive legislation and his attack on Nowak did not give him any immunity. His criticism of Senator Smith and his liberalism on other issues still made him suspect to conservatives. Some conservative Democrats claimed that the party had been taken over by the ADA and CIO, who they viewed as "subversive left-wing elements." The press and the Republicans picked up these charges. According to the *Detroit Free Press*, the governor received support from "the coral pink and the ruby red." The *Detroit Times* doubted the ADA's "loyalty to American principles," and urged its readers to "vote against socialism." The Republican nominee for governor, Harry F. Kelly, vowed to end "the socialistic tendencies of the ADA who have taken over the Democratic party by communistic methods." Williams denied that any of his programs were socialistic, but the insinuations continued. The election was extremely close, and after a recount, Williams squeaked out a victory.[24]

Two months later, the 1951 session of the legislature convened with strong GOP majorities, who were determined to continue the antisubversive effort begun the summer before. Both houses passed three bills without a negative vote. The first, an enabling act to the constitutional amendment outlawing subversion, set penalties for its violation. Another measure required school boards to publish an approved list of textbooks. The final measure that passed unanimously seemed to run counter to the principles of private property. It ruled invalid any will or codicil which made a bequest to any subversive person or organization. With only minor dissent, the legislature also passed a positive loyalty oath for public employees. More controversial was a two-fold proposal to require the registration of Communist members and organizations and to ban subversive organizations from the ballot. The measure was guided through the House by its sponsor, Representative Kenneth O. Trucks. The Senate Judiciary Committee remembered the controversy over the 1947 Callahan Act which required registration and killed the proposal.[25]

In the 1952 legislature, Representative Trucks introduced his bill again, this time with more success. In addition to the registration requirement and the ballot ban, it now made sabotage a felony, barred Communists from public employment, and declared that a public employee's use of the Fifth Amendment before a legislative committee would be considered "prima facie evidence" on the truth of the charges. The house passed the Trucks Act unanimously. The only debate concerned whether to include the death penalty as punishment for sabotage. The provision was deleted in favor of a maximum fine of $10,000 and/or imprisonment for ten years. While the senate was considering the measure, HUAC came to Detroit for several days of hearings. A few FBI undercover agents described leftist and Communist activity in the state, and gave the names of many radicals. Several witnesses, interrogated by the committee, invoked the Fifth Amendment concerning such activities. The press reported the hearings in a sensational manner; several "unfriendly" witnesses were physically attacked. This local event significantly intensified the restrictive political climate. Charles Potter, a congressman from the state and a HUAC member, proclaimed his support for state legislation like the Trucks Act, and Governor Williams praised the exposure of Communists. The state police commissioner urged that the CP be outlawed, although he admitted his inability to prove that any Communist presently sought the violent overthrow of the government. Shortly thereafter, the senate passed the Trucks Act unanimously. It defeated an amendment that would have required members of the Black Legion and the Ku Klux Klan to register as well. Governor Williams, asserting that Communists posed "a clear and present danger" to the society, signed the bill.[26]

In contrast to the executive branch's refusal to enforce the 1947 Callahan Act, administrative efforts began immediately on the Trucks Act. Subversives had to register within five days or face criminal penalties. The registration form asked not only for an admission of Communist affiliation but also about associates and CP activities. William Albertson, the state Communist party secretary, condemned the registration law as an "uncon-

stitutional monstrosity . . . framed arrogantly by Fascist-minded legislators."
He refused to register and, on behalf of the party, filed a suit challenging the
law's constitutionality. It allegedly restricted freedom of speech, denied due
process, and constituted a bill of attainder. Only two persons, neither CP
members, registered. At the same time, Attorney General Frank Millard
interpreted the ballot ban in the Trucks Act to include not only the CP but
also the Socialist Workers party (SWP), characterized as "a dissident
Communist group." The SWP state chairman, protesting that his organization was bitterly anti-Communist, filed suit against the ruling. He won a
temporary restraining order which allowed the SWP to appear on the
November ballot.[27]

The attorney general also launched an investigation of a union in Flint.
Influenced by the HUAC hearings in Detroit, Buick local 599 (UAW-CIO)
in Flint invited the committee to investigate "Communists and their
supporters" in the local. The local's president protested that the invitation's
sponsors were the "outs" who wanted to use the issue to help them win an
election coming in two months. Attorney General Millard announced that
HUAC's help was unnecessary, and sent an assistant attorney general and
two state policemen to begin an inquiry. At a closed meeting on March 18,
the three state investigators questioned ten members of the UAW local, who
identified seven or eight fellow workers as Communists. In another private
hearing a week later, the investigators heard twenty-nine more UAW
members. The attorney general studied the testimony, but took no immediate action. On April 20, the UAW-CIO regional director requested that
Millard either file formal charges of subversion or clear the local. The
attorney general responded ambiguously that disclosure of the information
would be "unfair" to the local. No state action ever followed.[28]

Meanwhile, State Police Commissioner Donald S. Leonard encouraged
the criminal prosecutions of Communists under the new state laws. He urged
the attorney general to summon a grand jury that could investigate,
subpoena, and recommend action. Millard, rejecting this proposal, declared
that the best antisubversive method was further exposure through legislative
hearings. Leonard angrily denied that exposure or even loss of employment
was sufficient punishment, and reiterated his original request. Since the
former CP state chairman, Carl Winter, had been convicted of violating the
Smith Act, surely his supporters had committed similar violations, the
commissioner concluded. Almost a month later, the attorney general agreed
to request the creation of a grand jury. On May 8, 1952, the Wayne County
Circuit Court rejected the attorney general's request because of insufficient
evidence.[29]

The period from the summer of 1950 to the summer of 1952 thus
marked the peak of the Scare. Despite an incredible amount of antisubversive action by the state legislature, the period ended with little direct results.

The Trucks Act was tied up in litigation; the investigation of the Flint UAW was unresolved; and the attorney general's call for a grand jury was rejected.

After this time, the Red Scare in the state gradually declined. Having enacted almost every type of restriction, the legislature in 1953 did not pass any new loyalty and security measures. It did put a few safeguards into the Trucks Act. It amended the definition of a Communist to include only those who knowingly associated with the CP. It allowed an organization accused of being a Communist front to have a hearing on the charge. Finally, it partially shifted responsibility for registration from the state police to the attorney general. These amendments, sponsored by Representative Trucks, were not controversial.[30]

The Trucks Act, which had passed unanimously in 1952, was limited further in the following years primarily by the courts. Less than a year after the attorney general had ruled against the Socialist Workers party (SWP) qualifying for the ballot, he withdrew his objection. The attorney general acknowledged that he had insufficient evidence to prove that the SWP was a Communist front organization. More strikingly, the CP after four years of legal procedures succeeded in its suit against the law. The court ruled the registration provision unconstitutional. A later Supreme Court ruling reversed the provision that considered a public employee's use of the Fifth Amendment to be "prima facie evidence" of the truth of the accusation and thus grounds for dismissal.[31]

Michigan's fight against subversive activities was characterized by the significant impact of national developments. HUAC influenced the creation of the Callahan Commission and its initial target, the American Youth for Democracy (AYD). Partially because of the Korean War, the legislature acted with bipartisan and often unanimous support for anti-Communist proposals. The Supreme Court, on the other hand, gutted the Trucks Act, thus ending the state's efforts to identify and prosecute subversives.

Although local developments did not play a determining role, they did interact with the national factors. Two attorneys general slowed the momentum of the Scare in 1947–1949 by refusing to enforce the Callahan Act. The Scare revived in 1950 partially because the state was unique in the Midwest in having legislative sessions in off-years. Moreover, the proximity of the primary and general elections in that summer increased the consensus on loyalty legislation.

The loyalty and security crusade had some overt results. The Callahan Commission prompted Wayne University and the University of Michigan to ban their AYD chapters. Governor Sigler's attacks on the United Public Workers (UPW) broke the strength of that union among state employees. The state barred the CP and tried to bar the SWP from running candidates for public office. Several public employees who invoked the Fifth Amendment before HUAC were confronted with the Trucks Act which pointed to the amendment's use as "prima facie evidence" of the truth of the charges. They were usually dismissed.[32] It took time, effort and money to block the Trucks Act in court. The broader effectiveness of the crusade on the general political climate is impossible to measure exactly, but certainly must have been profound.

Wisconsin

In Wisconsin, national developments did not determine the pattern of the Red Scare. Conservatives proposed antisubversive bills, but the legislature defeated them. The opposition was much stronger than in Michigan. Thus, no legislative committee questioned suspected subversives, and no laws caused dismissals or prosecutions.

The legislature's inactivity must be explained by local factors, the state's political culture. Such factors include the Progressive-La Follette tradition; the memory of excessive patriotic zeal during and after the First World War; the prestige of the state university; the liberal persuasion of two powerful newspapers, the *Madison Capital-Times* and the *Milwaukee Journal*; the opposition aroused by Senator Joseph McCarthy; the senator's fulfillment of conservatives' fears and anxieties; and the state's social stability. The interaction of various factors, rather than an emphasis on a single factor, is the proper interpretative key.

The 1947 legislature considered three antisubversive bills but passed none. Senator Bernard Gettelman, a conservative Republican from Milwaukee, introduced a measure to restrict individual Communists from running as independents. The state already barred the CP from appearing on the ballot, but in the 1946 election, a Communist had campaigned for governor as an independent. The *Madison Capital-Times*, which had strong ties to the Progressive faction in state politics, rallied the opposition. It lambasted Gettelman as the "Martin Dies of Wisconsin," and the bill never got out of committee.[33]

The senator did not become discouraged. Concerned about the American Youth for Democracy (AYD) chapter at the University of Wisconsin, Gettelman proposed to ban "avowed Communists" as university regents, administrators, instructors, and students. A former Communist testified on the treachery of all CP members and sympathizers, and announced the existence of Communist activity on campus. Opposition came from many sources, including the student board and teachers' union at the university. The debate on the bill's merits became diverted when the *Capital-Times* accepted a full-page advertisement from the CP attacking HUAC. Senator Gettelman characterized the advertisement as deceitful, and called the newspaper's editor, William Evjue, "the Communist mouthpiece in the United States." Evjue, noting that the advertisement had appeared in almost twenty other newspapers without incident, termed Gettelman a "dema-gogue." Insults flew back and forth for the next two weeks, and the controversy helped to swing opinion against the senator's bill. It remained in committee, and the AYD was never banned at the university.[34]

The *Capital-Times* also became involved in a third loyalty bill. This measure made it a crime to advocate, print, write, sell, distribute, or exhibit any material which advocated the overthrow of the government. Its sponsor termed it "a bill for Americanism" that would honor the sacrifices made in the war to save freedom. Another supporter claimed that the bill's opponents had "spotted" loyalty. Yet, critics pointed out that the bill probably would require schools and libraries to remove all books by authors such as Jefferson, Lincoln, and Marx. Its sponsor cut his own throat when he agreed that the bill could be used against the *Capital-Times* for its "un-American activities." Although most legislators had little love for the crusading newspaper and its prickly editor, they knew that the paper was not disloyal. On May 9, the assembly voted 57–25 to table the bill.[35]

Two years later, the legislature remained unconvinced of the need for additional loyalty and security measures. The assembly quickly consigned to oblivion bills to investigate un-American activities and to prohibit Communists from using public buildings. Receiving only slightly more attention was a proposed loyalty oath for public employees and all professionals, such as lawyers and doctors, who received licenses from the state. Opposition arose from even the GOP majority leader in the senate and a former American Legion state commander. The bill met defeat 27–4. The session's major antisubversive bill, sponsored by the American Legion, would have required Communists to register with the secretary of state or face criminal prosecution. If they did register, those who held a state job would be dismissed and those who held a state license would have it revoked. Liberal and radical groups testified strongly against the bill in two separate hearings. They condemned the bill for its self-incrimination features. The legislature did not pass the bill, and the session ended without additional loyalty legislation.[36]

The Communist issue by-passed the 1951 legislative session,[37] but reemerged in 1953. The major bill at that time proposed to bar Communists and those who used the Fifth Amendment when asked about their political affiliations from public employment. The bill also specifically included Trotskyists in its proposed ban, but excluded those "who only advocate the common ownership of any or all goods or property," thereby acknowledging the loyalty of the state's Socialists. Critics condemned the bill as harmful and "another McCarthy tactic," but for the first time in the postwar decade, one house of the legislature passed an antisubversive bill: 56–31 in the assembly. In the senate, the proposal got caught in the last-minute deadline, and was tabled with many others.[38] In 1955, the legislature did not consider any loyalty proposals.

The Wisconsin legislature acted quite differently from its counterpart in Michigan. Its inactivity reveals the importance of local factors. It also poses a direct dilemma for all historians who have examined the career of Senator Joseph McCarthy and, more broadly, the meaning of "McCarthyism." If the Wisconsin voters felt anxious about their status and thus voted for McCarthy, why was this not translated into state legislative campaigns and action? If the state GOP represented a conservative, anti-New Deal force that used the Communist issue to grasp for power, then why did the same conservative voters in the state fail to elect other "Fighting Joe's" to the legislature? Although the legislature's inactivity might be an aberration among all states, a tentative explanation of its behavior must still be attempted.

Although McCarthy was twice elected senator, he was less a state phenomenon than a national one. Throughout his career, critics, especially the *Madison Capital-Times* and the *Milwaukee Journal*, lambasted him for his various errors and excesses. The state Democrats were also not intimidated. Indeed, the senator acted as a negative reference point around which they waged a moral crusade. The Democrats kept building their strength throughout the postwar decade, and soon reversed the GOP domination. Even within the GOP, McCarthy had opposition, which ultimately led to the "Joe Must Go" recall movement of 1954. Although unsuccessful, the effort revealed widespread dissatisfaction with McCarthy within the state. The senator, in short, was not the political power on the state level that he was in Washington, D.C. McCarthy furthermore preferred to play on the national stage. Only rarely and off-handedly did he accuse persons and institutions in the state of being Communists. For example, he never even vaguely challenged the state university, which had a liberal reputation. Therefore, the state's political culture should not be characterized solely by his ideology or activities.[39]

Even considering the relative weakness of "McCarthyism" in the state, the legislature's inactivity is still puzzling. Every other midwestern state legislature launched an antisubversive campaign. Wisconsin, moreover, cannot claim a purer civil libertarian history. It experienced not only excessive patriotic zeal in 1917–1919 but also an investigation of the university in 1935 and the enactment of a law barring the CP from the ballot in 1943.

Why, then, during the postwar decade did the state refuse to begin more investigations and enact more laws? One tentative suggestion is that conservatives might have received sufficient satisfaction by Senator McCarthy's airing of their grievances. Possibly, the senator appealed primarily to frustration concerning foreign policy, and the voters—and the legislature—felt no similar anxiety about social and political trends in the state. Perhaps, Wisconsin residents considered their communities as stable, with no need for witch hunting. Between 1940 and 1950, when Illinois,

Michigan, and Ohio experienced rapid population growth due to migration, Wisconsin had a net out-migration. State population growth occurred only as a result of more births than deaths.[40] Throughout the period, moreover, the state's politics remained relatively constant. The Republican party held a solid grip on state government, a condition unique among the five mid-western states. Perhaps the conservatives felt their fears eased by GOP control, and believed more loyalty laws and investigation unnecessary.

These tentative suggestions would also help to explain the state's deviation from the national pattern. No single reason will explain the legislature's inactivity. In any case, this historical dilemma must be answered by local factors. Any attempt to explain Wisconsin politics during the Red Scare solely by consulting national developments must fail. It falls on the opposite end of the scale from Michigan.

2

State Politics:
Illinois, Ohio, and Indiana

Michigan and Wisconsin represent a stark contrast in their responses to the Red Scare. Three other Midwestern states—Illinois, Ohio, and Indiana—fall between these two extremes in terms of the number of loyalty proposals enacted. Each state passed antisubversive laws, as did Michigan, but each also defeated such measures, as Wisconsin did. Using other criteria to examine these states, they show no similarity in pattern. Illinois enacted loyalty laws early but soon developed a partisan struggle which blocked the crusade. The Scare in Ohio had partisan overtones in the beginning but these faded, and the state after 1950 adopted many restrictions. Indiana, by contrast, dealt with the Communist issue sporadically but on a consensus basis. The states' similarities and differences can be partially shown in table 2.

Illinois

The interaction of national developments and local factors shaped the pattern of the Red Scare in Illinois. Conservative Republicans led by Senator Paul Broyles pushed the loyalty compaign. Their early victories, such as the creation of a legislative investigating committee, showed some national influence. Just as on the national level, the Communist issue came to be personified by one person, in this case Senator Broyles. Yet by 1949, his excesses created a strong backlash. The opposition, largely Democratic and led initially by Governor Adlai Stevenson, amended some bills and defeated others. In contrast to Michigan and Wisconsin, the Communist issue was partisan and divisive. As a result of the strong opposition which included two vetoes, the state enacted no major loyalty proposals between 1949 and 1954. The Scare's development can be divided into two major phases: a sudden rise until the spring of 1949, and afterwards a basically partisan battle with little room for either side to compromise.

Table 2. Loyalty Laws Enacted

	Illinois	Ohio	Indiana
1947	Legislative committee Bar subversive organ- izations from Uni- versity of Illinois		
1949	Temporary legislative committee	Loyalty oath for unem- ployment compensation recipients	
1951		Legislative committee	Outlaw CP
1953		Legislative committee Require public employees to testify about CP Bar Communists from public employment Outlaw subversion Confiscate funds of sub- versive organizations Special attorney general	
1955	Loyalty oath for public employees		Loyalty oath for lobbyists

In the first phase of the Scare, the loyalty crusaders won easy victories, and Senator Paul Broyles emerged to personify the Communist issue. Republicans had just won a major victory in the November 1946 elections, and a strong anti-New Deal spirit animated the 1947 legislature.[1] Conservatives focused particularly on subversion in universities. Influenced by HUAC's attack on the American Youth for Democracy (AYD) as a Communist front organization, the student newspaper at the University of Illinois urged the banning of the local AYD chapter. This prompted Charles Clabaugh, a Republican who represented the university's district, to sponsor a bill to deny the use of university facilities to any subversive organization. The university president, George Stoddard, believed that the campus AYD was not "subversive or dangerous." Listening instead to Clabaugh's anti-Communist charges, both the house and the senate passed the Clabaugh Act with only one dissenting vote in each chamber. The university administration soon banned the student group.[2]

The legislature's concern about education also led it to establish a legislative investigating committee, partially influenced by HUAC. In the process, Senator Paul Broyles (R, Mount Vernon) came into prominence. The senator introduced a bill, suggested by the state American Legion, to establish a Seditious Activities Investigating Commission (SAIC). The senate passed the bill without a dissenting vote. In the house it began to encounter opposition from some liberal groups: the Chicago Civil Liberties Committee, Chicago Action Council, ACLU, and the AAUP chapter at the University of Illinois. These critics argued that the committee could restrict freedom of thought and degenerate into a witch hunt because of the bill's vague definition of subversive activities. The state CP and Civil Rights Congress also opposed the SAIC bill, but legislators stopped their officials' attempt to testify to the House Judiciary Committee when they refused to answer questions about their political activity. Senator Broyles, who would lead the fight for loyalty and security bills in the next several sessions of the legislature, stressed the immediate danger of the internal Communist threat. In June, the house passed the bill 87–24. It was not a party-line vote, but it does confirm the Republican character of the conservative movement in the state. Republicans voted strongly for the measure, 67–1, while Democrats split, 20–23.[3]

The SAIC resembled HUAC in its conservative ideology but not in its composition and method. The SAIC accepted the conservative attitudes of its chairman, Senator Broyles, a life-long Illinois resident. The devoutly religious senator believed that the loyalty crusade paralleled the Christian movement. Dividing the world into the saved and the damned, Broyles felt confident in the righteousness of his efforts and the errors of his critics. The SAIC strongly proclaimed the danger of the internal Communist threat. The committee, however, was not a perfect model of its national counterpart, HUAC. It was composed of five senators, five representatives, and five citizens appointed by the governor. More importantly, it held only closed hearings. During 1947–1948, it questioned no "unfriendly" witnesses and cited no one for contempt.[4]

The commission, following Senator Broyles' advice, focused on education and "over-liberals."

> Should we spread ourselves all over, or go after a specific group? It is my opinion that we should concentrate our efforts on a specific group. I think the greatest danger is in the over-liberal educators who have a tendency to glamorize the various -isms, especially communism, to our young people.[5]

In the hearings, some witnesses identified subversive professors, while several university presidents, state education officials, and PTA representatives gave a more general description of the loyalty of teachers. The SAIC investigator traveled to several campuses to question other university officials about subversive activities. Contrary to Broyles' expectation, the investigator found little leftist and even less Communist activity. The SAIC was also concerned about public schools, and it established a citizens' committee to review textbooks. It did not meet until November 1948, when the SAIC's life had almost ended, and it had no funding. As a result, it did nothing except debate whether to scrutinize teachers or textbooks.[6]

Broyles' use of terms like "over-liberal" reveals much about the SAIC's operations. The committee did not concern itself with the obvious target, the state CP, and only occasionally did witnesses label persons as Communists. The SAIC seemed to agree with one witness's view that "our greatest danger is not in the known Communist, but in those that taper off from a healthy pink." Witnesses and committee members used terms like "over-liberal" and "liberalist" as synonyms for "disloyal." According to one witness, a liberal was "in favor of the Kremlin, [but] not without friendly criticism." One university president denied that any significant difference existed between Socialists and Communists. Various witnesses declared that the ACLU, Chicago Housing Authority, American Education Fellowship, National Student Association, and the University of Chicago student newspaper had Communist sympathies or members.[7]

Because the SAIC held only closed hearings and released no public statements, none of these activities raised any controversy. The commission worked under the assumption that its activities constituted only the first step in a long antisubversive campaign. It spent most of its time debating the best method of restricting subversion. When one senator favored an emphasis on Americanism in the public schools, Broyles proclaimed it an ineffective method. "You can't educate people out of theft and murder," he concluded. When an American Legion representative suggested talking quietly with school officials about leftist student organizations, Broyles dismissed the proposal as "appeasement" and demanded a get-tough policy. In its effort to determine the best method, the SAIC sought information from other antisubversive agencies. It heard from officials in the Chicago police "red" squad, and examined its files, which had the names of 30,000 Chicago residents and 50,000 other Americans. The commission listened to two Illinois congressmen and sent its members to confer with HUAC, SISS, and the FBI. It also participated in the Interstate Legislative Conference on Un-American Activities, sponsored by the California and Washington investigative commissions.[8]

Its final report, taking a dark view of education, concluded that schools and colleges were the "most dangerous" area of subversion. Textbooks taught little patriotism; some radical teachers indoctrinated their students; and subversive organizations functioned openly on some campuses. Much needed to be done to combat the internal threat, and the SAIC recommended the enactment of new, restrictive laws.[9]

The 1949 legislature marked the turning-point in the Red Scare. In the beginning, the conservative movement repeated its successes of 1947. The legislature temporarily re-established the SAIC to investigate the University of Chicago and Roosevelt College. Yet the excesses of that probe and the release of the 1947–1948 SAIC report caused a strong backlash. As a result, the legislature ended without enacting any new antisubversive measures. The partisan fight which arose at this time would continue throughout the remainder of the postwar decade.

In the 1949 session, Senator Broyles sponsored several antisubversive bills and found initial success. With minimal debate, the senate passed the three Broyles' bills: to dismiss public school teachers who advocated any doctrine that would undermine the government; to require a loyalty oath from public employees and to dismiss anyone affiliated with a subversive organization; and to outlaw the CP. The senate passed the bills with broad bipartisan support: 42–7, 44–6, and 39–9, respectively.[10]

None of them passed the house, however. The mood shifted dramatically between March, when the senate acted, and June, when they came to the house floor. This change occurred because of an SAIC probe of the University of Chicago and Roosevelt College. On March 1, the Senate Judiciary Committee held a hearing on the pending Broyles' bills. Between 150 and 200 students from the two colleges came to Springfield to lobby against the bills. In the hearing, the students hissed at the bills' supporters and cheered their opponents, including a CP official. Later in the day, some of the black students were denied service at the restaurant in the Abraham Lincoln Hotel. With some whites, they staged an impromptu sit-in, occupying all of the chairs and sending out for sandwiches. The next day the conservatives were in uproar. Representative G. William Horsley, a Republican from Springfield, introduced a resolution to investigate the two colleges because the "students are being indoctrinated with Communism." Another representative suggested that the University of Chicago "should be disbanded and most of them sent to Russia for awhile." In an angry mood, the house voted to suspend the rules and then in an overwhelming voice vote passed the resolution to re-establish the SAIC. A week later, the senate also voted for the investigation. The few voices of opposition warning of emotionalism and praising academic freedom were drowned out by conservatives such as the senate minority leader. "I never have seen such a dirty, greasy bunch of kids like those ... Why, their hair wasn't even combed! How can they be clean on the inside if they're so dirty outside?" The conservative movement seemed unstoppable.[11]

Once again, the SAIC found life with Senator Broyles chairing the investigation of the two colleges. The students' activities had only confirmed his belief about the subversive nature of higher education, a conviction which had been expressed privately in the SAIC's first term. The hearings, which personalized Broyles even further with the Communist issue, nevertheless dealt for only a brief period with the students' lobbying effort and student activities generally. Almost all of the proceedings concerned the alleged Communist front affiliations of several professors. University of Chicago Chancellor Robert Hutchins and Roosevelt College President Edward J. Sparling both made strong defenses of the loyalty and integrity of their respective faculties. Hutchins in particular ripped apart the questioning of the SAIC counsel, J. B. Matthews, by continually interrupting, condemning guilt by association, terming the Broyles' bills "unnecessary," and pointing to "thought control" as the country's greatest danger. The charges against the professors were elaborated by two reporters from Hearst newspapers and a state representative. The six professors and one student who testified, all of whom were from the University of Chicago, showed that most of the alleged Communist associations did not exist.[12]

At the end of the proceedings, the SAIC split over its findings. The Democratic minority concluded that no documented evidence of disloyalty or indoctrination had been found. The Broyles-led majority issued a far different report. It termed the critics either communists, sympathizers, or dupes, and condemned the professors' affiliations and the leftist student organizations. It proposed the dismissal of any instructor who belonged to an organization on the attorney general's subversive list and the expulsion of any student who was a Communist or who refused to answer about his political affiliation. If any university did not adopt these policies, the majority report concluded that the legislature should remove its tax-exempt status and should dismiss its trustees if it was a tax-supported school.[13]

The SAIC investigation affected not only the two colleges but also the three Broyles' bills which were still under consideration by the house. Liberals perceived the investigation as directed not at subversives and traitors but at liberals and liberal institutions. They viewed Senator Broyles as a dangerously sincere politician who would curtail freedom of thought and expression. This perception seemed confirmed when the SAIC issued its 1947–48 report which contained testimony from the hearings, including Broyles' concern with "over-liberals." Throughout April, May, and June, liberal organizations rallied in opposition to the pending bills. Lobbying efforts came from the ACLU, American Jewish Congress, Independent Voters of Illinois, CIO, NAACP, Chicago Federation of Labor, state PTA, various AAUP chapters, as well as ad hoc groups. Governor Adlai Stevenson, a Democrat, rallied his forces against the bills. As a result, when the house considered a separate loyalty oath bill, the vote split almost perfectly down party lines: aye 63R, 2D; nay 1R, 59D. Although the bill received a 65–60 plurality, it was defeated because it needed a majority, or 77 votes, of the elected representatives. In the final days of the session, the house spent most of its time on a crime bill and a gasoline tax bill. The lower chamber never even voted on the three Broyles' bills that had so easily passed the senate only a few weeks before. If they had come up for a vote, it is doubtful that the house would have approved them, and if they had passed, it is almost certain that Governor Stevenson would have vetoed them.[14]

Two years earlier, the legislature had given consensus support to antisubversive legislation. The Clabaugh Act banning the AYD and the establishment of the SAIC had been passed by overwhelming margins. By contrast, in the 1949 legislature, the Communist issue aroused hostility and polarization. The conservative, self-righteous Senator Broyles acted as a negative reference point around which the opposition coalesced. This solidification process was aided by the prestige of Governor Stevenson (elected in 1948), the established ACLU chapter in Chicago, and the liberal press led by the *Chicago Sun-Times* and the *Saint Louis Post-Dispatch*. A final factor, cumulative voting, is a unique electoral device in the state that almost ensures that the minority in each legislative district will be able to elect a representative.[15] Local factors thus helped to turn the loyalty crusade away from its goal, and helped to set the pattern of the Scare in the state. For the remainder of the postwar decade, conservative Republicans continued to push for antisubversive legislation, but they were met by Democrats, who voted against such efforts. The 1949 session therefore set the pattern of the Scare in the state: a close, bitter, largely partisan fight.[16]

Illinois naturally did not exist in a vacuum, and national developments after 1949 intensified concern over loyalty and security. Alger Hiss was found guilty of perjury; eleven Communist leaders were convicted under the Smith Act; the Truman administration and the State Department were savaged by Senator Joseph McCarthy; and American forces were sent into the Korean War. Yet, just as in Wisconsin, none of these national events undermined the opposition in the state. It had already coalesced and would battle any proposal offered by Senator Broyles.

The 1951 legislative session again featured a controversy over a bill sponsored by Senator Broyles.[17] His proposal outlawed subversion, required a loyalty oath for all public employees, and established a special assistant attorney general to investigate and prosecute these matters. Supporters of the measure came primarily from veterans organizations, the Daughters of the American Revolution, and the Knights of Columbus. They argued that existing legislation was insufficient because Communists acted openly in the state. Especially now that Americans were fighting against Communists in Korea, they found it difficult to understand why any patriotic American would oppose restricting the Communist party. To a large degree, they accepted the argument of George Sokolsky, a leading conservative columnist, who wrote in the spring of 1951 that "any American who is not a fanatical anti-Red is just a no-good bum . . . and should be treated as such. There can be no half-way, half-hearted anti-Communism."[18]

The bill's opponents did not shrink from the fight. Unlike in Michigan, the liberal governor did not meekly accept loyalty legislation, and Stevenson rallied the liberal forces. By this time, the opponents formulated what can be called the liberal critique. They agreed with the Broyles' supporters on the dangers of the CP and on the proposed goal, restrictions on CP activity. Yet they criticized proposed state actions, such as the Broyles' bill, on several points. The liberals argued that the responsibility for the control of subversive activities should be left with the federal government. Since the Department of Justice and the FBI handled the job adequately, state efforts were unnecessary. Illinois, moreover, did not need further legislation because it already had protection with a "criminal syndicalism" law. Finally, liberals worried that the bill's vagueness would cause the harassment of non-conformists and liberals, the restriction of free speech, and the intimidation of teachers and the curtailment of academic freedom. Such fears seemed confirmed when one legislator exploded, "Let's stop quibbling. We shouldn't be too fussy. We are fiddling while Rome burns. I only wish that this bill could do something about the UN, the One Worlders, and all the others trying to undermine America." Broyles also occasionally became emotional, once claiming that "there are Communists everywhere, even in this state house."[19]

The debate between liberals and conservatives did not change many minds. Arguing that they supported national restrictions on Communist activities, the liberal critics insisted that the debate concerned means, not ends. Yet the supporters of the Broyles' bill found that difficult to believe. To them, the issue was indeed one of ends. They did not believe that liberals truly wanted to pursue Communists. The debate in the state legislature was thus a type of trench warfare. Both sides dug in, taking secure positions, and then launching fairly ineffective efforts to win the other side. The war would be a long one.

The controversy in the 1951 session concerned the Broyles' bill to outlaw subversion, require a loyalty oath from public employees, and establish a special assistant attorney general. It passed the senate easily on a partial party line vote, 34–15: aye 29R, 5D; nay 2R, 13D. After much more debate and a few technical amendments, the house also passed the bill, 88–41, on another relative party line vote: aye 69R, 19D; nay 10R, 31D. A few days later, Governor Stevenson vetoed the bill in a classic expression of the liberal critique. He argued that the bill would harm innocent citizens and that the antisubversive effort should be left to the federal government. An aide later reported that the latter argument had been confirmed in the governor's discussions with FBI officials in Washington, D.C. The next day, the Broyles' bill returned to the senate where it had received a two-thirds majority on its first passage, the amount needed to override the veto. The senate debate, which lasted for three hours, found harsh charges expressed by both sides. According to Senator Broyles, the veto would "bring great joy to the Communist conspirators, traitors, and the Kremlin." His critics repeated the governor's arguments in his veto message. Stevenson's action caused four senators, three Democrats and a Republican, to switch their votes, and the Senate sustained the veto. Broyles angrily charged that the governor insisted "upon following . . . [a] sympathetic philosophy toward Communism," and the *Chicago Tribune* echoed that sentiment.[20]

During this period, Broyles' main strength had come from his fellow Republicans. No other GOP leader had challenged the senator's leadership in the loyalty field. The state GOP had had a vacuum at the top since the incumbent Republican governor and U.S. senator had been defeated in 1948. This changed in November 1952, when a moderate Republican, William G. Stratton, won the governor's chair. The moderate-conservative divisions within the GOP would now become reflected in the 1953 session of the legislature.[21]

That session again featured two loyalty bills, sponsored by Senator Broyles, a dedicated and persistent man. One bill would re-establish the SAIC, and the other, a copy of his 1951 bill, would outlaw the CP, require a loyalty oath from public employees, and create a special assistant attorney general to investigate these matters. Both sides took their familiar positions, although the opposition successfully attracted an even wider variety of persons and organizations to its side:

League of Women Voters
CIO
AFL
American Jewish Congress
state PTA
various AAUP chapters
American Veterans Committee
Illinois Bar Association
Illinois Federation of Teachers
Illinois Council of Churches
Macon County Farm Bureau
Greene County Farm Bureau
Edward Ryerson, chairman of the board, Inland Steel
Harold H. Swift, chairman of the board, Swift and Company
Laird Bell, chairman of the board, Weyerhauser Timber Company[22]

The opposition, as strong as it was, had little immediate effect. In the upper chamber where Senator Broyles could guide the bills, they passed easily on party line votes: 33–11 for the SAIC and 35–11 for the other. The controversy heated up in the house. Governor Stratton began to drop hints that he felt that the bills were unnecessary. "The Broyles' bills were never part of the administration's program," he finally proclaimed. Edward Clamage, a prominent American Legion official, shot back that Stratton was "turning chicken." Two days later, Stratton's supporters on the House Judiciary Committee allied with the Democrats to recommend that the bill not pass. When that recommendation came to the house floor, the debate was fiery, and many conservative Republicans attacked their governor. By a vote of 83 to 55, the house rejected the committee's decision and revived the bills. Only twenty-one Republicans backed Stratton, while fifty-nine broke ranks to support both bills. Enthused, Broyles pronounced that he would not "crawl anymore" to the governor.[23]

The bills' opponents continued their efforts, and this time found more success. They succeeded in deleting the provision creating a special assistant attorney general. The house passed the remainder of the bill, which outlawed the CP and required a loyalty oath from public employees. Its vote, 87–51, again revealed a partial party line split: aye 68R, 19D; nay 12R, 39D. The opponents did not capitulate. A week later, the house defeated the Broyles' bill to re-establish the SAIC by a vote of 69 to 66. The liberal Democrats had been helped by Governor Stratton's quiet opposition which had caused several Republicans to switch sides. A few days later, Stratton stunned the conservatives even further by vetoing the first bill. Although he admitted that it contained some beneficial provisions, the governor argued that the loyalty oath section would cause administrative confusion because it conflicted on the number of public employees covered. The veto occurred on the last day of the session, and neither the senate nor the house had the time to consider the action before adjournment. In all probability, the veto would have been sustained in the house. A two-thirds vote, or 102 votes, was needed to override, and the bill had received only 87 votes when it passed. A few weeks later, the American Legion formally condemned Stratton's veto as giving "tremendous encouragement to the reds, pinks, and gullibles."[24]

The opposition was characterized by its antagonism to Senator Broyles, not by its aversion to loyalty bills per se. The 1953 legislature easily passed two such measures. One bill to require a loyalty oath from all public housing tenants was passed 27–11 by the senate and 89–27 by the house. Another measure, which required all prospective public school teachers to pass an examination of the U.S. and Illinois Constitutions before receiving certification, was sponsored as "an effort to offset the vicious effects of the infiltration of our schools by United Nations 'one world' propaganda." The legislature ignored the sponsor's inflated rhetoric, and passed her bill without a dissenting vote in each house. Neither bill caused much controversy.[25]

In the 1955 session, Senator Broyles found success by compromising slightly. He gave up his attempt to re-establish the SAIC and to create a special assistant attorney general. The senator also separated his two remaining provisions into separate bills: one to require a loyalty oath from public employees and the other to outlaw the Communist party. His critics again opposed both bills, but both passed the senate rather easily: 31–16 for the oath and 28–17 for the other. The party divisions were evident in both votes: on the first bill, aye 28R, 3D, nay 2R, 14D; and on the second bill, aye 25R, 3D, nay 3R, 14D. The house amended the loyalty oath bill slightly before passing it on another relative party line vote: aye 64R, 20D; nay 12R, 43D. Broyles' supporters in the house then let the bill to outlaw the CP die since its chances for passage were considered poor. On July 18, 1955, Senator Broyles finally won his victory when Governor Stratton signed the loyalty oath bill into law.[26]

At least seven public employees did not sign the oath. A philosophy professor at Southern Illinois University resigned and later took a job at Bradley University. Two University of Illinois staff members, neither instructors, also resigned. An employee of the Chicago Land Clearance Commission, a Quaker, was dismissed. Three Chicago public school teachers—a teacher of retarded children, a high school mathematics teacher, and a substitute elementary teacher—filed suit against the law. They were allowed to continue to teach, but were denied their salaries according to a provision in the bill. In March 1956, a district court upheld the oath.

> There is no undue infringement of civil liberties . . . In the desperate battle for youth's minds, the State must protect the integrity of its schools. . . . The danger is here and threatening. . . . These are critical times. We are all in a fight for survival.

In November, the Illinois Supreme Court affirmed the decision, and the teachers were dismissed.[27]

The pattern of the Red Scare in Illinois was set by an interaction of national and local developments. Conservative Republicans led the loyalty crusade and won early victories in the 1947 legislature. The Clabaugh Act, which denied the use of University of Illinois facilities to subversive groups, reflected not only HUAC's attack on the American Youth for Democracy but also local attacks on that campus chapter. The latter factor explains why the law was limited to a single institution. The creation of the SAIC was influenced by HUAC, but it was not a true reflection of its national counterpart since it included citizen members, held only closed hearings, heard only "friendly" witnesses, and scrutinized education.

The conservatives' easy successes ended in 1949 primarily because of local factors. This second phase of the Scare continued for the remainder of the postwar decade. A strong opposition formed after the SAIC probe of the University of Chicago and Roosevelt College. Liberal opponents not only defeated all of the 1949 proposals for antisubversive legislation, but also coalesced into a strong force for the next several years. Indeed, the divisions in the state legislature remained relatively constant in the next three sessions (see table 3).

Table 3. Degree of Party Unity on the Broyles' Bills
(Republicans voting aye, Democrats nay)

	Senate		House	
SB 102, 1951	94%R	72%D	87%R	62%D
SB 102, 1953	94%R	75%D	85%R	67%D
SB 58, 1955	92%R	82%D	84%R	68%D

Neither international events such as the Korean War nor national developments such as the rise of Senator Joseph McCarthy significantly changed the basically partisan divisions in the legislature, which had been primarily created from local factors.

Among the five Midwestern states, only in Illinois did a politician, Paul Broyles, come to personify the Communist issue. In this way, he came closest to being a "little McCarthy." While both were conservative Republicans, Broyles differed from the Wisconsin Senator in some ways. McCarthy spent little time trying to pass new legislation; he focused on exposing individuals. Broyles, on the other hand, was intimately involved in the legislative process, and did not attack specific individuals as Communists. To become a "little McCarthy," Broyles would have needed a vehicle for continual publicity—a permanent SAIC. The few months of the legislative session were insufficient to give Broyles the same type of power McCarthy had in the national arena. The legislature's refusal to create such a permanent SAIC points out that at least in this way the Scare at the state level was less severe than on the national level.

The loyalty crusade nevertheless had some effectiveness. The Clabaugh Act forced the University of Illinois to ban the campus AYD chapter. The SAIC did not cause the dismissal of any instructor, but it certainly sent a warning to state university officials, which possibly led to increased administrative surveillance and pressure. The only Broyles' bill which became law, the loyalty oath for public employees, probably did not generate any increase in political conformity since the opposition had been so vocal and effective. Yet, the law did cause the dismissal or resignation of a few state workers. While the conservatives' successes did not equal those in Michigan, they surpassed Wisconsin's. Illinois thus falls between the two extremes.

Ohio

In Ohio, the pattern of the Red Scare was again set by the interaction of national and local factors. Conservative Republicans led the loyalty campaign and succeeded most prominently in establishing a legislative investigative commission modeled after HUAC. The effort to pass loyalty legislation neither received consensus support as in Michigan nor caused partisan divisions as in Illinois. In particular, the response of Democratic Governor Frank Lausche fell between the opposition of Stevenson in Illinois and the support of Williams in Michigan. In 1950, the opposition was weakened both by local factors, such as an exposé of Communists in the Cincinnati area and the senatorial campaign of Robert Taft, and national developments, such as a HUAC probe in Cincinnati and the outbreak of the Korean War. The Scare thus can be divided into two phases: a slowly increasing concern with the Communist issue until 1950, and afterwards a sharp intensification.

The first phase of the Scare from 1946 to 1950 was relatively quiet. Conservatives made some efforts, but were not too successful in legitimizing the Communist issue. The 1947 legislature enacted no loyalty measures, and the 1949 session passed only a loyalty oath for unemployment compensation recipients. In 1948, the Progressive party's effort to get on the ballot was initially blocked by an anti-Communist law, but the courts cleared the way.

The 1947 legislature passed no loyalty measures. In two separate bills, conservatives proposed the creation of a commission to investigate Communist activity in the schools and colleges. Two months earlier, Senator John Bricker had asserted that "subversive elements" existed at Ohio State University. The University, however, had banned its AYD chapter in early 1946, and thus the Ohio legislature did not consider Bricker's alarms real. Both bills remained in committee.[28]

In the next year, the legislature was not in session, but the executive branch activated a 1941 law barring Communists from the ballot. In the summer of 1948, the Ohio Wallace for President Committee attempted to qualify for the November ballot. It filed a petition with 46,000 names, more than the legal minimum, as well as an affidavit required by the 1941 law that the committee did not advocate the overthrow of the government. On June 4, Secretary of State Edward J. Hummel ruled against the petition, but gave no reasons for his action. When the Wallace committee challenged the ruling in court, Hummel charged that three of the eleven executive officers who had signed the affidavit were Communists and that three others were sympathizers. Hummel believed that this invalidated the affidavit, and thus the Wallace committee did not qualify for the ballot. On June 19, the Wallace committee formally became the Ohio Progressive party. At the convention, Henry Wallace pledged to "stop the philosophy of Hitler, Himmler, and Hummel." A month later, the Ohio Supreme Court overturned Hummel's decision in a six-to-one ruling. The court declared that the three alleged Communists had not been proven to advocate the overthrow of the government. To deny a place on the ballot, moreover, would require proof that the group, not just a few individuals, supported such violent action. The Progressive party thus qualified for the ballot, although the incident reflected the party's difficulties in the campaign.[29]

In the 1949 legislature, conservatives raised the Communist issue with slightly more success than in 1947, but still did not meet with bipartisan approval. One bill to outlaw the Communist party died in committee, but a loyalty oath bill aroused more controversy. The measure required the accuser to file formal charges of disloyalty against a public employee in court, but the house deleted this restriction 65 to 30. It then passed the bill 104 to 15. This bipartisan support was not repeated in the senate though. The Senate Rules Committee sat on the bill for nearly a month in an effort to kill it. On the next-to-last day of the session, the senate Republicans attempted to pull the bill out of the committee, but lost on a party-line vote,

12–15: aye 11R, 1D; nay 15D. Angered, some Republicans blasted the Democrats for being soft on communism.[30]

The Communist issue also touched two other bills in the 1949 session. When the house considered a revision of the unemployment compensation statute, conservatives proposed a loyalty oath for all recipients. Those who did not sign would be denied compensation. The House passed the amendment 69–56 with the Republicans giving it the margin of victory: aye 59R, 10D; nay 1R, 55D. The senate did not vote on the amendment separately, but did approve the house bill.[31]

The second bill caught up in the Communist issue proposed the creation of a Fair Employment Practices Commission (FEPC). After the Communist party endorsed the bill, the Small Businessman's Association (SBA) declared that such action was "sufficient evidence that its [the bill's] principles are unsound." Civil rights groups wrote many letters to the editor ridiculing such arguments, but the SBA stuck to its guns and some legislators echoed its point of view. The bill was defeated in a controversy over its enforcement powers.[32]

During this first phase of the Scare in Ohio, the Communist issue had some prominence, but the legislature and the courts had not yet jumped on the antisubversive bandwagon. Conservatives had been successful with only the loyalty oath for unemployment compensation recipients. The legislature had rejected the oath for public employees, a legislative investigative commission, and the outlawing of the CP. In 1950, this relatively mild political atmosphere became more stringent due to a combination of local and national developments. In February, the *Cincinnati Enquirer* launched a two-month exposé of Communists in that area. Its sensationalistic series was followed by an invitation to HUAC to investigate the situation. The Committee came in July, two weeks after the beginning of the Korean War, and found its usual quota of recalcitrant witnesses. Emotions grew higher during the U.S. senatorial campaign. Senator Robert Taft did not directly red-bait his opponent, Joseph Ferguson, but he painted the campaign as a struggle between "right" and "left" even though Ferguson was not a liberal. The Ohio press drew a similar picture in dark, forbidding colors. After the Communist party rejected both candidates, the *Mansfield Journal* headlined "Ohio Reds After Taft" and did not mention the CP's denunciation of Ferguson. Actually, the Democratic party was neither liberal nor unified. Despite some mud-slinging by Ferguson, Taft easily won re-election. More importantly for our story, the Republicans regained control of both houses of the legislature in a stunning victory:[33]

	House			Senate	
1949:	69D	66R		19D	14R
1951:	36D	97R	1I	7D	26R

A new phase of the Scare now began. Whereas in 1949 the Democrats had been able to block the loyalty oath bill on a party-line vote, now they would be unable to do so. In the next two sessions, conservatives succeeded in establishing an un-American activities committee, outlawing the Communist party, and creating a special assistant attorney general. The opposition arose only occasionally, and did not have the strength even to sustain a veto by Governor Frank Lausche.

The 1951 legislature, filled with new Republicans, immediately confronted the Communist issue. Terming the 1950 HUAC investigation of Cincinnati's Communists "limited and cursory," a Republican representative sponsored a resolution to create a legislative committee, the Joint Anti-Subversive Investigating Committee (JASIC). Its hearings would be held during the 1951 session and would determine the need for further legislation or investigation. Both houses passed the resolution unanimously.[34]

The JASIC did not remain a consensus vehicle. Composed of eight Republicans and four Democrats, the committee held eight open and five closed hearings during its two-month existence. Several conservative witnesses, pointing to the Korean War, urged the creation of a permanent loyalty commission. "A war situation makes it imperative that we adopt new thoughts that are the antithesis of our normal attitudes," asserted the executive director of the Ohio Manufacturers Association. A few witnesses, agreeing with the need for surveillance, identified persons as Communists and subversives. One such witness, admitting that he no longer distinguished between Communists and leftists, gave the names of those who had opposed the 1950 Internal Security Act. On the other hand, liberal representatives from the CIO, NAACP, Urban League, B'nai B'rith, and Cleveland Civil Liberties Union rejected the need for further investigations or legislation. They argued that the legislature could best curtail Communist activity by enacting social and economic reforms, such as the FEPC. The conservatives, however, received a boost when four other witnesses invoked the Fifth Amendment about their Communist affiliations.[35]

The JASIC's conclusion revealed sharp partisan differences. The majority report, signed by all eight Republicans, asserted the real danger of Communists working in defense industries, deceiving people in the peace movement, and agitating minority groups. It recommended a permanent investigative commission, modeled after HUAC, to probe such activities. The minority report, signed by three Democrats, denied the need for further hearings designed to expose individuals. It asserted that such commissions brought headlines but no constructive results. Instead, the minority report favored a legal study to determine the necessity of enacting additional loyalty laws. The Republicans quickly translated the JASIC majority report into a bill to create a permanent Ohio Un-American Activities Committee (OUAC). The senate passed the bill 23–7 on a straight party line vote: aye

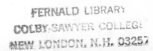

23R, nay 7D. The house voted 79–39 on a strong partisan basis: aye 78R, 1I; nay 10R, 29D. The Democratic legislators thus had a greater unity than their counterparts in Illinois. Yet they did not have a responsive governor, like Adlai Stevenson, to veto the bill. Instead, Governor Frank Lausche, a conservative Democrat, signed the bill and the Scare gathered momentum in Ohio.[36]

The OUAC, chaired by Speaker of the House Gordon Renner, recruited a former FBI agent as its counsel, and established good contacts with the FBI, HUAC, and SISS. Its initial hearings, which began in January 1952, featured Communists who had left the party in the last several years: Charles Baxter in 1945; Matthew Cvetic in 1950; Harvey Matusow in 1951; John Janowitz in 1952; John and Martha Edmiston in 1941; and John DeLong in 1946. Some therefore had rather dated information. A few attempted to be precise in their identification of Communists, but others were sloppier. After Martha Edmiston named many people who had opposed the American entry into the Second World War, a senator demanded to know what criteria she used to determine CP membership. In another case, after hearing the names of many liberals identified as suspects, a representative suggested that "names of persons that are not members of the Communist party, or who have not associated with more than two or three front organizations be omitted from the record." Although the committee seemed to agree with his suggestion at the time, the transcripts remained verbatim reports of the testimony, and the OUAC retained this information in its files.[37]

The OUAC functioned like its national counterpart, HUAC. It asked witnesses about their political affiliations and associations. These inquiries were occasionally brief, occasionally overtly hostile. In 1952, the hearings featured four "unfriendly" witnesses in Columbus, four in Dayton, and three in Columbus again. All used the Fifth Amendment in refusing to answer the questions, and the OUAC cited them for contempt. Since it seemed that the committee was interrogating witnesses with clear Communist connections, it received favorable publicity from these proceedings. A few of these leftists lost their jobs, but one "unfriendly" witness underwent an unusual trauma. At Oscar Smilack's arraignment for his contempt citation, he pled not guilty. The prosecutor rose to assert that Smilack had psychiatric problems since the recent death of his mother. Without hearing any evidence or testimony, the judge ordered Smilack to the Lima State Mental Hospital for thirty days. Smilack's attorney immediately filed suit to free his client, and two weeks later, the court of appeals unanimously reversed the initial order.[38]

The OUAC aroused more controversy in its October investigation of Communists in the Cincinnati area. The hearings themselves were fairly quiet as six witnesses refused to answer questions about their affiliations. The uproar came when someone, probably OUAC chairman Gordon Renner who lived in Cincinnati, released testimony that had been taken in executive session. The witness was Cecil Scott, a former Communist who had worked closely with the *Cincinnati Enquirer's* exposé of Communists in 1950. Scott's testimony had not been officially released because of his unreliability, but now his accusations were splashed all over the city's newspapers. Scott not only accused the labor movement of being dominated by Communists but also identified many persons as Communists. His claim was challenged, and after a two-month delay, the OUAC returned to the city to hear eight persons deny any association with the CP. They also condemned the committee for letting Scott's testimony leak out. The Cincinnati episode marked the low point for the OUAC in its first term, but it still received a generally favorable press. Public opinion was hostile toward "unfriendly" witnesses, and the OUAC seemed to have current information on leftist activities.[39]

The OUAC affected not only the individuals it questioned but also the 1953 legislature. Specifically, the Democratic opposition grew even weaker. The committee made several legislative proposals, most of which received bipartisan support. The senate had more debate and a stronger Democratic opposition than the house, but it did not defeat any bills. The OUAC's first recommendation, an extension of its own life for another year, revealed its public approval. Whereas in 1951 the parties split over the establishment of the committee, in 1953 the OUAC bill passed easily: 123–4 in the House and 27–2 in the Senate.[40]

The chances for other loyalty legislation in the session were increased when HUAC opened an investigation. In March 1953, HUAC questioned Byron Darling, a professor at Ohio State University (OSU) who invoked the Fifth Amendment about his Communist associations. The OSU president immediately suspended him and three weeks later dismissed him. The Darling case seemed to confirm the infiltration of subversives into sensitive positions and the need for further restrictions.[41]

While the Darling case developed, the legislature continued giving consensus approval to loyalty proposals. A bill to dismiss any public employee "or teacher" affiliated with a Communist or subversive organization was passed 30–1 by the senate and 109–1 by the house. Another measure declared that a public employee's refusal to testify about his affiliations would mean "prima facie evidence" of the truth of the accusation. Its sponsor praised the measure for putting the burden of proof on the accused. On June 17, when HUAC came to Columbus to question Darling for the second time, the house passed the bill 108–13. In the senate, critics protested that the bill was unconstitutional, and the upper chamber amended it so that use of the Fifth Amendment would constitute "unfitness" for public employment rather than "prima facie evidence." Even then, the senate passage of the bill revealed partisan differences: aye 21R, 1D; nay 1R, 9D.[42]

The final OUAC legislative recommendation aroused even more controversy. Known as the Devine bill after its Republican sponsor, Representative Samuel Devine, it outlawed subversion and membership in a subversive organization, confiscated any funds belonging to a subversive group, and established a special assistant attorney general to investigate and prosecute these matters. The ACLU, CIO, Progressive party, and Ohio State University Religious Council opposed the Devine bill as an infringement on personal freedom, but they received harsh criticism. One prominent Republican linked the ACLU and CP in the old saying, "birds of a feather flock together," and the *Ohio State Journal* lambasted the OSU Religious Council for "serving the cause of the subversives." On the day of HUAC's second interrogation of Darling, the house passed the Devine bill 119–2. The senate experienced a greater fight over the bill, but on July 13 it passed the measure 21–11. Two weeks later, Governor Frank Lausche finally used his veto power. Relying on the liberal critique, the governor asserted that the OUAC had been ineffective in controlling Communist activity and that the task should be left to the federal authorities, especially the FBI. The bill was "violative of the Bill of Rights," and could "destroy the reputation and the security of innocent citizens," Lausche proclaimed. Lausche's effort to kill the bill was overriden in the house 92–26 and in the senate 20–12. Democrats formed the basis of the opposition, especially in the upper chamber, but they were simply outnumbered.[43]

The OUAC, having another year to function, again focused on the exposure of Communists and leftists. Its hearings in Akron, Canton, and Cleveland claimed victims, but did not cause further restrictive action by either the legislature or the particular communities. In September 1953, the OUAC questioned four former Communists from the Akron area. Three admitted that they had never heard any Communist advocate the overthrow of the government, but all identified persons to the committee. For once, a newspaper, the *Akron Beacon-Journal*, did not sensationalize the hearings. Rather than listing the names of the accused, the paper tried to contact the persons. Some refused to comment, but other responses ranged from the incredulous to the confessional.

> Don't tell me I'm a Communist? I've never heard of such a thing. I'm not a bit worried.

> [I supported the Communists because it was the Depression.] I had a family to feed and no one would help me. I didn't want charity, just a job . . . [The Communists] were a group fighting for jobs . . . I can't believe that a man can be blasted for that.

The newspaper concluded that the OUAC had caused "embarrassment to innocent people." A month later, the committee returned to question eight people, all of whom invoked the Fifth Amendment. The *Beacon-Journal*, unimpressed, editorialized that the hearings had served no purpose. Nevertheless, at least one "unfriendly" witness lost his job.[44]

The OUAC's two remaining hearings similarly threatened a few individuals but left the communities relatively untouched. In October 1953, the committee questioned five Canton area residents, all of whom invoked the Fifth Amendment. The *Canton Repository* found nothing sensational in the hearings, but one "unfriendly" witness lost her job. A few weeks later, the OUAC summoned nine Cleveland area residents. Their refusal to testify about their affiliations did not even make the front page of the *Cleveland Plain Dealer*. This time, at least two people lost their jobs.[45]

The OUAC cited for contempt twenty persons in 1952 and twenty-two in 1953. The maximum penalty was a $500 fine and ten days in jail for each count. In the case of Anna Morgan, one of the first defiant witnesses and thus a test case, the state supreme court upheld her conviction. Her use of the Fifth Amendment was invalid because, according to Ohio law, evidence derived from such legislative investigations could not be used in prosecution but only in legislative recommendations. The witnesses thus had an immunity from state prosecution and could be directed to testify, the court concluded. Morgan and three other defendants appealed to the U.S. Supreme Court, which in 1959 overturned the conviction because the witnesses had not been advised of the immunity provision while before the OUAC. On technical grounds, the Court sustained the conviction of one defendant, who later served his time in jail. In a separate case decided in 1961, the Supreme Court overturned two contempt convictions but sustained three others on technical grounds. The OUAC, despite these setbacks, was the state's most potent antisubversive weapon. None of the other laws was ever enforced.[46]

In Ohio, the pattern of the Red Scare was set by a combination of local and national factors. The period before 1950 showed only a gradual move into the loyalty and security arena. The legislature did not enact any laws in 1947; the courts allowed the Progressive party on the ballot; and the 1949 senate defeated a loyalty oath for public employees. The crucial change in the political atmosphere came in 1950. Local factors—the *Cincinnati Enquirer's* reports of the area's Communists, the Taft senatorial campaign, and the massive GOP victory in state elections—interacted with national developments, HUAC's investigation, and the Korean War. The immediate result was the establishment of the OUAC in 1951, and the final result was the enactment of several restrictive laws in 1953. In the latter session, HUAC again played a role in its interrogation of Professor Darling, once in the state capital.

Ohio's battle in the loyalty and security arena occasionally had partisan overtones, but this tendency never fully developed due to the 1950 GOP landslide and the conservatism of Governor Frank Lausche. When Lausche finally vetoed the Devine bill, there were too few Democratic legislators to sustain his action. The OUAC, it should be noted, did not act in a partisan manner as the SAIC in Illinois did. The latter's probe of the University of Chicago caused a liberal backlash, while the OUAC, after a year of activity, found overwhelming support in the 1953 legislature.

Ohio's antisubversive effort was not quite as extensive as Michigan's but much more so than Wisconsin's. The legislature required recipients of unemployment compensation to sign a loyalty oath, and it required public employees to testify about their political affiliations. Its most effective effort, the OUAC, caused the exposure of more than forty persons, some dismissals from employment, and a few fines and jail sentences. Only the dedication of the witnesses and their attorneys as well as the responsiveness of the U.S. Supreme Court limited the punishment. Although the OUAC's scope was directly limited to forty-two persons over a two-year span, it increased the anti-Communist consensus in the state. Local developments thus interacted with national events to form the Scare in Ohio.

Indiana

Indiana repeats the pattern of the Red Scare being set by a combination of local and national factors. Conservatives first raised the Communist issue in a 1946 probe of Indiana University. When the investigation proved groundless, it inhibited the development of the Scare for four years. The outbreak of the Korean War reinvigorated the loyalty campaign. It prompted the executive branch to dismiss a few state employees and the 1951 legislature to outlaw the Communist party. After this flurry of activity, the Communist issue again declined until the 1955 legislature acted to restrict a leftist lobbyist. In other words, the Red Scare affected state political life in a sporadic manner. Although the state's senators, William Jenner and Homer Capehart, were leaders in the national loyalty crusade, the state legislature enacted only two antisubversive laws and refused to create a legislative investigative commission. This relative inactivity was not caused by a strong or partisan opposition, as in Illinois. Rather, it resulted from the legislators' conservatism, the belief that Communists did not constitute a threat in the state.

In the postwar decade, the Red Scare first raised its head in Indiana's political life when the CP petitioned to qualify for the November 1946 ballot. Several prominent liberals requested that the State Election Board allow the freedom of expression. Although these liberals specifically declared their anti-Communist beliefs, the state American Legion urged the governor to investigate four liberals who were professors at state universities. The governor, even though he had voted with the other members of the election board to approve the CP petition, referred the Legion request to the trustees of Indiana University. In December, after the election had been held, the trustees heard from several university personnel, all of whom denied the existence of any Communist instructor. The trustees' report to the governor confirmed this testimony.[47]

As a result of the 1946 probe, the Scare was slow to develop in the state. There seemed little or nothing subversive to restrict. Whereas in 1947 Michigan established the Callahan Commission and enacted a registration law, the 1947 Indiana legislature saw no loyalty bills introduced. Two years later, conservative legislators proposed the creation of an un-American activities committee. This measure, influenced by HUAC and the Illinois SAIC, featured a unique plan—private financing by the American Legion. The senate passed the resolution by voice vote when it was introduced. In the house, though, opposition arose over the scheme of private financing and the potential abuses of such a commission. One prominent sponsor withdrew his support, and a house committee killed the resolution.[48]

The political atmosphere changed dramatically after the outbreak of the Korean War. First the administration and later the legislature took action to ensure loyalty and security. On July 8, 1950, the *Indianapolis Star* discovered that two state employees, La Rue Spiker and Iola Klaas, had been distributing the Stockholm peace petition:

> We demand the absolute outlawing of the atomic bomb, a frightful weapon for the mass extermination of the populace.
> We demand the establishment of a rigorous international control in order to assure that this outlawing will be carried out.
> We consider that the government which would first use the atomic bomb against any country whatsoever would commit not only a war crime but a crime against humanity, and should be treated as a war criminal.
> We call upon all men of good will in the world to sign this petition.

The leftist origins of the petition aroused charges that it was a Communist plot. The petition drive in the city was sponsored by the Civil Rights Congress, accused of being a Communist front, and Spiker and Klaas both admitted their CRC membership. These two child welfare consultants immediately came under scrutiny by the state welfare department. The press sensationalized the incident, and the governor encouraged the department's investigation. Four days later, the welfare director fired both women for "aiding and abetting" a subversive organization and for causing "discord . . . [and] public criticism . . . [which] destroyed confidence in your effectiveness."[49]

Once aroused, the Scare did not go back to sleep. The governor declared that "a person who assists the program of subversive organizations is just as guilty as the Communist who shoots at our troops." The attorney general began surveillance of other state employees, and he urged that all sign a loyalty oath. That same day, thirty-six workers in his department signed such an oath. Soon, other departments issued their own oaths.

Theoretically, workers took the oaths voluntarily, but they knew the threat of investigation and perhaps dismissal if they did not sign.[50]

The controversy particularly swirled around the welfare department. On July 19, a supervisor in the children's division, Naomi Gillespie, resigned after it was learned that her husband had distributed Communist literature. On the same day, resignations came from Louise Gilbert, another welfare supervisor, and Raphie Berman, a consultant. Gilbert, the secretary of the Indiana Committee for Alternatives to War, had supported the Stockholm peace petition, and both women had attended a fund-raising meeting for the Progressive party, featuring Mrs. Paul Robeson, a few months earlier. Their resignations probably prevented their suspensions or dismissals. Everyone else in the welfare department signed a loyalty oath. A month later, the board issued its report about the investigation. It declared that the Communist sympathizers had been rooted out.[51]

When the state legislature convened five months later in January 1951, it was prepared to take bipartisan action against the state's subversives. The most important bill made a crime of subversion, outlawed the Communist party, and barred subversives from public employment. According to one conservative legislator, "we don't want our state to become a refuge, a sanctuary for Communists. We don't want our state to lag behind the others in stamping out" the CP. The house passed the bill without a dissenting vote. Before the senate acted, the *Indianapolis Times* added more fuel to the hostile atmosphere with an exposé of Communist activity in the state. Its front page headline screamed "500 Commies Plot Sabotage in State." It is doubtful that the senate needed such encouragement, for a few days later it passed the bill with only one dissenting vote. The action was symbolic; the state never attempted to enforce the law during this period.[52]

The 1951 action of only symbolic impact shows the difficulty that the loyalty crusaders had in enacting real restrictions. This was confirmed in the 1953 session. Conservative legislators revived the proposal of an un-American activities committee, which had failed in previous sessions. While conservatives wanted a little HUAC, liberals made two counter proposals. The commission should investigate the Ku Klux Klan and the Silver Shirts, and it should have procedural rights for the witnesses, such as the opportunity to cross-examine one's accuser. The house defeated both proposed amendments 63 to 19, and then passed the bill 81 to 7. The senate received the bill four days before the end of the session, and did not vote on it due to the logjam of other bills. The 1953 legislative session therefore showed that the momentum of the Communist issue, which had been strong after the beginning of the Korean War, had now slowed again.[53]

This was confirmed when another controversy, occurring slightly after the end of the session, ended inconclusively. Senator William Jenner, a Republican, charged that Leon Kroll, the painter of three murals in the state senate chamber, belonged to a group on the attorney general's subversive list. When Jenner demanded the removal of the murals, the Senate Advisory Committee began an inquiry. In its report, the Committee admitted that the choice of Kroll to be the painter was "unfortunate," but it found nothing un-American about the murals, which portrayed the state's industry, agriculture, and history. "We're not going to burn great literature, music, and art," the committee unanimously concluded. "That's the favorite trick of the Communists, and we're not going to fall for it."[54]

In the 1955 legislative session, the Communist issue revived slightly though not fully. Conservatives led by the American Legion again proposed the creation of a legislative investigative commission. Its critics argued that the antisubversive effort should be left to the federal authorities, especially the FBI, but the house passed the bill by a 71–6 vote. Yet just as in 1953, the senate received the proposal only a few days before the end of the session, and never voted on it due to greater concern about other bills.[55]

Conservative legislators were more successful when the target was more specific. In late January 1955, a CIO official charged that Victor Pasche, a lobbyist for the United Electrical Workers (UE), was a Communist. Since the CIO had expelled the UE for alleged Communist domination in 1950, the two unions had been bitter rivals. The CIO official sent a list of Pasche's activities and affiliations to several legislators. Before the Senate Internal Security Subcommittee (SISS), Pasche had taken the Fifth Amendment about his Communist membership, although he presently denied his affiliation. One legislator suggested an investigation of Pasche, and another formally proposed that all lobbyists sign a loyalty oath, declaring that they neither had been a Communist nor had used the Fifth Amendment on questions of political affiliation. In a hearing on the loyalty oath bill, Pasche condemned legislative committees like the SISS for exercising "tyranny by headline." He urged the legislators to judge him by his activities, "not gossip." The UE lobbyist refused to state if he had been a Communist, and this refusal ensured the passage of the oath bill. The house passed it 75–7, and the senate also gave it overwhelming approval 40–3.[56]

In Indiana, the Red Scare was formed by both local and national developments. The 1946 probe of professors defused the Communist issue for several years because the charges were so unfounded. The Korean War changed the political atmosphere. Executive action caused the dismissal and resignation of a few employees, and the 1951 legislature outlawed the CP with only one dissenting vote. The legislature's action nevertheless was symbolic in some ways. The state never prosecuted anyone for subversive activities, and the legislature even refused to create an un-American activities committee. Only another local incident, the Victor Pasche incident of 1955, reawakened the legislature from its usual somnambulant state.

Indiana acted on the Communist issue therefore in a sporadic manner.

Its two major actions of 1951 and 1955 were interspersed with periods of relative calm. Its limited output was caused primarily by local factors. Although a state Commmunist party existed, it was weaker and less flamboyant than the party in large metropolitan areas such as Cleveland, Chicago, and Detroit. It thus caused less of a reaction. Another cause of the legislature's inactivity was its own short session of sixty-one days, the shortest in the Midwest. The short session meant that fewer external events would occur to energize the legislators and that bills would more likely become caught in a last-minute logjam. Finally, the legislators' conservatism also helped to restrain its output of antisubversive bills. Conservatives' desire for a balanced budget conflicted with proposals to fund a legislative investigating commission. Realizing this, the American Legion once offered to fund the commission itself, but the legislature rebuffed the suggestion. In 1957, the legislature finally did create such a commission, but it did not appropriate any funds. The commission was limited to attending a HUAC hearing and writing a general report on the evils of Communism.[57] It had no impact on leftist activity or on the legislature. In conclusion, national factors helped to form the Scare, but local developments limited it in Indiana.

Summary

Midwestern state politics in the postwar decade confirms the existence of a conservative movement, composed primarily of Republicans, dedicated to the restriction of Communists and leftists.[58] This GOP leadership had mixed effects in the states because of their different approaches. Some, such as Governor Kim Sigler of Michigan and Senator Paul Broyles of Illinois, made reckless accusations that hurt the momentum of the loyalty crusade. Other Republican leaders, such as the head of the Ohio Un-American Activities Committee, used more restraint and won more victories as a result. Yet these differences in rhetoric should not mask similarities in objective and motivation. In each state, conservative Republicans worked hard to promote their brand of Americanism. Those GOP leaders who believed in the internal Communist threat joined with those who only realized the electoral viability of the Communist issue. Midwestern state politics, therefore, confirms the antipluralist theory, which finds the greatest support for McCarthy among conservative Republicans.

This state political activity also reveals a liberal movement. This response to the Red Scare was not only weaker but also less coherent than the conservative one. Its greatest strength was in Wisconsin and Illinois, but opponents of the loyalty crusade appeared in every state, reciting the liberal critique. Yet with the possible exception of in Wisconsin, liberals remained on the defensive throughout the Midwest. Governor G. Mennen Williams' actions in the summer of 1950 provide a classic example of this. He first refused to let the legislative special session, dominated by Republicans, consider loyalty proposals. He then agreed to allow consideration but harshly criticized the GOP measures. Finally, the governor endorsed all the bills that the legislature passed. Williams' actions seem to contradict the strong determination of Stevenson in Illinois, but actually both men had a basic liberal outlook. Both believed that government was the agency to solve social problems, just as it had done in the Depression. Their support for an activist government differed only over whether that agency entrusted with the loyalty effort should be the federal government alone (as Stevenson believed) or a federal-state partnership (as Williams supported by the summer of 1950). Because of this division, liberals did not have as coherent a movement as the conservatives. Yet their responses to the Scare differed enough from the conservatives to form a separate movement.

Conservative efforts to impose the Red Scare had definite effects. The loyalty campaign had successes in two goals. First, some laws claimed real victims, usually people associated with the CP. Ohio's Un-American Activities Committee had the most obvious effectiveness in questioning more than forty people. Some lost their jobs; others had to endure a lengthy appeal process before they were cleared of contempt charges; and a few were jailed for their defiance. Michigan's Callahan Commission and the Illinois SAIC directly threatened Wayne University, and the University of Chicago and Roosevelt College, respectively. Other laws affecting public employees, such as Ohio's requirement that teachers testify before legislative committees, also caused dismissals. These laws also carried a second, more subtle meaning. Laws are enacted not only to create public order but also to legitimize political norms. These antisubversive laws, in other words, played a symbolic role in condemning Communist beliefs and activities.

Yet it is impossible to measure repression exactly—and possible to overestimate the damage. Although some states enacted laws and prosecuted individuals, other states did not. "Little HUACs," for example, did not exist everywhere, nor were the ones established long-lasting. Some states, such as Indiana, never attempted to enforce their laws. The federal courts furthermore blocked some efforts at enforcement. Just as these overt restrictions had some limits, so did the effort to reinforce a general negative feeling toward reform activities. During these years, reformers won control of the Democratic party in Michigan and Wisconsin, and they began an ultimately successful campaign to control state politics. None of these caveats deny the existence of repression. They merely suggest that repression did not operate in a uniform or total manner.

The analysis of the Scare in the Midwest clarifies the relationship between federal activities and state developments. Both Robert Griffith and Robert Goldstein have theorized that "federal law and precedent and . . . national leaders" played the determining role in forming the Scare.[59] Their model might be visualized as follows:

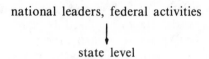

national leaders, federal activities

state level

These chapters have pointed to the weaknesses of the Griffith-Goldstein theory. It is erroneous to search for origins of the Scare in the actions of a single national politician, even President Truman, or even in the variety of federal antisubversive activities. Instead, two sets of interactions should be posited. First, a conservative and a liberal movement existed. These loose alliances of voluntary organizations affected the national and the state levels simultaneously. Their primary strength derived from the diffused and nonideological character of the two political parties. Secondly, the national and the state levels interacted. It is not necessary to repeat the experiences in each state in order to conclude that they clearly exhibited both similarities and differences. The influence of federal activities on the state level, contrary to Griffith and Goldstein, was not a consistent phenomenon or always the determining factor in forming the Scare. Rather, the pattern of the Communist issue at the state level was set by the interactions of various factors.[60]

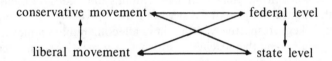

conservative movement   federal level

liberal movement   state level

This emphasis on the federalist character of American politics parallels the general thesis offered by Samuel Patterson:

> Obviously the states are highly influenced by national policy, and politics in the United States has become increasingly nationalized. Yet, the states can be treated for analytic purposes as relatively independent political systems with political cultures at least somewhat distinctive to themselves.[61]

In other words, Griffith and Goldstein's emphasis on the similarities should not mask the differences that the states show. The complexity of the Red Scare is more important than neatly tying up all the loose threads.

3

Local Level: Elections and Government

If Paul Broyles and Matthew Callahan are little remembered today, then even more forgotten are Thomas Coleman, Henry Bettman, and Albert Kauffman. These "unknown" people, and others like them, played parts in the Red Scare on the local level. It is a drama rarely examined. The next three chapters will examine the local level: elections and government, schools and libraries, and voluntary organizations, respectively.

This chapter analyzes city elections and governental actions that were influenced by the Red Scare. After a brief survey of small towns and medium-sized cities, it focuses on three larger cities, Detroit, Chicago, and Cincinnati. With some minor variations, each city experienced similar controversies touching political leaders and city workers.

	Election issue	Investigation of city employees	United Public Workers	Loyalty oath
Detroit	x	x	x	
Chicago	x		x	x
Cincinnati	x	x		x

Detroit had a bitter mayoral campaign in 1945; launched its own loyalty commission in 1949; probed tenants of the Detroit Housing Commission; and broke the United Public Workers (UPW), a left-wing union. In Chicago, the Communist issue arose in the 1947 mayoral election over a proposed loyalty oath for employees of the Chicago Housing Authority, and concerning recognition for the leftist UPW. Cincinnati experienced the Scare in various elections from 1947 to 1953 and in a loyalty oath controversy.[1]

In each city, the conservative movement, led by Republicans and the press, worked to establish the restrictive climate. They magnified the small contingent of radicals—and sometimes even included moderates and liberals—into a dangerous threat to the social and political order. Although the conservatives usually succeeded, they nevertheless met counterpressures in these large metropolitan areas. Not every candidate or party who used the

Communist issue won; not every restriction against "subversives" was enacted; not every suspected city worker was dismissed. The variations in the pattern point to the significance of local factors, while the similarities reflect broader patterns.

In contrast to large cities such as Detroit, Chicago, and Cincinnati, the loyalty issue was rarely controversial in small and medium-sized towns. Because of their greater homogeneity, smaller cities had fewer potential targets of attack. Throughout the Midwest, these city governments confronted the Communist issue, but usually passed symbolic measures with little or no overt effect.

Smaller cities gave consensus approval to various types of loyalty proposals. In January 1949, the city council of Saginaw, Michigan, quickly passed a loyalty oath for its six-hundred employees. The only debate concerned whether to use the specific term "Communist" or the more general description of those favoring the violent overthrow of the government. The council decided to accept the latter term. In June 1949, the city council of Columbus, Ohio, unanimously passed a loyalty oath for its employees and officials, even though no one could cite any suspected leftists or subversives. The same occurred in Lorain, Ohio, in February 1950. In September 1950, Wyandotte, Michigan, unanimously required a loyalty oath from its public employees. The city's newspaper found the action distinctly unnewsworthy and buried the resolution in a list of city council proceedings on an inside page. In a few places, such as Evanston, Illinois, in January 1951 and Indianapolis in June 1951, the mayor issued an executive order for a loyalty oath.

A few cities attempted to take sterner action against subversives. Lafayette, Indiana, made it illegal to advocate communism within the city, and soon thereafter Wabash and Terre Haute enacted similar restrictions. In each case, the punishment was 180 days in jail and a $500 fine. Yet even these measures were symbolic. The *Terre Haute Star* reported the resolution's enactment in a bottom paragraph on a story about the city council's debate on gambling. In small and medium-sized towns, loyalty proposals just did not generate much debate or controversy. No one was ever prosecuted or dismissed. The law's enactment was an easy way for the town leaders to declare their Americanism. Loyalty in these towns was not an issue; it was already assumed.[2]

On rare occasions, medium-sized cities experienced brief controversies over restrictions. Such incidents occurred in Peoria, Illinois; Indianapolis, and Evansville, Indiana. The Peoria controversy involved the visit of Paul Robeson, the noted black singer and leftist, in April 1947. Three days before the concert, a columnist for the *Peoria Star* claimed that Robeson included Communist songs and speeches in his performance. Outraged by this information, conservatives, led by an American Legion post, worked to stop the concert. An alderman characterized the upcoming appearance as "a direct insult to our boys who fought and died for the principles of America." The city council then unanimously passed a resolution, sponsored by the alderman, that condemned the appearance of "any artist or speaker who is an avowed propagandist for un-American ideologies." The concert's sponsor decided to cancel the performance. A few of Robeson's supporters requested the use of the city hall for a reception in his honor, but the mayor rejected this proposal. Robeson came to the city on schedule but only spoke at a private home to his few supporters.[3]

Such controversies in medium-sized cities at other times did not result in definite restrictions. In September 1950, an Indianapolis councilman proposed that all Communists register with the city clerk and pay a peace bond of $1,000. He denied that the city had to wait on federal authorities to take such action, especially since the country was at war. After other councilmen expressed doubts about the measure's constitutionality, the council referred it to the city's legal counsel. When the counsel confirmed the critics' doubts, the council tabled the measure. At the same time, Evansville, Indiana, experienced a similar incident. An ad hoc group proposed making it illegal for Communists "to enter, reside, or work" in the city. The council passed the measure, but the mayor vetoed it because of its unconstitutionality.[4] These incidents in Peoria, Indianapolis, and Evansville were exceptions to the general rule that municipal actions in small and medium-sized cities were consensus decisions with only symbolic effect.

Detroit

Red Scare controversies tended to occur in larger cities, such as Detroit. In the Motor City, the Communist issue had arisen in the 1930s, but after 1945 it re-emerged with renewed intensity. Although initially the Scare affected liberal politicians in the 1945 mayoral campaign, basically the targets were individual leftists. Detroit was unique in creating its own Loyalty Investigating Commission (LIC), which formally accused one city worker of subversive activities and pressured others. Conservatives also broke a leftist union for city employees, the United Public Workers, and evicted radical tenants from city-owned buildings. After the 1945 election, all of this restrictive activity occurred during a protracted convulsion between 1949 and 1952.

In Detroit, the Communist issue dominated the first mayoral election after the end of the Second World War. The incumbent used the issue to put his challenger, a CIO official, on the defensive. The press vigorously supported this effort. The city conducted its local elections on a nonpartisan basis, and it did not have a strong local machine like Chicago (Democratic) or Cincinnati (Republican).

The mild mayoral primary during the summer of 1945 did not give a preview of the general election. The incumbent mayor, Edward J. Jeffries, Jr., was challenged by Richard Frankensteen, the vice-president of the United Auto Workers (UAW-CIO), and by James Friel, the county auditor. The two challengers severely criticized Jeffries' handling of many city services, especially garbage collection, bus service, and education. Their criticisms found some response from the voters. In the August 7th primary, Frankensteen polled 44% of the vote, Jeffries 37%, and Friel 19%, with the highest two qualifying for the general election in November. Friel's supporters would probably back Frankensteen since both candidates had been critical of Jeffries. Yet, since only twenty-six percent of the electorate voted in the primary, Jeffries could still win the race if he could create a larger turn-out.[5]

Frankensteen's major strength lay in his position as a UAW-CIO official and the union's active support for his campaign. Soon after the August primary, he received an endorsement from the Wayne County Democratic Committee, which had been influenced by the UAW. This support was not without its price, however, since the election was held on a nonpartisan basis. Jeffries pictured Frankensteen as a tool of narrow, partisan interests, while claiming that only he could represent all citizens. Jeffries' charge put Frankensteen on the defensive, a position that intensified during a wave of CIO strikes that occurred in September and October after the war's end. At various times, Ford had to shut down; General Motors had to lay off workers; the city had to curtail its bus service; and other strikes hit smaller factories. The press interpreted the strikes as selfish actions, and the public anger put Frankensteen and the CIO officials in a dilemma. On the one hand, the union supported the strikes, even though the public backlash hurt Frankensteen. On the other hand, the CIO wanted its candidate to win.[6]

Jeffries played this dilemma both ways. At plant gates, he distributed to CIO members a pamphlet entitled "Spending Our Dues for Frankensteen's Deal":

> Why should union officers and paid organizers spend their time in electioneering for Frankensteen, when they are supposed to take care of workers' grievances? . . . Instead of throwing union funds into the election campaign, this money should be kept in reserve as a strike fund.

To other Detroit citizens, Jeffries emphasized the danger of the union controlling the city. When the Communist party and the Socialist Workers party endorsed Frankensteen, Jeffries exploited the issue of a radical take-over of the city, and made it his dominant topic for the remainder of the campaign. He continually asserted that Frankensteen would use Detroit "as a guinea pig . . . to try out many crackpot and new-fangled ideas."

Reminding audiences of the CP endorsement, Jeffries claimed that "PAC bosses in New York and Washington" wanted to control the city in order to start a social and economic uprising. Detroit would become "a battleground of class warfare," the first step in a national revolution, Jeffries warned.[7]

Jeffries' attacks found echoes on the far Right and in the press. Gerald L. K. Smith, a prominent right-wing spokesman who lived in the city, spoke repeatedly during the campaign. He found Communists and subversives throughout Frankensteen's supporters and viewed Jeffries as the city's last hope for salvation. A few suburban newspapers owned by Floyd McGriff made similar changes:

> [This election] is being manipulated by some of the most sinister forces ever permitted to operate. . . . The Communist-backed candidate, Richard Frankensteen, is a foxy playboy of Stalin's gang. . . . Voters who want to see the hands of Russian Quislings kept out of managing Detroit will be aroused to get out the American vote.

The larger newspapers were only slightly more restrained, and criticized Frankensteen as either a radical or a dupe. According to the *Detroit Free Press*, outsiders and union bosses were attempting to end freedom and create tyranny in the city. The police would be turned into a goon squad in order to force acceptance of Frankensteen's policies, the paper predicted. The *Detroit Times* viewed Frankensteen's campaign as a radical effort to establish "a one-party system" oriented toward "Communist theories."[8]

To this boiling pot was added the issue of race. In the middle of the campaign, the Detroit Housing Commission (DHC) reaffirmed its policy to maintain "the racial characteristics of a neighborhood." Frankensteen, who had swept ninety percent of the black vote in the primary, was urged by black leaders to skirt the segregation policy as an issue. Although they were angry at the ruling, especially since a housing shortage existed, they remembered the 1943 riot, feared another white backlash, and decided to focus on Frankensteen's election. The issue could not be ignored though. Jeffries openly supported the DHC policy, and his assertions of a social revolution subtly used the racial issue without being openly racist. Some of his supporters chose to exploit the issue. According to the McGriff newspapers, Frankensteen's black advisors included one of the "most active Communist front figures in America." Anonymous cards and pamphlets predicting a black invasion if Frankensteen won were widely distributed in white neighborhoods. Some were supposedly from Frankensteen's camp:

Negroes Can Live Anywhere
In Any Area—Any Section of Detroit
WITH FRANKENSTEEN MAYOR
Negroes—Do Your Duty Nov. 6

As recommended by his advisors, Frankensteen tried to sidestep the issue. He favored a program of increased housing which would presumably end the racial conflicts without ending white neighborhoods.[9]

At the campaign's end, Frankensteen remained on the defensive. Pamphlets accusing him of being Jewish were distributed in Protestant neighborhoods, and in Jewish areas, he was accused of friendship with the anti-Semitic Father Charles Coughlin. Frankensteen desperately attacked Jeffries as reactionary and fascist, terming him Gerald L. K. Jeffries. Instead of presenting a coherent program, Frankensteen used his final campaign appearances and newspaper ads to refute his opponent's charges. He denied his Communist affiliation and any desire to fill city offices with CIO officials or Communists. On November 6, Jeffries won a fourth term with fifty-six percent of the vote. "A Challenge Was Met: Detroit Remains Free," trumpeted the *Free Press*.[10]

Jeffries' successful campaign appealed primarily to whites and non-CIO members. He swept the upper and middle classes, and also won endorsements from rival unions, the AFL and the Teamsters. His eight years as councilman and six years as mayor gave him a recognized name and the endorsement of "Establishment" groups. Support also came from the three major newspapers, which were crucial in airing and prolonging some of the charges during the campaign. In retrospect, it is doubtful that Jeffries needed the Communist issue to win. His use of it and his tacit acceptance of those who exploited it even further reveals his realization of its viability. He had seen its effectiveness in the 1937 mayor's race, and had used it himself in 1943. It was another weapon designed to make people vote against Frankensteen. A close race turned into a fairly comfortable victory.[11] Once elected, Jeffries ignored the Communist issue, and did not establish any regulations to ensure loyalty in the city. While he did not further exploit the issue, his campaign pointed the way to other political leaders and the press.

While Detroit in the early postwar years experienced the Scare in the struggle within the CIO, the city government grappled with the issue in the summer of 1949. A controversy surrounding one public employee touched off a chain of events, which led to the peak of the Scare. In this three-year period, the city took various restrictive steps, including the establishment of a committee to investigate all city workers, the disruption of the United Public Workers, and the formal "trial" of one employee.

The initial loyalty controversy was touched off by George Shenkar, a twenty-four-year-old city worker in the Water Commission. In December 1948, Shenkar passed the written exam to become an assistant mechanical engineer for the Water Commission, but was denied the position because of his identification as a Communist. Shenkar appealed to the Civil Service Commission (CSC), but at the hearing refused to answer if he was a Communist. He denied that he favored the overthrow of the government, and maintained that he would defend the U.S. if it was attacked. The CSC upheld the Water Commission's ruling, and the case went to the Detroit Common Council, where Shenkar again refused to answer the crucial question about his affiliation. The council ordered its legal counsel to find a way to fire the employee. The city had no obvious grounds to dismiss Shenkar because the City Charter prohibited discrimination on the basis of political beliefs.[12]

Although the city already had a police "red squad" and a loyalty oath for city employees, the Shenkar case created momentum for new restrictions on subversives. The Civil Service Commission secretary, Donald Sublette, claimed that at least 150 Communists or sympathizers held city jobs. When asked to document his assertion, Sublette was forced to admit that the figure was one-half percent of all city workers. Even then, his arithmetic was incorrect for the actual figure would have been fifteen radicals. Nevertheless, the newspapers urged action, decrying the debate over the precise number of Communists. The *Free Press* wanted Shenkar's dismissal and further investigations. The *Times* declared that any Communist or anyone who refused to declare his political affiliations forfeited the right to a hearing or probation. The *News* urged an amendment to the City Charter that would permit the dismissal of Communists and would establish a permanent loyalty board. On July 7, 1949, Mayor Eugene I. Van Antwerp named a three-member committee, chaired by Police Chief Harry S. Toy, to draft an amendment to the City Charter that would force the dismissal of disloyal persons. Less than two weeks had passed since Shenkar's hearing before the Civil Service Committee.[13]

The council charged ahead on its own. Charles G. Oakman proposed his own amendment to create a loyalty board to investigate "unfriendly and hostile" city employees. Councilman Edward Connor argued that such a vague proposal would create a "thought police." He urged a public hearing, but his suggestion was defeated. The mayor's commission reported that thirty-four Communists or sympathizers held city jobs, and it agreed with Oakman for the need of a permanent loyalty board. On July 13, Oakman and Connor met for four hours and Oakman agreed to drop his vague language from the proposed amendment. For example, the term "unfriendly and hostile" employees was discarded in favor of "those seeking to alter the government by unconstitutional means." George Edwards, a liberal and council president, also wrote a draft amendment that included various guarantees for the defendant, including the right to cross-examine the accuser. On July 15, the council unanimously passed the loyalty amendment based on the Edwards' draft. Citizens would vote on its ratification on September 13, the date of the mayoral primary.[14]

This schedule became scrambled when Governor G. Mennen Williams, a Democrat, vetoed the proposed loyalty amendment on August 8. According to the governor, the amendment unconstitutionally delegated legislative authority because the council used the attorney general's subversive list as its definition of subversion, rather than making a precise definition of its own. Councilman James H. Garlick angrily charged that the governor was "playing into the hands" of the Communists. The *Free Press* asserted that Williams, a dupe of the CIO and ADA, "does as he is told and so the reds are protected." The council had two alternatives. Either it could override the veto by a two-thirds majority and keep the loyalty amendment on the September ballot, or it could delete the provision and schedule the ratification vote for the general election in November. Although the difference of two months might seem slight, the council debated the issue in a heated session on August 9. On a motion to override the veto, the council tied four to four, and then postponed further action. Three days later, the solution came in the legal counsel's ruling that the governor's veto was illegal. The veto letter had been sent by the governor's legal advisor rather than by the governor himself. Since the act of veto was the sole responsibility of the governor, it could not be delegated to a subordinate, the counsel concluded. In this roundabout way, the loyalty amendment was again set for ratification for September 13.[15]

While the loyalty amendment controversy developed, conservatives also raised the Communist issue against the United Public Workers (UPW-CIO), a left-wing union which had locals in several city departments. Civil Service Secretary Donald Sublette charged that Communists controlled the UPW and warned of possible sabotage. Yale Stuart, the Detroit president of the union, retorted that Sublette only wanted to bust the UPW or at least to obscure the issues of wages and working conditions. Councilman Oakman demanded that Stuart appear before the council to testify if he was a Communist. Reporters questioned other UPW officials, including Margaret Foster, if they were Communists. When Foster refused to answer, her supervisor declared that he would fire her if she did not reply. On the next day, she denied the affiliation. A rival union, local 25 of the State, County, and Municipal Employees (AFL), supported Sublette's charges against the UPW, and urged the Civil Service Commission to refuse to bargain with the UPW. Yale Stuart refused Oakman's demand to appear before the council, and the union's executive board supported him in a vote of confidence. Councilman Edward Connor declared that Stuart was "at least a fellow traveler," and encouraged the union's rank-and-file to oust him. Councilman Oakman wanted a subpoena to force Stuart to come before the council, and his resolution was passed. Stuart avoided the subpoena by temporarily leaving the city. In response, four of the nine council members announced that they would no longer accept Stuart as a bargaining agent for city workers.[16]

Once the council passed the loyalty amendment, the situation for the

UPW only worsened. Several city workers, most of whom were UPW officials, challenged the amendment in court because it violated the City Charter's provision against dismissals for political reasons. The regional UPW president, Mort Furay, decided to run for mayor to help the campaign to defeat the amendment. Such actions only tended to confirm the popular impression that radicals controlled the UPW and that the city should take restrictive measures. Some UPW members quit the union for fear that they would lose their jobs. One local voted to withhold its dues from the state and regional offices until all of the UPW officials signed a loyalty oath.[17]

UPW officials claimed that the city was trying to bust the union, and Stuart began a counterattack. On August 15, he proposed his own loyalty oath:

> My loyalty is pledged to the principles of political, social, and economic democracy. It is pledged to the fight against all those who would restrict or deny those principles. . . . My loyalty belongs to my fellow Americans; it is not for hire to scheming politicians and special interests.

Three days later, Stuart finally went before the Common Council, but the Spanish Civil War veteran refused to answer if he was a Communist. Under heated questioning the next day, Stuart again refused to answer the question. In a compromise move, a councilman suggested that he sign a city loyalty oath, which did not inquire specifically about CP membership but only about organizations that advocated the overthrowing of the government. Stuart agreed to sign, but this did not quiet the UPW controversy. Members continued to quit the union, and a few locals disaffiliated. In December, Stuart resigned his position in an attempt to reverse the union's decline. The UPW's fate was sealed soon afterward when the CIO expelled it for being Communist dominated.[18]

The campaign to ratify the loyalty amendment in September 1949 generated more controversy. The CIO, Federation of Teachers (AFL), and National Lawyers Guild opposed the measure because it was unnecessary and would encourage spies and hysteria. Veterans groups, the Detroit Municipal Employees Association, and the three newspapers supported the proposal. The *News* interpreted the ratification vote as a vote for or against Communism. The *Times* agreed that the only opponents of the amendment were Communists or "suckers for sugar-coated Communist propaganda." Despite Mort Furay's race for mayor, the amendment was not an issue in that campaign because all four major candidates endorsed the proposal. On September 13, 1949, the amendment passed easily, receiving over seventy-five percent of the vote. It did not ensure the election of the mayor, however. Two challengers defeated him.[19]

George Shenkar, the fuse that lit this dynamite, still had his city job.

Waiting for the loyalty amendment to be drafted, passed by the council, and ratified by the voters, the Water Commission had given Shenkar a six-month leave of absence. In January 1950, after the ratification vote, Shenkar asked for an extension of his leave. Before the Civil Service Commission could act on Shenkar's request, the Water Commission fired him for insubordination. The relationship between the city and its employees had been undermined by Shenkar's distribution of literature criticizing the city administration and the Water Commission. The commission's general manager later admitted that it would have been difficult to prove that Shenkar was a Communist. The employee appealed his dismissal, but this was rejected.[20]

A few months later, the outbreak of the Korean War intensified the Scare in the city even more. It brought a censorship policy and the formal "trial" of a city worker. When the war began, the *News* emphasized the need for greater vigilance. In a front page banner headline, it proclaimed that "Unguarded City Utilities Offer Shining Targets for Saboteurs." On July 18, Mayor Albert Cobo approved an increase in the size of the police "red squad." On the same day, Councilman Oakman introduced a resolution to ban newsstands which operated on city property from selling subversive newspapers and magazines. Four newsstands sold the *Michigan Worker*, the CP organ. The Detroit Newspaper Guild, ACLU, and ADA protested that the resolution could lead to police harassment since it lacked a definition of subversive material. Yet, with Oakman calling the *Worker* "treasonable," the council approved the measure seven to one. One news dealer, Izzy Berenson, refused to quit selling the *Worker*. On July 25, the council ordered him off of city property, and when he refused, the police removed his stand.[21]

The Korean War also saw the actual implementation of the loyalty amendment approved in September 1949. The amendment created two separate committees. The Loyalty Investigating Commission (LIC), composed of citizens, investigated the charges against city personnel. Its complaints were heard by the Loyalty Commission, composed of five elected officials. The LIC had not begun its activities because of a pending suit challenging its constitutionality. After the war's outbreak, Mayor Cobo ordered the LIC to begin its investigation of all workers except for the plaintiffs in the suit. The LIC chairman, George Schudlich, encouraged all citizens who had suspicions about a city employee to relay their information to the commission.[22]

In the fall of 1950, the LIC filed its first charges against Thomas J. Coleman, an employee for twenty-three years and a UPW official who had recently led a garbagemen's strike. The proceedings before the Loyalty Commission did contain some legal safeguards for the defendant. He had the right to see written charges against him, to be represented by an attorney, to have a hearing within thirty days after the charges were presented, to know his accusers, to have his attorney cross-examine all witnesses, and to present defense witnesses. On the other hand, the amendment did not specifically define disloyalty, though it referred to membership in an organization on the attorney general's subversive list. Accusers, moreover, could remain anonymous if publicity "would seriously affect security precautions."[23]

Coleman's hearings before the loyalty commission were heated. The accusers—two former Communists, two members of the police "red squad," and one CIO official—charged that Coleman attended meetings of the Progressive party, Civil Rights Congress (CRC), and CP; associated with Communists and subversives; belonged to the UPW, which had been expelled by the CIO for Communist domination; and was a member of two organizations on the attorney general's list, the CRC and the National Negro Labor Congress (NNLC). When Coleman's attorney cross-examined the accusers, they all admitted that they did not have any direct evidence that Coleman belonged to the party. Coleman denied ever being a Communist, and maintained that his associates were not disloyal. The CIO's expulsion of the UPW was not based on its Communist domination, he declared, but on the issue of local union autonomy. He acknowledged close ties with the CRC and NNLC, but he doubted that he held current membership. The charges against him were false or misleading, he concluded. Seven character witnesses, including two prominent ministers and the editor of a black newspaper, confirmed Coleman's loyalty and integrity. After several weeks of deliberation in early 1951, the Loyalty Commission unanimously found Coleman not guilty of the charges.[24]

Coleman's victory did not slow the LIC's investigations. Shortly after his hearing ended, the court ruled against a suit challenging the commission. Soon afterward, the LIC proposed that it be given subpoena power, and the city council approved. On April 2, 1951, the voters ratified the amendment with more than seventy percent approval. Coleman's victory did not clear the UPW either. The final nail was driven into the union's coffin when Councilman Oakman sponsored a resolution which barred it from any negotiations with the city. With little debate, the council passed this on April 20, 1951.[25]

With only a slight pause, the Scare continued to claim new victims. Less than a year after the UPW ban, the city evicted two leftist tenants, and after a HUAC visit, pressured a city worker to resign and revoked the tax-exempt status of a few groups that had rented their buildings to "subversive" groups. The conservatives' only defeat came in an attempt to remove paintings from the Detroit Art Institute.

Besides its own employees, the city also had control over the tenants who lived in its subsidized low-income housing. Beginning in February 1952, public controversy swirled around the Detroit Housing Commission (DHC) and one of its tenants, William Allan, an admitted Communist. The reporter for the *Michigan Worker* had lived in city-owned housing for six years, with part of his rent being paid by the city. The DHC assistant director criticized this arrangement, but declared that the DHC could not take action against Allan since he satisfied the regulations. Other leftists had been evicted because they had not followed the requirements, but the apartment manager admitted that Allan had been a model tenant. "I watch that fellow like a hawk, but he never makes a slip. He pays his rent on the day it is due, and keeps his place neat and clean."[26]

On February 15, 1952, Councilman Oakman introduced a resolution barring Communists from public housing. DHC officials indicated that they suspected only five or six tenants. They met with officials from the Federal Housing Authority and the Office of Rent Stabilization, but confessed that they could not "find some loophole for evicting Allan." The Detroit Common Council nevertheless adopted the Oakman resolution and promised to pay for the court costs when Allan challenged its constitutionality. Several days later, the DHC gave a thirty-day eviction notice to Allan and to Gustave Jurist, who had been named as a Communist before HUAC three days earlier. Jurist, the president of the Detroit Public Housing Tenants Council, had recently led a successful fight against a proposed twenty percent rent increase. The eviction notice was not based on either city or federal regulations, but on a state statute which allowed eviction "with or without cause." Allan and Jurist challenged the action, but several months later the courts upheld the DHC's action.[27]

The HUAC hearings at which Jurist had been identified as a Communist took place in Detroit beginning in late February 1952. Sensationalized by the press, the hearings generated the last restrictive action taken by the city government. Only one city employee, Mildred Franklin, was identified as a Communist before HUAC. The secretary in the Department of Purchases and Supplies had signed the city's loyalty oath and worked hard according to her supervisor. The LIC felt that it had sufficient evidence against her, and filed for a hearing before the Loyalty Commission. Rather than fighting the charge in a public hearing, Franklin resigned on the next day.[28]

One county employee, Frank Novak, was also identified as a subversive. The clerk for a probate judge found his private life disrupted. He received almost 100 telephone calls a day, most of them abusive; acquaintances avoided or snubbed him and his wife; and children taunted his son at school. The Civil Service Commission began an inquiry, and on January 29, 1953, Wayne Salisbury, a former Communist working for the state police, testified that in 1945 Novak spoke to an organization that was later listed as subversive. Novak confessed no memory of the incident, questioned how he should have known the group's affiliation, and denied being a Communist. Shortly afterward, the Civil Service Commission cleared him, and HUAC expunged his name from its report.[29]

In the suburb of Dearborn, the city dismissed John Gallo from the recreation commission after he invoked the Fifth Amendment before HUAC. A fireman, Daniel Zahari, was also named as a Communist, but he did not appear before HUAC. The Dearborn Civil Service Commission investigated the case, and Zahari agreed to sign a new loyalty oath that he had never been a CP member. On that basis, he retained his job. Shortly afterward, the city council voted to require a loyalty oath from all city employees. They signed the oath on "Loyalty Day," which featured a parade and the crowning of "Miss Loyalty."[30]

The HUAC proceedings also prompted the Detroit Common Council to act on two separate loyalty issues. "Friendly" witnesses before HUAC had identified the buildings where Communists had met, and the city determined the organizations that owned the buildings. At the same time, the council was considering a proposed tax break to charitable and fraternal groups. On March 19, 1952, the council denied a tax reduction to four groups that had rented their halls to subversive groups, and warned six other clubs never to rent their facilities again.[31]

On the same day, Councilman Eugene I. Van Antwerp, the former mayor, proposed that the murals painted by Diego Rivera, the Mexican artist, at the Detroit Institute of Art be "ripped off or covered up" because they were "pure Communist symbolism." Another councilman disagreed, and termed them "beautiful religious paintings." The council referred the resolution to the Arts Committee, a four-member citizens group. The director of the Detroit Institute of Art, warning against hysteria, noted that a similar controversy had erupted in 1933 when the murals were first installed. The murals were fine art, he argued, portraying Detroit as a modern city based on technology and mass production. He also indicated that the murals were the institute's most famous and most valuable possession. The *Free Press* felt that the murals were Communist propaganda, but argued against taking them down because they should be viewed as "a historical curiosity— an example of the shallow thinking that was so prevalent in the country a decade or so ago." On March 25, 1952, the Arts Committee defended the murals in its report, and later the council agreed to keep them.[32]

The mural affair reveals a desperate search for new ways to prove one's loyalty, but it also points out that most councilmen refused to be led down that path. Having broken the UPW, established the LIC, and continued to fund the police "red squad," they were now willing to withdraw from the hunt a bit. Naturally, surveillance of leftist citizens and public employees continued unabated. The "red squad" watched leftist activities in the community, such as a rally supporting clemency for the Rosenbergs on December 20, 1952. The police not only identified those in attendance, but also listed the license plates of fifty cars "in the immediate vicinity" in order to widen their net. The LIC brought no new cases before the Loyalty

Commission for the remainder of the postwar decade, but it continued to check everyone who became certified for employment by the Civil Service Commission. If the person was identified in its files in any way, the LIC would subject the person to a full investigation. The committee performed fifty such inquiries in 1953 and sixty-two in 1954, which indicates either the immense efforts of Communists to obtain public employment or the huge number of files on non-Communists. The LIC claimed that its activities also forced the resignations of several city workers.[33]

Another indication of the LIC's continuing effort to ensure loyalty came in a controversy involving public school teachers. In January 1953, the Senate Internal Security Subcommittee (SISS) issued its report on subversive influences in education. The only reference to Detroit was that "Communist activity took place among teachers in . . . Detroit" and other cities. No elaboration nor any date was given. The statement was probably based on testimony given by Bella Dodd, a former Communist, and concerned a prior period. In relating the SISS report, the *News* also interviewed anonymous LIC officials. The result was a sensationalized front page story with the headline: "150 Suspected as Reds in City School System." The Detroit Teachers Association and Federation of Teachers (AFL) cried foul, and the Board of Education requested the names of the suspects. The LIC admitted that it had some files, but announced that it could neither disclose the names nor investigate the charges because the teachers were not city employees. It announced that the files had been generated only as a by-product of other inquiries, and were not intended to prove disloyalty. By this time, even the *News* urged disclosure of the suspects' names, and liberals criticized the LIC as irresponsible. The Board of Education created an ad hoc group—its own legal advisor, the police commissioner, and the Wayne University provost—to inspect the files of SISS and HUAC. Their report indicated that the federal committees had no proof of Communist activity against any Detroit teacher. While the incident gave the LIC a black eye, it did not generate any efforts toward its abolition. The Red Scare had been institutionalized in the city.[34]

During the postwar decade in Detroit, the conservative movement won notable successes, particularly Jeffries' victory in 1945, the creation of the LIC, and the evictions of Allan and Jurist. Their defeats were relatively minor. In these controversies, the press significantly aided the conservative cause by sensationalizing the security threat. The development of the Scare was influenced by both local events, such as the George Shenkar case, and national developments, such as the Korean War and HUAC.

Chicago

In Chicago, the Red Scare affected political and governmental activity in a more sporadic manner. The Communist issue occurred in three unconnected incidents: an election campaign in 1947, a union recognition dispute in 1951, and a loyalty oath controversy in late 1952. In the first case, Republican "outs" used the loyalty issue in the mayoral campaign, but unlike in Detroit, were unsuccessful. More successfully, the county welfare department broke a UPW local, and the Chicago Housing Authority required a loyalty oath of its employees. These incidents were generated by the conservative movement, led by the Republican party, the American Legion, the *Chicago Tribune*, and the *Chicago Herald-American*, a Hearst newspaper.

The 1947 mayoral campaign featured the Communist issue. A few months earlier, the Republicans had made significant gains in the congressional elections in the Chicago area, and this buoyed their hopes for the spring mayoral election. The losses shook the Democratic machine, and partially as a result, the party selected an outsider, Martin Kennelly, as its mayoral nominee. In the campaign, the Republicans used the loyalty issue in two ways. First, GOP leaders stressed that the race had national significance. Russell W. Root, the Republican candidate, argued that a Democratic defeat would send a message to President Truman to quit coddling the Communists at home and abroad. According to Root, the election was "a referendum on the question of this country's appeasement of Russia." GOP speakers repeatedly warned of the danger to the country if the Democrats won the local election.[35]

The Republicans also used the Communist issue on local issues in the campaign. The Republican governor of the state claimed that Communists actively supported the Democratic candidate. According to the state auditor, the Chicago Democrats exhibited "un-American and un-Christian conduct." Root charged that Kennelly had not repudiated Communist support, and challenged him to do so. The former American Legion national commander asserted that Kennelly's supporters included the Independent Voters of Illinois (IVI), which was led by "starry-eyed pacifists, party liners, and communist sympathizers." If Kennelly became mayor, he would make the IVI president the head of the board of education, where he could use the school system for subversive propaganda. As election day drew near, Root continually interpreted the election as a referendum "for or against Communism." Echoing this, Senator Wayland Brooks concluded that the election would "determine whether representative government will survive in the world." For his part, Kennelly rejected all claims that national issues had any significance, and he focused on other local issues and on strengthening the Democratic machine. On April 1, 1947, Root received more votes than any previous Republican candidate, but Kennelly won the race with fifty-nine percent of the vote. His easy victory was caused by his personal integrity and the power of the Democratic organization. Although the Republicans used similar attacks in later elections, the Communist issue never reached the same intensity in a political campaign.[36]

The Scare was used more successfully against the United Public

Workers (UPW), even though the conservatives never proved its disloyal sympathies. The left-wing union, which the CIO had expelled in March 1950, still had a local in Cook County Bureau of Public Welfare. This group included one-third of the case work staff and even some supervisors. In January 1951, its immunity ended when the *Chicago Tribune* launched an attack. The paper charged that welfare workers who belonged to the UPW put Communists on the rolls and stirred up loyal recipients against the county. It recommended the dismissal of all UPW members. American Legion officials, especially Ellidor Libonati, followed up the *Tribune's* story and filed a complaint against the local with the Cook County Board of Commissioners. Libonati's information might have come from a former UPW official, then working for a rival public employees' union affiliated with the AFL.[37]

The conservatives had a difficult time in proving their charges. In a Commissioners' hearing, welfare director Joseph Moss denied that the local was a subversive organization, and proclaimed his satisfaction with the ability and dedication of his staff. The Legion officials attacked Moss for allowing the UPW to use welfare offices for its meetings and to post notices, such as one concerning the Warsaw Peace Conference, on the bulletin board in their office. Irate, the commissioners ordered Moss to keep the UPW from using county property. They referred the other charges of Communist affiliation and sympathy to the state's attorney, who later refused to confirm them in a legal opinion. He concluded that while the CIO had expelled the union for being under Communist domination, the attorney general had not listed it as a subversive organization. The commissioners asked the attorney general to make a determination on the union's loyalty, but this request was denied.[38]

In the meantime, a Republican state legislator from Chicago introduced a resolution to investigate the welfare program and the UPW. Both houses quickly passed the proposal, which established a commission of five senators and five representatives. Its report, issued on May 15, 1951, revealed nothing new. It alleged that the national UPW was subversive, primarily because of its expulsion by the CIO, and the local was subversive because of its support for the UPW national organization. It found no conclusive evidence that any member of the UPW local was subversive. The commission urged a further investigation by the county commissioners.[39]

A few weeks later, the UPW local officials made their defense to the commissioners at a public hearing. They argued that the UPW had not been expelled from the CIO for any Communist leanings and that none of its national officers were disloyal. Other UPW locals had come under similar attacks, they acknowledged, but theirs was an autonomous unit composed of competent employees who should not be judged by their relationship to other UPW locals or to the national office. They helped a few persons accused of being subversive only because of union brotherhood, and they allowed an allegedly subversive organization to use their meeting hall only for the rent. The officials denied authorizing the notice about the Warsaw Peace Conference. Although the local's defense had been strong, it could not alter the political climate which associated leftist activity with Communism and disloyalty.[40]

Two months later in September 1951, the commissioners cut the Gordian knot. They decided to skip the factual question of the disloyalty of the local's members and even the relationship of the local to the national UPW. Without giving a reason, they ordered the welfare director to break off all relations with the local, which he did. The commissioners did not dismiss any employees affiliated with the UPW, but the conservatives had made their point.[41]

While the UPW controversy found the county commissioners united, a loyalty oath controversy split the board of the Chicago Housing Authority in December 1952. In accordance with federal requirements, the board required a loyalty oath for its 8,500 tenants. The furor erupted when a CHA board member cited some previous attacks on the employees as subversives,[42] and proposed a loyalty oath for the agency's staff. Other board members protested that an oath would be ineffective, and they defeated the resolution three to two. The American Legion, *Chicago Tribune*, and *Chicago Herald-American* protested the oath's defeat, and the resolution was resubmitted to the board. Its legal counsel declared his opposition to the proposed oath. It was unconstitutional because it would penalize unknowing membership in a subversive organization. As a result, on December 22, the CHA board again defeated the oath three to two.[43]

The American Legion intensified its pressure, especially on the CHA chairman, Wayne McMillen, a professor at the University of Chicago. McMillen, who had been interrogated by the state Seditious Activities Investigating Commission in 1949, allegedly belonged to many subversive organizations. The Legion passed a resolution that urged the mayor to dismiss McMillen and to investigate the other two board members who had opposed the oath. On December 30, the city council debated the controversy and recommended by a unanimous vote that the CHA pass the oath. As a result, the CHA decided to consider the proposal for the third time. On January 14, 1953, the CHA held a public hearing at which the ACLU, CIO, Independent Voters of Illinois, and American Friends Service Committee criticized the oath as ineffective and as needlessly smearing loyal citizens. A week later, a compromise oath, which only included knowing membership, was introduced and passed by a vote of three to two. Only one employee refused to sign the affidavit. Two months later, McMillen, who had voted for the compromise oath, resigned his position.[44]

In Chicago, the Communist issue did not develop as fully as in Detroit.

The incidents, occurring in 1947, 1951, and late 1952, had no related or continuing effect. The city not only did not create its own investigative commission, but liberals rejected GOP attacks on Kennelly and initially fought against the loyalty oath. Only the conservatives' persistence brought them victories.

Cincinnati

In Cincinnati, the final big city to be examined, the Red Scare featured similar cases: election campaigns, investigation of city workers, and a loyalty oath dispute. Again, the conservative movement was led by Republican leaders and the press. The Scare first appeared in the 1947 and 1949 elections, but sharply intensified in 1950 after an exposé in the *Cincinnati Enquirer* of "Communist" activities. As a result, the city passed a loyalty oath, and HUAC investigated the area's leftists. Three years later, the Republicans sensationalized the Communist associations of a city employee in an effort to win the city council elections, but they were unsuccessful.

Cincinnati's political structure differed from that of Detroit and Chicago. It had a city manager form of government, and the city council elected the mayor. The council itself was elected by proportional representation (PR), a complicated electoral device.[45] The city had adopted this method in the 1920s in an effort to break the power of the Republican machine. In the process, a coalition of Democrats and reform Republicans had formed the Charter group. The Charterites and Republicans both ran nine-member slates for the city council, and independents usually had little chance of getting elected. In elections from 1947 to 1953, Republicans repeatedly used the Communist issue to woo or to scare the Charter Republicans back into the traditional GOP fold.

The Communist issue emerged strongly in the 1947 council campaign when the Republicans sponsored a referendum on the repeal of PR. GOP leaders warned that PR could be used by subversives and Communists since council members did not need to obtain a majority, but only the quota, to be elected. A minority therefore could block-vote and elect one of its supporters. The conservatives alleged that this had already happened in New York City, where two Communists and two fellow travelers had been elected to the city council. Even if the Communists did not win a majority on the council, they could still disrupt city operations by receiving confidential information and by holding the balance of power on the council. The GOP, supported by the *Cincinnati Enquirer* and the *Times-Star*, urged the repeal of PR.[46]

These attacks obviously smeared the Charter candidates who defended PR. Republicans also attacked the Charterites after they received endorsements from the CIO and the Progressive Citizens Council, two allegedly "pink outfits." The Charter candidates ridiculed the idea that Cincinnati would elect a Communist, defended their endorsements, and emphasized their own success in providing good government in the previous years. In November, the PR repeal lost narrowly, and the Charter group won a five to four majority on the council. The vote margin indicated the divisions within the community, and promised a resumption of the attacks in the next election.[47]

The 1949 campaign did not feature another referendum on PR, but the loyalty issue reemerged with the Republicans leading the banner. Shortly before the election, Republican Councilman Carl W. Rich introduced a loyalty oath for city employees and the creation of a loyalty board to investigate any charges. Workers would be dismissed not only if they refused to sign the oath but also if they committed "another act or circumstance indicating disloyalty." The resolution, which had been suggested by the county American Legion, met stiff opposition from the Charterites. They argued that the resolution would not weed out Communists, but would leave innocent city workers open to unsubstantiated accusations. These councilmen suggested that the task be left to the FBI. One Charter councilman, the swing vote, nevertheless did indicate his support if the oath was written acceptably. All four Republican councilmen praised the oath, and condemned the four Charterites for their refusal to support Americanism. The council held two heated debates in September, but decided to postpone any action until the city manager had issued a report on the resolution.[48]

With the election only five weeks away, the campaign swung into high gear. Republicans continued to attack the Charterites for opposing the oath, and raised new accusations because of the CIO-PAC endorsement and because a Charter candidate had once belonged to the National Lawyers Guild. Charging that left-wing Democrats now controlled the Charter coalition, the Republicans raised the specter of socialist control. The *Times-Star* bluntly editorialized that its "chief interest in the present campaign is in the return of a Republican majority in the council. We've had enough of the New Deal and the Fair Deal in Washington, and we don't want to see a similar order and way of thinking established" in Cincinnati. On November 8, 1949, the Charter group retained its five-to-four majority on the council. A few days later, the city manager issued his report on the loyalty resolution, which doubted its constitutionality. The Scare had not yet reached its peak.[49]

The Red Scare nevertheless had only just begun. In 1950, the sensationalistic press generated enough fear to pass the oath and to get HUAC to investigate leftists in the area. In February, the *Enquirer* began an exposé of the area's Communists and leftists. "Communists Mark 12 City Plants for Sabotage! 178 Reds in Cincinnati," the banner headline screamed. The story also claimed that the city had more than 2,000 "crypto-Communists" who, with their leaders, secretly worked to dupe the innocent, promote violence, and hasten the destruction of freedom. Fear and suspicion increased in the city because the newspaper story did not list the names of the suspects. Two days after the article, the city manager changed his mind and announced the need for a loyalty oath. The series was the talk of the town, and each Sunday new front-page articles appeared: "Reds Bore Into Politics," "Commies Control Two Big Cincinnati Unions," and "Many Liberals Are Sucked In By Communists."[50]

The Republicans pressed again for the loyalty oath resolution. They and the American Legion officials referred often to the *Enquirer's* series, but various union and liberal organizations repeated their claims that oaths were ineffective and potentially harmful. A CP official hurt the liberal opposition when he refused to answer if any city workers were Communists. The *Times-Star* supported the loyalty oath, but the *Post* and ironically even the *Enquirer* opposed it. In mid-March, the council decided to restrict the oath to new employees and to delete the provision requiring dismissal for any "act or circumstance indicating disloyalty." Meanwhile, the *Enquirer's* series came under severe attack from the other two papers. They pointed out that the *Enquirer's* major source, Cecil Scott, was a former mental patient whose testimony had been deemed unreliable by HUAC. They also criticized the withholding of the names of the "Communists" since it smeared innocent people. The *Enquirer* defended its reports as factual, and began a campaign to get HUAC to follow up the investigation. In this fluid but emotional situation, the city council on March 22, 1950, approved the loyalty oath by a vote of six to three. It defeated a proposal that defined a subversive organization as one that had been so determined in a judicial hearing. A few weeks later, the county commissioners ordered all of their employees to sign a similar oath. This chain of events concluded when HUAC questioned several persons from the area in July. The hearings were much less sensational than the *Enquirer's* reports primarily because the newspaper had so exaggerated the Communists' strength. Nevertheless, these exposures prompted the city council to require a loyalty oath from all city workers.[51]

Although calm returned to the city for a while, the Communist issue erupted for a final time during the 1953 election campaign. This incident, which centered on a city worker, equaled the intensity of the 1950 controversy, but conservatives met with less success. In late September 1953, a GOP councilman leaked an FBI report that the city planning director, Sidney H. Williams, had belonged to a Marxist study group several years earlier. The City Planning Commission (CPC), which was composed of five unpaid citizens, the city manager, and one councilman, became the center of the 1953 council campaign. Prior to Williams' appointment as director, he had informed two CPC members, Henry Bettman and Wallace Collett, of the association. Bettman and Collett, both Charter appointees, had not relayed the information either to the other CPC members or to the city council. The disclosures rocked the city, and Republicans called for the resignation not only of Williams but also of Bettman and Collett.[52]

On September 30, as the CPC debated Williams' fate, it became known that he had belonged to the Young Communist League in the early 1940s, and that his wife allegedly still had Communist associations. Williams explained his YCL membership as the result of an "inquiring mind," and declared that none of his associates ever favored the overthrow of the government. He claimed to have broken with Communism in 1946, but he refused to discuss his wife's activities because they did not pertain to his own qualifications for the CPC job. The Republican critics found his defense unconvincing, and maintained that public officials needed the absolute trust of the people. Williams' past behavior had cost him that trust, they concluded. One charter CPC member accused the GOP of exploiting the minor incident for political gain, and another termed Williams' accusers as "jackals . . . [who] feast on freedom of thought." The debate culminated on the next day when the CPC by a strict party vote asked for Williams' resignation. The *Enquirer* supported the decision, while the *Post* defended Williams' ability, hard work, and loyalty for the last seven years. Five days later, Williams resigned.[53]

Bettman and Collett, who as CPC members had voted to retain Williams, defended their initial decision to withhold the information about Williams' past activities as irrelevant, but Republican critics accused them of "dereliction of duty" and the destruction of public confidence in city government. The issue now became Bettman and Collett, and on October 7, the city council debated their fate. On a strict party-line vote, the council asked for the resignations of both men. They refused, and the election which was less than a month away became a referendum on the Bettman-Collett affair.[54]

The Republicans were jubilant about their chances for victory. All of their campaign material emphasized the Bettman-Collett affair. Their newspaper advertisements were particularly vitriolic:

> Should Cincinnati Hire Ex-Communists for Key
>   Jobs in the City Hall?
> The Charter Democrats   Republicans
> Say: Yes!   Say: No!
>
> We Republicans are for destroying Communism
> whenever and wherever it is discovered—and
> that includes Cincinnati, Ohio.
> We believe Communism is deadly dangerous to
> life, liberty, and religion. It is not to be
> coddled or excused.
> We won't be soft-talked or loud-talked into
> accepting less than 100% Americanism.
> That is our position today, tomorrow, and forever.

Anti-Protestant!
Anti-Catholic!
Anti-Jewish!
Anti-Negro!
Anti-God!
This is what members of Marxist study groups are
taught, Charter Democrats. Is this the "Study
Group" you are excusing?

YOU—be the jury
Are Republicans right or wrong in opposing
Communist-Coddling in Public Office?
Do you approve of the "New Style" Charter-
Democratic Party with its present day
influences and control?

Another GOP ad asked if the defenders of Williams, Bettman, and Collett had "read the Korean death list," and it ended with a row of crosses at the bottom of the page.[55]

The Charterites fought back by trying to divide the issues. They rejected GOP claims that Williams would be rehired if they won, thus making him a sort of "fall guy." Instead, they focused their campaign on Bettman and Collett, two long-time Cincinnati residents. Bettman, an architect, had been a CPC member since 1947, and Collett, a businessman, was vice-president of the Junior Chamber of Commerce. Supporters of the two men formed the Committee of 150 for Public Morality and they launched a series of their own ads in the newspapers. They characterized the GOP attacks as "character assassination." They also condemned the lack of due process since the council had demanded Bettman and Collett's resignations before any formal charges had been brought against the men. Their ads attempted to defuse the Communist issue:

Should Cincinnati citizens be condemned without
fair trials?

| The County Republican | The Charter Committee |
| Machine Says: Yes! | Says: No! |

Their candidates have been willing to subvert
the truth to exaggerate errors of judgment and
to vilify outstanding citizens who have given
years of service to Cincinnati without a cent
of payment. . . .

Communism is no issue in this campaign . . .
You abhor it, we abhor it, every decent citizen
abhors it. For the county machine to say otherwise is to libel thousands of decent patriotic
citizens of our great city.[56]

No other issue appeared in the campaign. The *Times-Star* and the *Enquirer* supported the Republican position, while the *Post* backed more charter candidates. On November 2, the Charter group regained control of the council by a five to four majority. Its narrow but convincing victory resulted from several factors. Some voters were repulsed by the pilloring of two prominent civic leaders. Others rejected the attack on the nine Charter candidates because of Bettman and Collett's action. Still others feared that the traditionally nonpolitical planning commission would become a political tool in control of one party. Timing also was a key. Although the initial attacks had occurred only a few weeks before the election, there was sufficient time for the Charter group—aided by the Committee of 150—to mobilize. Indeed, the issue helped to unify the Charter movement. Morally aroused, Charter volunteers poured out to work the city in a door-to-door campaign. The Charter candidates were also willing to let Williams fade away and to publicly avow their anti-Communism. The election did not result in a voter realignment. The Charter Committee had won similar five-to-four councils in three of the previous four elections, the only exception being a five-to-four GOP council. The close divisions remained in the city, and the Charterites were able to sway the independents to their side once more.[57]

Summary

Neither Detroit, Chicago, nor Cincinnati can be termed perfectly representative of the Red Scare on the local level. No one city can be such a model. Yet these three reveal certain key characteristics. First, the events in one city did not directly influence the development of the Scare in another. Further, the events in the nation's capital did not create local controversies. The Scare's emergence in cities was caused by the existence of a conservative movement. Loosely structured, it operated in various locales, ready to exploit local circumstances into a loyalty controversy. The conservatives, usually Republicans, probably believed in the issue, but they used it primarily as a political tool to win or maintain power. They used it regardless of the type of electoral process.[58] Detroit had a mayoral system based on a non-partisan ballot; Chicago's mayor campaigned on a party ticket; Cincinnati voted on its city council by proportional representation.

The conservative movement tended to be successful. It forced the dismissal of several city workers, broke the UPW, and initiated some loyalty oaths. Yet these larger cities should be distinguished from the smaller towns which gave consensus approval to loyalty measures. These larger cities, with their heterogeneity, had a liberal movement which showed occasional displays of strength. It put significant safeguards into the Detroit loyalty program, and it resisted the attacks on Bettman and Collett in Cincinnati.

Basically however, the liberal critics were weak. In the fights in the state legislatures, the liberals could argue on principle; the fights did not concern a specific individual. On the local level, the controversies were more directed; the conservatives used victims such as George Shenkar, Wayne McMillen, and Sidney Williams to put the issue on a more immediate and emotional basis. As a result, they were often more successful on the local level.

4

Local Level: Schools and Libraries

If the loyalty crusaders were concerned about leftists employed by the city—a Thomas Coleman or a Sidney Williams—they were even more anxious to weed out non-conformists in the public schools. "Protect the children" was their cry. These Red Scare incidents involving education again reveal the key aspect of the conservative movement: the lack of a unified structure coinciding with the unity built around similar motives, rhetoric, and methods. Conservatives believed that Communists and their sympathizers had become teachers and writers of textbooks. Almost always, conservatives accused teachers of political activity outside of the classroom rather than indoctrination of students. Yet these right-wing critics dismissed the distinction between classroom and outside activities since the actor was the same and a role model for students. They viewed children as "plastic," easily molded by educators.[1] The conservatives thus justified dismissals of teachers and censorship of books.

In most cases, the conservatives succeeded in their restrictive efforts. School officials, dependent upon local financing, reacted harshly against anyone or anything controversial, even when Communist ties were tenuous. In the state legislatures, liberals could debate abstract principles with the loyalty crusaders; on the local level, the issue was more immediate and emotional. The cases examined in this chapter show the excesses of the conservative movement as they imposed "loyalty."

These incidents affecting teachers and textbooks seem to confirm the severity of the Scare. According to one historian, "the young and their mentors learned silence. The fear was tangible." Another has concluded that "truth, freedom, and integrity became the first casualties."[2] This chapter refrains from such exaggeration. In the first place, educational controversies occurred before the Second Red Scare. In 1936, Howard Beale had surveyed the restrictions in public schools. His book, *Are American Teachers Free?*, strongly implied that they were not. The Scare did not change an educational utopia because none had ever existed. Second, neither students nor teachers were plastic. Just as they were not molded by "subversive" influences, neither were they molded by little Joe McCarthys. Their response was not automatic fear and conformity, but a mixed reaction. The public schools mixed anti-Communism with idealism and civic responsibility. This chapter, in other words, points out both the excesses and the limitations of the conservative movement.

Educational controversies occurred throughout the Midwest, although more arose in larger cities than in smaller towns. The loyalty of teachers was subjected both to general scrutiny and specific investigation. The former came in the guise of loyalty oaths, while the latter originated from sources on the federal, state, and local levels. Controversies involving textbooks occurred both in schools and libraries. This chapter analyzes disputes affecting teachers (generally and specifically) and books (both in schools and libraries). None of these incidents involved support for the violent overthrow of the government. Instead, the issue concerned the community's desire to have the schools express its values versus the teacher's or textbook writer's freedom to express political ideas freely.

Teachers

Teachers, as public employees, were often under general scrutiny from government agencies: state and local. Positive oaths of loyalty were widespread before the Second Red Scare, but in the postwar decade, conservatives tried to impose specific anti-Communist oaths. Although they occasionally succeeded, there was not a tidal wave of oaths at this time. Generally, government and school officials did not believe that an anti-Communist oath would be an effective screening method.[3] Only Illinois made such a requirement for its public employees, and this law was not enacted until 1955. The varied success of loyalty oath proposals can be shown in two cases: Cleveland and Chicago.

In Cleveland, the loyalty oath received consensus approval. In May 1949, the school board adopted the oath on the same day that it was introduced. One board member suggested that the oath include a definition of a Communist, but another member maintained that the definition was self-evident. No one needed to define "burglar," he concluded. Accepting a different suggestion, the board included in the oath a denial of membership in a Nazi or Fascist organization. Leftists challenged the oath in court, but it was upheld.

> Could anyone who really loves the Constitution or his country have an objection to such an oath? . . . Would a teacher who objects to taking that oath be qualified sincerely to lead his class in the Pledge of Allegiance to our Flag, by which there is so frequently and beautifully engendered a love of this country?

The Cleveland action prompted Canton and Massillon, fifty miles to the south, to adopt similar oaths.[4]

A more divisive loyalty oath controversy occurred in Chicago. In August 1950, a school board member proposed an oath because of the need to affirm anti-Communism during the Korean War. The oath's sponsor felt that all loyal employees would be glad to sign, but debate broke out on whether to include a denial of Ku Klux Klan membership and whether to bar persons who had formerly been associated with a subversive organization. The board president pointed out that few if any teachers were suspects. The Chicago Principals Club supported the measure, but the Chicago Teachers Union and the Citizens Schools Committee opposed it as unnecessary and ineffective. At one public hearing, an American Legion official accused an opponent of the oath of being a subversive. The Legion official concluded that he was "glad to find out who are the people so opposed to Americanism in the schools." Despite such rhetoric and conservative pressure, the Chicago Teachers Union and the Citizens Schools Committee were able to exert sufficient counterpressure that the board never approved the oath.[5]

The oath controversy nevertheless reappeared in Chicago four years later. In 1955, the Board of Examiners quietly decided to require prospective teachers to declare their membership in any organization on the attorney general's subversive list. In one case, the board denied certification to a former member of the Young Communist League, even though he declared his present non-Communist status. The ACLU, Chicago Teachers Union, Citizens Schools Committee, American Jewish Congress, and City Club protested the use of the list to screen teachers. While this local dispute developed, the state legislature enacted a loyalty oath for all public employees. The Chicago school board then substituted the state oath for the questions based on the subversive list. This oath, after being upheld by the courts, claimed as victims three teachers who refused to sign the oath.[6]

More common than general scrutiny through loyalty oaths were investigations of specific teachers. These educational controversies arose from "external" developments: federal investigative committees (HUAC) and a state legislative body in Ohio. Furthermore, Ohio and Michigan enacted laws which in effect required public employees to testify about their political affiliations to such committees. This caused the emasculation of the Fifth Amendment, and institutionalized restrictive attitudes toward leftists and non-conformists. In other words, "unfriendly" teachers were dismissed. These externally caused controversies, usually involving the use of the Fifth Amendment, occurred in Cleveland, Dayton, and Massillon, Ohio, and Detroit (and suburbs).

The Cleveland school board, which had promulgated an anti-Communist oath, encountered a loyalty controversy when a teacher defied a state legislative committee. In December 1953, the Ohio Un-American Activities Committee (OUAC) questioned Edward Likover, who taught science and driver's education at the Cleveland Trade School. Likover, who had taken the school board's loyalty oath, refused to answer questions about his political affiliations. He relied only on the First Amendment partially because, according to state law, a public employee's use of the Fifth Amendment constituted his "unfitness" for employment. The Cleveland Board of Education did not rule on the suitability of Likover's leftist affiliations, but unanimously suspended the teacher for "unbecoming" conduct. Likover condemned the board's lack of support for constitutional guarantees, and argued that judgment on employment should be based solely on his ability as a teacher. The board remained unconvinced and two weeks later dismissed Likover.[7]

In Detroit, teachers were the targets of two "external" investigations from HUAC, in 1952 and 1954. The first time, the state had not yet enacted the law requiring testimony from a public employee, but this seeming tolerance made no difference in the final determination of the case. In February 1952, a witness before HUAC identified Elinor Maki, an art teacher in elementary schools since 1929, as a Communist. The Detroit Board of Education suspended her without pay. Her fellow teachers at the school indicated that Maki was a good teacher who had never spoken about her political beliefs even to other teachers. The school's principal acknowledged that he had never had a complaint against her. A few days later testifying before HUAC, Maki refused to answer questions about her alleged Communist affiliations and associations. In a hearing with Superintendent Arthur Dondineau, Maki argued that judgment should be based on her teaching ability, rather than her outside activities or her "unfriendly" testimony before HUAC. She pointed out that she had willingly signed the loyalty oath required of all teachers. Unswayed by her arguments, Dondineau recommended her dismissal to the board. To the superintendent, her refusal to refute the allegations indicated their truth, and her distinction between school and outside activities was abstract and immaterial.[8]

Maki decided to appeal, and went to the Detroit Federation of Teachers (DFT) for support. At a DFT meeting, she denied that she had ever taught subversive material to any student, broken the law, or advocated the overthrow of the government. She maintained her ability as a teacher and concluded that the government acted improperly in its inquiries into her political beliefs and associations. The DFT acknowledged the charged political atmosphere in the city when it passed a resolution asking reporters to omit the names of those who spoke in support of Maki's position. A few DFT members did approve of her arguments, but her critics argued that HUAC's investigations were legitimate and that Maki had an obligation to parents and to other teachers to cooperate. The DFT voted 261 to 103 to reject her request for support. Later, the Board of Education came to a similar conclusion and dismissed her.[9]

Two years later, HUAC returned with a wider net and created a similar furor in Detroit and surrounding areas. Four "unfriendly" witnesses—

Evelyn Gladstone, George Miller, Shirley Rappoport, and Paul Baker—
were former teachers in various Detroit suburbs. Each had either resigned or
been dismissed within the past year as their respective school boards became
aware of the HUAC investigation. As the proceedings began, three witnesses
still held positions as public school teachers: Blanche Northwood, a grade
school teacher in a Detroit suburb; Sidney W. Graber, a social studies
teacher for five years in Detroit; and Harold Rosen, a music teacher for
seventeen years. Each invoked the Fifth Amendment before the Committee.
By this time, a new state law declared that refusal to testify would mean
"prima facie evidence" of the truth of the accusation. A week later,
Northwood was dismissed. The Graber and Rosen cases took slightly longer
to develop. In a hearing with Superintendent Arthur Dondineau, they
refused to answer if they had ever participated in Communist activities. As a
result, they were suspended. Several weeks after HUAC had left the city, the
Board of Education held a hearing on the two men. Both denied being CP
members or attending any Communist meetings since the passage of a 1952
state law which required all Communists to register with the Michigan State
Police. They refused to testify about their activities before 1952. Attacking
HUAC, Graber and Rosen claimed that they had the constitutional right to
refuse to testify about their private activities. Their arguments, just like
Maki's two years before, did not convince the board, which unanimously
dismissed them.[10]

The 1954 HUAC probe in Detroit even caught a school board member,
Tom E. Bryant, from suburban Garden City. Three days after his use of the
Fifth Amendment before HUAC, the school board held a mass meeting with
more than 1,000 attending. Many parents, including some of his campaign
supporters, begged him to answer the questions about his affiliations. Bryant
declared his opposition to the overthrow of the government, but he refused
to state if he was or had been a Communist. The latter question was a private
political affiliation, he concluded, and he would not "play the game of fear
and smear." A few supported his stance, but critics at the meeting began a
recall drive against Bryant. A few days later, he resigned.[11]

Even when a teacher had publicly broken with the CP, his use of the
Fifth Amendment could activate conservative pressure in the community. In
September 1954, HUAC visited Dayton, Ohio, and questioned Joseph
Glatterman, an elementary school teacher for four years. The teacher, who
had been identified as a Communist before HUAC, invoked the Fifth
Amendment on his party membership. Earlier, Glatterman had given an
affidavit to the superintendent that he had been a party member until 1950
but had broken with the CP at that time. Glatterman asserted that he had
never broken any laws, and declared his willingness to fight for the U.S. in a
war against the Soviet Union. The day after his "unfriendly" testimony, the
school board suspended the teacher. Some who had supported his employ-

ment despite his former Communist affiliation were now critical of his refusal to cooperate with HUAC. They argued that he should have identified other Communists if he had truly broken with the party. Other critics cited the Ohio law that refusal to testify by a public employee constituted "unfitness." A week later, Glatterman resigned.[12]

Finally, an "external" investigation could brand a teacher as an undesirable even without a hearing before HUAC. In 1954, the Massillon, Ohio, school board planned to hire Keve Bray as a junior high school teacher. Five days before the opening of the schools in September, the board rescinded the contract, although it did promise to pay the salary. No reason was given, and Bray demanded a hearing. Two weeks later, the board met in closed session, and unanimously denied Bray's request for a hearing. The termination was probably caused by a HUAC investigation, which culminated in Bray's interrogation in July 1955. Bray willingly answered all questions. He denied belonging to the CP and knowingly attending any Communist meetings. Obviously, the hearing came too late to rectify the Massillon incident, but it probably cleared Bray for other teaching positions.[13]

Besides "external" agencies probing teachers, educational controversies also could arise from "local" events: students' complaints of classroom behavior and the teacher's political activities. Such "local" incidents occurred in Chicago, due to classroom behavior, and in Muskegon and Sunfield, Michigan, due to outside activities. These teachers actively fought the accusations of disloyalty, rather than trying to protect themselves from self-incrimination. They found occasional success.

In Chicago, a teacher became the target of a "local" controversy because of her alleged classroom activities. Students made the initial accusations against the high school civics teacher with twenty-four years of experience. The students claimed that the teacher, Emily Noack, had criticized capitalism for producing unemployment and war, and that she had praised the Soviet Union. When students attempted to challenge her views, they alleged that she had ridiculed them. One student asserted that Noack had publicly admitted her Communist beliefs. These charges became sensationalized in reports by the *Chicago Herald-American*, a Hearst newspaper. Noack denied any Communist sympathies, although she acknowledged that she did not hate the Soviet Union since such hostility would only cause wars. Her loyalty and teaching ability were defended by other students in the class, former students, more than 100 fellow teachers at the high school, and the Chicago Teachers Union. Superintendent Herold Hunt interviewed the students who had made the complaints, and questioned Noack about the class. She again denied her Communist beliefs and affiliations, and willingly signed a loyalty oath. Several days later, the superintendent cleared the teacher, whom he described as an "idealist" but not disloyal. According to

Hunt, the civics class which Noack taught did not promote Communism, but showed the advantages of the American way of life.[14]

These "local" controversies usually did not result from a teacher's activities inside the classroom but from outside the school. Muskegon, Michigan, experienced a "local" controversy over an avowed socialist teacher, Eugene L. Howard, who tried to publicize his beliefs in the community. In 1932, the school district had transferred Howard from teaching civics to mathematics because of his socialist beliefs, and for the next fourteen years no further dispute arose. In 1946, Howard wrote a book critical of capitalism, and conservatives began to complain to the school board. Shortly before the city voted on a special appropriation for the school district, the board issued the math teacher a one-year terminal contract. Several months later, Howard asked for a reconsideration of the decision. He denied any indoctrination of socialism in his math class, and he denied any Communist sympathies. The local American Federation of Teachers (AFT) supported his efforts, and at a public hearing, most citizens criticized the termination. One referred to it as an action that reflected the policies of Nazi Germany. The president of the school board denied that freedom of expression was being curtailed. He argued that Howard's views were legitimate as private opinions, but that the school board did not have to continue to employ him. The job was a privilege, not a right, he concluded. The school board reaffirmed its decision, and Howard was terminated in the summer of 1948.[15]

The final "local" controversy involved a superintendent whose political views expressed outside of school alienated many conservatives in the community. In July 1949, a small school district in central Michigan hired Rev. Albert W. Kauffman, a Congregational Church minister in a nearby town, as superintendent and as a Latin and English teacher. Shortly after school began in the village of Sunfield, Kauffman wrote a letter to *Soviet Russia Today* in support of the magazine's peace proposals:

> [I oppose] the capitalistic ideology that is promoting war against Russia. If only we can live through the present Truman administration and until the fervor of the radical and foolish patriotic organizations cools off, I am sure there will be no war. . . . The greatest promoter of war with Russia is the Vatican and the hireling priests that swarm over the United States in an effort to put the Roman Church in power here.

The magazine denied any ties with the Soviet government, but HUAC claimed that it was a Communist front organization.[16]

Since few people in rural Michigan read the magazine, Kauffman's letter did not cause an immediate controversy. All this changed on November 29, 1949, when George Sokolsky, a nationally syndicated conservative columnist, lambasted Kauffman in his daily report, entitled "Twisted Thinking of a Clergyman." Bypassing the minister's anti-Catholic sentiments, Sokolosky demanded to know "how can patriotism or a patriotic organization be foolish? Is it foolish to love one's own country?" The state American Legion demanded an apology, and a local Legion post picketed his church, protesting that he was unsuitable to guide the school system. The minister denied that he was a Communist, socialist, or pacifist, but the dispute split the small community.[17]

The five-member Board of Education reflected these divisions and uncertainties in a series of contradictory actions over the next two weeks. On Sunday, December 4, the board held an emergency meeting, and suspended Kauffman. Critics felt that anyone even suspected of Communist leanings should not be retained, while Kauffman's supporters pointed out that one statement did not make the superintendent into a subversive or end his abilities. They argued that Kauffman was entitled to express his political opinions regardless of his employment by the schools. On the next day, the board reinstated Kauffman until a public hearing could be held. Two days later, the board cancelled the mass meeting, and by a three-to-two vote dismissed Kauffman for bringing "unfavorable publicity" to the schools. According to one board member, "it's pretty bad when our basketball team comes out on the floor, and the opponents say, 'Here come the Communists.'" Yet, the drama had not ended for on the next day, the board president switched his vote on a motion to reopen the case. On December 10, the board by a three-to-two vote reinstated Kauffman. The Congregational Church also rejected any action against the minister.[18]

Throughout the Midwest, conservatives thus scrutinized the loyalty of teachers and administrators in both general and specific ways. In the first case, conservatives tried to impose loyalty oaths, but were not always successful in getting them passed or in weeding out the leftists. The HUAC cases did not begin until 1952. Educational controversies involving specific teachers arose from both "external" and "local" developments. HUAC claimed the most victims as several teachers unsuccessfully tried to defend themselves and to defy the committee. "Local" controversies had a less immediate or overt effect, but this was probably due to the non-Communist status of the accused. All in all then, the Scare affected leftist teachers directly and indirectly.

Books

Educational controversies involved not only teachers but also books in schools and libraries. Conservative critics condemned some social studies textbooks as subversive, and specifically singled out *American Government*, a high school civics textbook by Frank Magruder. None of the books under attack actually reflected leftist sympathies, but they often raised questions and issues which challenged the beliefs of the right wing. These attempts to ban textbooks, which frequently succeeded, occurred in Chicago, Lafayette, and Indianapolis.

The Chicago schools had a series of controversies throughout the postwar decade involving textbooks and courses. The first such uproar occurred when the *Chicago Tribune* launched an exposé of more than fifty textbooks in 1947. Although the *Tribune* acknowledged that the Chicago schools did not use the books, its series revealed its readiness to screen textbooks throughout the area. The newspaper alleged that the books portrayed America as a class society rather than as a land of freedom and opportunity. The solution to the country's problems, allegedly according to the texts, was either a continuation of the New Deal or an adoption of the British socialistic system. Support for the welfare state coincided with indoctrination of union sympathies.

> A union is not a political organization for class warfare. It is not an instrument for revolution. It is not a lawless combination to redistribute wealth. . . . It is an honest attempt . . . to improve working conditions and to raise wages.

Such texts not only ignored property rights but also used the term "democracy" rather than "republic" to describe the American system. Finally, the "subversive" texts libelled American Patriots. The colonial period was not characterized as oppressive; revolutionary heroes were not viewed as fighting against English tyranny; and the Founding Fathers were described as speculators. Not only did the schools have such un-American and "pro-British" propaganda, but some school libraries also held overtly Communist books. The leftist beliefs in these textbooks were reinforced, the *Tribune* concluded, by leftist teachers who had been indoctrinated by the National Education Association. The result was subversion of the American way of life.[19] (See fig. 3.)

The *Tribune*'s attacks, especially its hostility toward Great Britain, reflected its deeply held conservative convictions. Yet the timing of this series of reports was caused by a local incident, a project sponsored by the newspaper's liberal competitor, the *Chicago Sun*. The *Sun* had arranged for one student from every public and private school in the city to visit the United Nations in New York City. The *Tribune* could not prevent the project which had already been planned, but it did want to energize its conservative readers and to warn school officials throughout the area that it would investigate any hint of leftist tendencies in the schools. More directly, however, its reports did not cause the removal of any textbooks because the paper had so exaggerated moderate and liberal statements.[20]

Conservatives in Chicago continued to express their concern over specific textbooks and general educational policy. In the fall of 1949, conservatives attacked *American Government* by Frank Magruder, which

DOES THIS CONSTITUTE 'ACADEMIC FREEDOM'?

had been approved as one of the four possible texts for the required high school civics course. This time, the effort to ban the textbook was led by the Conference of American Small Business Organizations (CASBO), a conservative group with its headquarters in the city. CASBO officials charged that the Magruder book "follows the CP line" in its discussion of the capitalistic system. The *Tribune* did not think that the book was communistic, but agreed that the book should be replaced because it was not sufficiently anti-Communist. Superintendent Hunt defended the objectivity of the book, which had been in circulation since the 1920s, and it remained on the approved list.[21]

At the same time, however, the Chicago superintendent began a policy of consultation with the conservative critics. He suggested that the administration official in charge of textbooks (the director of instructional materials) join one of the right-wing groups, the Freedom Club. Supposedly, the administrator would then be able to better present the viewpoint of school officials. Obviously, he would also receive the conservatives' criticisms more directly and more often. Superintendent Hunt also appointed two hard-line conservatives to the advisory committee on controversial subjects. According to one appointee, a CASBO official, "there isn't a decent civics textbook in Chicago. They're all tainted with statism, New Dealism, and socialism. Most of our teachers have been made unconsciously disloyal by the teachers' colleges."[22]

These conservatives were not pacified by the consultation, but continued to push for the implementation of their beliefs. They focused particularly on the high school civics course and the Magruder textbook required for the course. In 1950, CASBO officials found fault with the primary learning objective of the course, which was as follows:

> to create an awareness of the certainty of change; to develop in students the habit of looking for such changes and to develop the ability to analyze them; . . . . to quicken the realization that our Constitution is a living document which contains within itself the machinery for adjustment to change.

This educational goal, according to a CASBO official, was another example of "socialism and even communism." They pushed for its replacement, and later the statement was quietly dropped.[23]

The conservatives scored a similar success when the Magruder textbook came up for review in early 1953. Although the textbook committee held no hearings, it decided to drop the book from the approved list. The committee gave no reasons for its action, but the director of instructional materials stated that the other books gave "a more typical interpretation of American life." Superintendent Hunt asserted that the decision of the textbook committee was based on their professional judgment and not on conservative pressure. A CASBO official nevertheless claimed credit because his organization had "caused so much furor."[24]

The Magruder textbook aroused controversy elsewhere as well, especially in Indiana. The state was unique among the five midwestern states in having a State Textbook Commission which approved two or three books for each course. The local school board could then choose among the approved texts. In 1947, the state commission approved the Magruder book, *American Government*, for high school civics, and gave it a five-year contract. Criticism of the book did not arise immediately, but in the early 1950s, conservatives in Lafayette and Indianapolis successfully attacked the book.

In Lafayette, conservatives quickly and quietly succeeded in censoring the book. In late 1951, the city's Chamber of Commerce objected to the Magruder text as socialistic. The school board quietly agreed to an investigation. In its report, school officials declared that the book favored nationalization of industry and socialized medicine. The *Journal and Courier* found that the text also supported "public housing, subsidized education, extension of public power projects. . . . all [of which] are socialistic." The school board dropped the Magruder book and selected the other approved text for the civics course. The ban caused no controversy because the Chamber of Commerce and the school board had acted quietly, withholding information until after the decision had been made to withdraw the book.[25]

The Lafayette ban had ramifications in Indianapolis and on the State Textbook Committee (STC). Just as in Chicago, the controversy in Indianapolis was sensationalized by one newspaper, the *Star*. From December 22, 1951, to January 13, 1952, the paper printed seventeen stories critical of the Magruder text. Allegedly, the book gave a favorable view of socialism and the Soviet Union as well as a critical picture of free market capitalism and the Republican party. Many times, the *Star's* quotations from the book were incomplete and thus misleading. The paper condemned defining socialism as "the use of government to bring abut equality of opportunity among citizens," but it did provide Magruder's entire context. "When a democracy owns and operates industries there is likely to be more inefficiency than when individuals compete with each other in business. Also when the many learn to tax the few for the benefit of themselves there is danger of their consuming the nation's wealth." The newspaper's attacks implied that the status quo should never be changed. As a result of the reports, the school board decided to quit using the textbook.[26] (See fig. 4.)

The Magruder book had been published since the 1920s. The 1948 edition was influenced by the Depression and pointed out the problems in the society. Conservatives were troubled by questions, such as those in the "Problems for Discussion" section:

1. Why has unemployment been called "America's Public Enemy No. 1?" Do you believe that private industry alone can prevent it?
2. Do you think that your town should own its water system? Electric power system? Gas system? Bus system?
3. Has the State in which you live been "gerrymandered" for the advantage of either party, or the advantage of the rural districts over the cities?
4. "Democracy will survive only as long as the quick whims of the majority are held in check by the courts in favor of a dominant and lasting sense of justice . . . ?" Do you agree or disagree?

The book's message was not influenced by the New Deal as much as by governmental action during the Second World War. The tone of the 1948 edition was quite optimistic, and its implicit message was that government and business could work together to solve problems, just as they had done during the war. Only in this sense was it a "liberal" book.[27]

Despite the reality of the book, the pressure from the Lafayette and Indianapolis controversies struck the State Textbook Commission (STC). The state superintendent of public instruction asked the attorney general if the STC could break its contract with Magruder's publisher, but the attorney general rejected the proposal. At a special closed STC meeting in December 1951, representatives from the publisher defended the book and promised legal action if the STC broke the contract, which had one more year to run. As a result, the STC refrained from any formal action, noting that local school boards could switch to the other approved textbook as the two cities had done. The next year marked the end of the Magruder contract, and the STC action was predictable. On December 11, 1952, it unanimously approved other books for high school civics, a decision which the press correctly interpreted as a ban on the Magruder book. Officially, the STC gave no reason for its action.[28]

Ironically, the 1953 edition under consideration—which was the same as the one banned in Chicago—was quite different from its 1948 predecessor. Its praise for the free enterprise system and its condemnation of socialism and communism was more unequivocal. The new preface also raised a more direct concern. "Today, as in years past, loyal Americans feel that there must be no letup in our attack on subversive movements. . . . Agitators never cease their efforts to overthrow our cherished institutions of government." Perhaps the most obvious difference in tone and message was reflected in the final paragraph of both books:

(The 1948 edition)
Great progress toward understanding has already been made in the meetings of the United Nations. Differences of opinion are inevitable, but time will convince the various members that compromise is necessary for world peace which is so much desired by all.

We can keep our powder dry; but patience is a great virtue. Whom the gods would destroy they first make mad.

(1953 edition)
We have become a leader among nations and we have accepted the responsibilities that this position has thrust upon us. We are firmly committed to the cause of world peace and the brotherhood of man. We face the future secure in the knowledge that our cause is just.[29]

The ban of the 1953 edition can be compared to the dismissal of teachers who had formerly had "subversive" affiliations even though they presently professed their loyalty to the U.S.

Censorship attempts occurred not only in schools but also in public libraries. The issues, of course, remained the same. Such controversies occurred in Indianapolis, Indiana; Madison, Wisconsin; and Peoria, Illinois.

The Indianapolis library established its policy on "subversive" books in the early years of the postwar decade, and then saw it tested. According to the policy, all periodicals were checked against the attorney general's subversive list. The *Daily Worker* was retained but only for the study of propaganda. The library withdrew books not because of the author's affiliation with a subversive organization but because of the book's support for subversive activities. The head librarian justified the policy because in "a national emergency, when the printed word may be used in such a way to constitute danger to the state and society, it is the duty of the library to limit the freedom it normally exercises." In 1952, this policy was tested when conservatives criticized an adult education book. *English for Workers* by Eli B. Jackson, published in 1928, allegedly portrayed the U.S. as a class society in which workers were poor, overworked, and exploited. This was "pro-Communist poison," declared a critic. On learning about the book from an English tutor, the librarian pulled the book from circulation. The *Indianapolis Star* praised the policy and denied that it constituted "book burning."[30]

A brief censorship episode occurred at the library in Madison. In the spring of 1953, the head librarian decided against purchasing *McCarthy, The Man, The Senator, The Ism* by Jack Anderson and Ronald May. The book criticized the Senator, and Westbrook Pegler, a conservative columnist, had implied that the authors had Communist leanings. When the *Madison Capital-Times* discovered the story, it was outraged by the ban. The head librarian denied that the book had been censored, and cited financial limitations as her reason for not buying the book. After the publicity, the library decided to purchase both the Anderson-May book and Senator McCarthy's own *McCarthyism: The Fight for America.*[31]

Films, rather than books, created the uproar at the Peoria library. In 1950, an American Legion post criticized "Boundary Line" and "Brotherhood of Man," two films on American race relations, as "hostile to democratic thinking." Legion officials also claimed that "Peoples of the USSR" was Communist propaganda, and that "Now the Peace," which discussed the United Nations, was distributed by a company with a "questionable patriotic nature." A few members of the Library Board denied that the films were subversive, but the majority decided to shelve "Peoples of the USSR." The next month, similar action was taken on the two films about race relations. The board did not label the films as subversive; it simply gave no reason for its action. All three films could continue to be shown but only in the library and with the permission of the librarian. The fourth film, "Now the Peace," was returned to an American Legion Auxiliary post which had donated it. A week later, the library received new information from *Counterattack* and HUAC that the film distributor of "Brotherhood of Man," the International Film Foundation (IFF), had "very definite Communist leanings and connections." As a result, the librarian further restricted the film to only "bona fide students of propaganda."[32]

The film's producer, the UAW-CIO, began a counterattack. In November, a board member who was also a UAW official defended the films, and he invited the national UAW film director to appear before the board. By a vote of five to three, the board refused to hear the director, and also refused to give an official reason for its action. Next, the minister of the First Methodist Church took up the gauntlet. In January 1951 he showed the three films to his congregation, and the church voted that the films were not subversive. When the minister asked the Library Board to reverse its censorship, it again refused.[33]

Despite such incidents, overt censorship in libraries was not common. In a poll of Ohio libraries in cities with more than 15,000 population, only four of sixty experienced any attempt to censor a "subversive" book, and only one complied. A California poll noted no increase in complaints about "subversive" books during the postwar decade. Moral objections outnumbered political ones by 49 to 22 percent. More difficult to measure, however, is covert censorship, or self-censorship by the librarians. As one critic pointed out, librarians never censor, just "'screen,' 'select,' and 'guide.'"[34]

Summary

Throughout the Midwest, educational controversies involved both teachers and books. Since education is often run on a nonpartisan basis, it cannot be said that the conservative movement was unified or led by Republicans. Yet the arguments and the tactics of the conservatives remained the same as on the state level and in city government. Moreover, some of the agencies which generated the Scare in schools and libraries—HUAC, *Chicago Tribune*, CASBO, *Indianapolis Star*, and the American Legion—had definite Republican tendencies, as expressed in earlier chapters.

The loyalty crusade was more successful in educational incidents than in other disputes. Loyalty oaths perhaps did not weed out leftists, but they gave a symbolic victory to the conservatives. This chapter has indicated that conservatives usually won in Fifth Amendment cases, "local" controversies, and textbook disputes. In short, the Scare had a noticeable effect on schools and libraries.

The imposition of loyalty oaths, the dismissal of teachers, and the censorship of books seem to confirm the severe repressive nature of the Red Scare. During the period, many liberal educators pointed to "the reactionary temper of our times" which would lead to the "destruction" of freedom in the public schools. When a progressive superintendent of schools was fired in Pasadena, California, the worried cry arose that similar purges could happen anywhere.[35] Echoing these concerns, some historians have argued that the reaction of teachers and students was fearful conformity, resulting in a distortion of the educational process.

Yet the Scare's effect should not be exaggerated. This chapter, like many other studies on education, has primarily discussed the incidents of dismissal and censorship, thus leaving the impression that such was the norm. For example, one historian has characterized an Indiana woman's attack on the Robin Hood legend as communistic as "an all too typical illustration" of conservative pressure. Yet the charge produced more laughter than concern, and the book was not banned.[36] Taking an overall view, the teachers who lost their jobs constituted a tiny percentage of the whole, and the censoring of a few textbooks did not produce a significantly more conservative view of American history and society.

These caveats do not ignore the conservatives' desire to use public education for their own ideological purposes. Their pressure certainly resulted in excesses and injustices, as this chapter amply shows. This caused some conservative tendencies to be exhibited in schools and libraries, but it did not cause those institutions to become agencies of conservative in- doctrination. Teachers reflected the society, but that society was not totalitarian. The anti-Communism expressed by teachers and librarians should not be interpreted as fearful conformity but as a broader attitude that ranged from hard-line conservatism to ardent liberalism.

Just as the overt repressive effects of the Scare had limits, so did the subtler effects. Some commentators have noted that the subtle effects—the creation of a conservative atmosphere so pervasive that it did not seem unusual—had more significance than the overt effects.[37] Even this argument has its hidden complexities since it incorrectly views students as passive recipients. While schools produced anti-Communists, they did not produce blind conformists who believed only in the status quo. The school taught not only American superiority but also civic responsibility, the need to maintain the superiority, the need to avoid repressive actions (that is, the need to avoid being like Communists). Such attitudes could be channeled into reform activities.[38] To take one example, many student protestors of the 1960s grew disenchanted with racism and the Vietnam War precisely because they had been taught a faith in American ideals, a faith which they saw as being corrupted. The use of nonviolence was more than a tactical effort; it also reflected the belief that others held that faith in American ideals and it was possible to appeal and to awaken those people. The 1950's inculcation of the superiority of the American system was not taken to its logical extreme, that the U.S. was perfect. The teaching of civil responsibility allowed many to turn to reform efforts, though, of course, many others remained opponents of such activities. Education did not mold little lumps of clay; it reflected the society and its end-product reflected the divisions and the unity of that society.

5

Local Level: Voluntary Organizations

Locally, the loyalty issue operated not only on the governmental level but also on the private or organizational level. Besides affecting institutions from state legislatures to city governments and schools, the conservative movement also forced voluntary organizations to formulate their response to the Communist issue. This chapter, which examines both conservative and liberal organizations, reveals the non-governmental restrictions on leftists.

Voluntary organizations played a crucial role in the development of the Red Scare. They responded to the Scare by limiting their membership to non-Communists and by attempting to limit Communist expression in the general society. These internal and external activities do not confirm the "elite" nature of the Scare because American politics generally is influenced by organized pressure groups. Attempts to explain the development of the Scare through analyses of "masses" and "elites" have largely failed. The examination of voluntary groups in this chapter therefore views them as part of traditional political expression.

In the postwar decade, conservative and liberal organizations responded differently to the Communist issue. The conservative movement included a few ad hoc groups, but it featured the American Legion. These groups tried to prevent meetings where leftists entertained and spoke, and they sponsored educational meetings on the CP threat. No single liberal group matched the Legion's strength, and thus it is necessary to analyze various liberal organizations. These liberal groups reacted to the Communist issue by purging themselves of Communist and leftist members, but as earlier chapters have shown, these groups did not always join the crusade to restrict general leftist activity. Both the conservative and liberal movements were anti-Communist, but their tactics and purposes in the loyalty campaign differed. These organizations' similarities and differences are not without debate for the line between them is blurred, not clear-cut. Yet the line is there, however blurred.

While the conservative movement was led by the American Legion, it also featured ad hoc groups and spontaneous actions designed to ensure loyalty. Operating on the local level, these voluntary organizations tended to last for just a brief period of time.[1] Such local or ad hoc groups arose in Yellow Springs, Ohio, and in northern Wisconsin. Occasionally, violence resulted from these confrontations.

Conservatives in the Yellow Springs, Ohio, area formed their own local group to promote loyalty and to expose subversives. They were upset at two liberal institutions in the area: Antioch College and the *Yellow Springs News.* The newspaper, which supported socialist positions, declared that the Red Scare caused the country to "drift to totalitarianism." The conservatives began to meet secretly in January 1953, and two months later formed the Association for Civic Action (ACA). The ACA wanted to publicize its cause by starting its own newspaper. At first, it tried to buy the *News*, but the owner would not sell. The conservatives then formed the Greene County Printing Company, bought out two newspapers in small, nearby towns, and on June 11, 1953, launched the *Yellow Springs American.* Its initial editorial denied any animus toward the *News*, but the same issue encouraged HUAC to "keep after the reds." The *American* was concerned not only with the CP threat but also with the "socialistic" trends in government. "Socialism Eats Tax Money" and "The Case Against Socialized Power" appeared in the first few issues. "No country can long exist half socialist and half free. . . . One must be victorious," the newspaper concluded. After a Republican official from Cincinnati became editor, the newspaper's focus shifted from promoting loyalty to exposing "parlor pinks." It issued a warning that people associating with the "security risks" in the area would be named in the paper. It labeled Antioch College as "pink," full of "pseudo-liberal 'eggheads.'" By April 1954, the charges became more direct as the front page headline screamed "Antioch College—Threat to National Security."

> Battles could be lost. . . . Defenseless women could die in the bombed ruins of their homes because there exists the possibility of the betrayal of the U.S. through the delivery to the enemy of secrets and important data by persons connected with Antioch College.

No names were given, but the exposé was to be continued in the next week's edition. That plan was not met for the *American* folded with that salvo. Its extreme stance alienated subscribers and advertisers alike. Its supporters continued their efforts in the other two newspapers which they had bought, but they remained unsuccessful.[2]

Just as the Yellow Springs episode represented strains arising over educational policy, so ethnic and religious differences could become translated into a political dispute. In northern Wisconsin, the conservative movement coalesced into an ad hoc group, led by the Catholic priest. In early 1949, the Civil Rights Congress (CRC), a leftist group, began to organize in the rural area, which had a large anticlerical minority. In Barron County, the CRC recruited Lumir Subrt, the president of the ZCBJ

(Western Czech Benevolent Association), as its secretary. The CRC requested the use of the ZCBJ hall, and after some heated debate on the CRC's Communist affiliation, the ZCBJ approved the request. The Catholic priest in Haugen, the county seat, decided to fight the CRC activity. He circulated a petition to ban any meetings "not in conformity with American ideals and principles." After he spoke with the editor of the *Rice Lake Chronotype*, the newspaper charged that the CRC was a Communist front and that the proposed speaker was an admitted CP member in the process of being deported. The priest made plans to pack the CRC meetings and have his supporters sing patriotic songs and give anti-Communist speeches. The CRC adherents got wind of the plan and decided not to use the ZCBJ hall. They went instead to the sales' pavilion, where they had a peaceful meeting. The divisions in the area remained throughout the postwar decade. The CRC supporters continued their leftist activities, subscribing to the *Daily Worker* and protesting the Rosenbergs' verdict, and the conservatives remained vigilant.[3]

As the CRC incident indicates, the possibility of direct confrontation between the two opposing groups was present. In some cases, such "local" disputes turned violent. Before the Korean War, leftists and peace proponents had endorsed the Stockholm peace petition:

> We demand the absolute outlawing of the atomic bomb, a frightful weapon for the mass extermination of the populace.
> We demand the establishment of rigorous international control in order to assure that this outlawing will be carried out.
> We consider that the government which would first use the atomic bomb against any country whatsoever would commit not only a war crime, but a crime against humanity and should be treated as a war criminal.
> We call upon all men of good will in the world to sign this petition.

Although the petition itself was relatively mild, its leftist origins caused a strong backlash after the war broke out. In Milwaukee, three workers at the Seaman body plant signed and tried to distribute the petition, but other workers forcefully asked them to leave. A few days later, five sympathizers of the original three got the same treatment. Officials of local 75 (UAW-CIO) urged the workers to refrain from mob action, but their warnings came too late to calm the emotions. The next day, one of the original three leftist-peace supporters reported for work. Other employees grabbed him, threw him down the stairs and out of the plant. He received a fractured back. The other two petition signers did not show up for work and were fired. Their five sympathizers agreed to a thirty-day leave of absence in the hope that tempers would cool.[4] Violence also marked a Chicago rally sponsored by the Council of American-Soviet Friendship. The 1953 meeting, scheduled to honor the eighth anniversary of Franklin Roosevelt's death, was picketed by an ad hoc group composed mostly of Ukranian and Slavic ethnics. The conservative pickets initially taunted and red-baited those who entered the auditorium, but soon they charged into the building. Fighting broke out, and the police had to restore order.[5]

The conservative movement was not characterized by either ad hoc local groups or violence, however. The most typical conservative organization was the American Legion. Although the Legion was a fraternal group which did not endorse political candidates, it entered the political arena to lobby for antisubversive proposals. On the local level, it acted to ensure loyalty in two ways. "Negatively," the Legion worked to prevent meetings at which leftists entertained or spoke. Such efforts created controversies concerning the following activities:

entertainment: *Death of a Salesman*
                     The Weavers
                     Limelight (Charlie Chaplin's film)
                     Salt of the Earth

meetings: American Peace Crusade
                     Methodist Federation for Social Action
                     ACLU

The Legion also acted "positively" in its sponsorship of educational efforts to awaken the public to the CP threat. Its most famous "positive" effort occurred in Mosinee, Wisconsin. Although the Legion was frequently successful in both "negative" and "positive" efforts, their leaders felt that the task was enormous and pictured themselves as lonely voices in the wilderness.

In Peoria, Illinois, *Death of a Salesman* became the target of a Legion boycott. This "negative" action resulted from a "positive" effort, a local Legion post's sponsorship of a two-day Conference to Combat Communism. Its featured speakers, including Benjamin Gitlow and Rabbi Benjamin Schultz, warned of the immediate danger of Communists within the nation, and even in Peoria. Vincent Hartnett, the founder of Aware, Inc., which probed the entertainment industry, focused his attack on *Death of a Salesman*, which was scheduled to play in the city later that month. Hartnett charged that author Arthur Miller, touring producer Dermit Bloomgardner, and actor Albert Dekker were affiliated with several Communist-front organizations. Moreover, the Communists sent seven and one-half percent of their earnings to the CP. Soon afterwards, the Legion post and the Junior Chamber of Commerce passed resolutions urging a boycott of the play. Miller, Bloomgardner, and Dekker responded that they did not have Communist affiliations and did not donate money to the CP. They also noted that this was the first effort to boycott the play. The theater owner did not break the contract, and the play was shown. Yet the Legion's action was partially successful since the audiences filled less than one-half of the seats.[6]

In Ohio, the Legion twice worked to ban the Weavers, a popular folk group. In the summer of 1951, the Ohio State Fair scheduled the Weavers. Before their appearance, a conservative magazine, *Counterattack*, charged that the four singers had Communist affiliations. The Legion immediately lodged a protest to the fair's directors. The Weavers denied the charges, asserted their loyalty, and announced that they performed only as musicians, not as political spokesmen. The fair manager nevertheless cancelled the concert.[7] A few months later, a similar incident arose in Cleveland. The Press Club sponsored a television benefit for the Heart Society, and scheduled the Weavers to perform. The Legion and the Knights of Columbus quickly protested, but the Press Club responded that no member of the group had ever acted illegally and that no political speeches would be made during their performance. As a result, they were able to play.[8] The blacklist against the group would soon become more universally effective.

Perhaps the Legion's major target among entertainers was Charlie Chaplin, who released *Limelight* in the spring of 1953. Throughout the Midwest, the veterans' group had mixed success in boycotting the film. The Legion ignored the content of the film, but criticized Chaplin's "contemptuous attitude toward American patriotism." In Detroit, the Legion boycotted and picketed the theater. The controversy probably convinced some to stay away, but it drew others to the film. One night, about 350 Wayne University students came. In Milwaukee, the county American Legion passed a resolution asking the theater owner to refrain from showing the film, but he refused and the film went on without picketing. In Columbus, Ohio, the film also played despite Legion protests, but it stayed for only three days due to poor attendance.[9]

That same year, the Legion took on *Salt of the Earth*, a movie which had been produced with the assistance of the Mine, Mill, and Smelter Workers Union, a left-wing union. The major theme of the prounion film concerned the role of Mexican-American women in a strike in New Mexico. After its opening in New York City and Silver City, New Mexico, the distributors tried to break into the Midwest by opening in Detroit and Chicago. After they had booked a theater in Detroit, Legion officials visited the owner, charged that the film was a Communist effort, and promised picketing if he showed it. The distributors, worried that the pressure might work, arranged for a preview for the UAW-CIO educational directors and the Legion officials, who had not seen the film. After the screening, all agreed that the film did not support radical or violent efforts to change the government, but the Legion officials still favored its ban. Not only had the Mine, Mill, and Smelter Workers Union been ousted by the CIO for being Communist-dominated, but film director Herbert Biberman, producer Paul

Jarrico, and writer Michael Wilson had all taken the Fifth Amendment before HUAC on questions about their Communist affiliations. The distributors argued with the Legion officials about their reasoning, but to no avail. The theater owner decided to break the contract, and the film was not shown in Detroit.[10]

In Chicago, the Legion also worked to block *Salt of the Earth*. The film was scheduled to open at the Hyde Park Theater beginning May 14, 1954. The Legion protested privately to the theater owner, and on April 30, he cancelled it. The film's distributors were caught off-guard, and tried again at the Cinema Annex. On May 12, the Legion wrote to the theater owner that the film was Communist propaganda put out by persons with Communist sympathies and affiliations. The owner refused to give in to the Legion's demands, and was prepared to show the film on opening night, the Friday evening of Memorial Day weekend. Although 2,000 persons arrived at the theater, no projectionist came. The Chicago Moving Picture Operator's Union (IATSE-AFL), which represented all Chicago projectionists, had decided to boycott the film. Four thousand more persons came over the next three days to the theater, but the film was never shown to the general public. Private screenings were given to the ACLU, a Unitarian church, and students at Northwestern and the University of Chicago. The distributors sued the union, seeking an injunction and damages. The union countered with interrogatories which inquired about the Communist affiliation of several persons connected with the film. After the court ordered them to answer, the distributors withdrew their complaint. No other effort was made in the Midwest to show the film, and only ten theaters in the country ran the picture.[11]

The Legion worked "negatively" to halt not only leftist entertainers but also meetings of liberals and leftists. Two such incidents occurred in Chicago. In June 1951, the American Peace Crusade scheduled a rally at the Coliseum in Chicago. The Legion urged the Coliseum's management to cancel the meeting, but they replied that they could not break the contract and the rally was held. A few months later, the Methodist Federation for Social Action (MFSA) planned to hold its annual convention at the First Methodist Church in Evanston, a suburb of Chicago. The county Legion and the *Chicago Tribune* protested that the MFSA was a Communist front, and suggested that the church withdraw the use of its facilities. The church refused to do so. At other times, the Legion was more successful. It was able to force the cancellation of two of the four Chicago meetings in support of the Rosenbergs.[12]

Perhaps the most controversial "negative" effort by the Legion was its opposition to an ACLU meeting in Indianapolis. Liberals in the state, concerned about the restrictive climate, decided to form a chapter of the ACLU. They proposed to hold their first meeting in the War Memorial Building, a state-owned monument dedicated to those who had died in the

First World War. The American Legion and another conservative group, the Minute Women, urged the rejection of the ACLU's request. The Board of Trustees, appointed by the governor, had strong ties to the Legion's leadership. The board refused the ACLU's proposal, and the board's executive secretary charged that the group was a "front for Communists." The ACLU denied the accusation, and arranged to meet in a church. The denial of free speech and assembly was criticized by the Indianapolis *Star* and *Times*, conservative newspapers which had emphasized the Communist danger in earlier times. The incident received national publicity when Edward R. Murrow televised the ACLU meeting and a Legion gathering. The War Memorial Board nevertheless remained convinced of its correct decision. Six months later, it again barred the ACLU from the War Memorial Building, even though the scheduled speaker was the chairman of the board of Studebaker Corporation, Paul G. Hoffman. In July 1955, the War Memorial Board issued new regulations which denied the facilities to groups that "were identified, directly or indirectly, actively or remotely, with communist or subversive groups." The board denied ACLU's requests again in 1957, 1962, and 1967. Although the Legion was able to block the meetings being held in a public building, the controversy over the ban helped to publicize the issue of freedom of assembly. It also did not stop the organization of an ACLU chapter, which recruited more members because of the Legion's actions.[13]

Besides such "negative" efforts aimed at restricting activities, the Legion also sponsored "positive" events aimed at educating the public. The Wisconsin Legion sponsored a Seminar on Subversive Activities in Madison in 1948; the Michigan Legion held the Wolverine All-American Conference in Lansing in 1950; and the Indiana Legion conducted conferences in 1954 and 1955. Conferences were also held in other places. Speakers included former Communists, such as Benjamin Gitlow and J. B. Matthews, and politicians, such as William Jenner and Paul Broyles. Speakers not only emphasized the dangers of Communism, but also characterized the general public as lazy, apathetic, and ignorant. From their viewpoint, the Legion was a lone voice with little power.[14]

Perhaps the most famous "positive" incident was the "Communist" take-over of Mosinee, Wisconsin, on May Day, 1950. In April, state Legion officials had approached the town leaders about the plan, and they immediately agreed with the proposal. The town was selected because of its small size, a population of slightly more than 2,000. The editor and publisher of the town's only newspaper became the chairman of "A Day Under Communism," and he sold the idea to other citizens. The technical advisor to the "coup" was Joseph Zack Kornfeder, a Communist who had quit the party in 1934 and had become a fervent anti-Communist. Reporters came from throughout the country, including CBS, NBC, and *Life*.[15]

On May 1, before dawn, a Communist combat team arrested the mayor and police chief. They quickly took control of the telephone building and the power house at the paper mill, the major industry in the town. By mid-morning, the reds were in complete control. They put up road blocks, distributed the "Red Star," and raised their flag over the city hall. At a public meeting, the Communist chief proclaimed the United Soviet States of America with Moscow as its capital. All land and industry was confiscated; all political parties except for the CP were abolished; and the Constitution was eliminated. Religion was to be tolerated, but with restrictions: no further printing of religious materials, no teaching of children, and no ministers. Policemen were executed; all firearms were confiscated; and a new "military security police" with power to arrest suspects without a warrant was established. Everyone was issued an identification card and a ration card. Strikes were prohibited as treason against the state, and wages—with CP dues already deducted—were based on piece work. Communist films were shown at the theater, and the schools taught Communist beliefs as students were required to wear CP uniforms. Sunset brought the end of Communist control; the "Day" was over. The American flag was raised while citizens sang the "Star Spangled Banner" and "God Bless America." All "Communist" materials were burned, and Legion officials spoke to the mass meeting on the glories of American freedom.[16]

A year later, a similar event occurred in Rushville, Indiana, but without the massive publicity. Occurring after the U.S. had lost the war to the Soviet Union, "the conquering hordes of Reds" occupied the small town quickly. Religion "felt the first whip of the lash" as all ministers were arrested. The Communists ordered everyone to say a new version of the Lord's Prayer: "Our Father who art in Moscow. . . ." Library books were burned; the newspaper was banned; and students were forced to attend classes in Communist ideology. Farms were collectivized. Anyone who criticized the new regime was arrested. "Later it was learned 476 bodies of men, women, and children were buried in a makeshift grave. . . . All had been tortured, then shot. Many had been forced to dig their own graves."[17]

Although the Legion worked at both "positive" and "negative" activities, there was some tension between the supporters of each type. These internal strains became evident in the mid-1950s in the Illinois and Indiana Legions. The "negative" supporters won in Illinois, while the "positives" succeeded in Indiana.

In 1954, the "negative" supporters controlled the Illinois American Legion, and they attacked an unlikely target, the Girl Scouts. This caused a brief backlash, but later the "negatives" came back into power. The Girl Scouts' handbook recently had been revised, and the conservative Legionnaires felt that it contained subversive passages on foreign affairs and the United Nations. One suspicious section dealt with the founding of the Girl Scouts because the handbook noted that Juliette Gordon Low had gotten the idea while in England. "The concept of 'One World' had taken shape in her lively mind many years before the phrase became common. She was one of the first true internationalists." The state convention approved a resolution urging the suspension of funds and members from the Girl Scouts "until such time as they restore the time-honored American patriotic and historical ideals in its teaching to American youth." The resolution was met outside of Legion ranks by widespread laughter, and many Legionnaires were embarrassed at the "overkill" mentality. The incident was even more ridiculous because the Girl Scouts had agreed two months earlier to make certain changes in the handbook.[18]

The following year, the supporters of the "positive" approach made a brief comeback. The new state commander, Irving Breakstone, decided to deemphasize the "negative" efforts of the Legion and promote educational activities. He began an Education for Freedom program, based on materials from the American Heritage Council. Local Legionnaires studied American history and such issues as the meaning of the Declaration of Independence and the Bill of Rights. According to Breakstone, the FBI was fully capable of handling subversive activities; it did not need the help of the Legion. To brand people and organizations as Communists was often a smearing activity which only harmed freedom. Breakstone's other controversial move was to support a report that cleared UNESCO of charges of communistic influence.[19]

Breakstone's policies caused a backlash. The American Heritage Council received funds from the Fund for the Republic, whose president was Robert Hutchins. In early 1955, conservative columnist Fulton Lewis, Jr., condemned the fund for its opposition to Senator McCarthy and other anti-Communist efforts. Breakstone's critics took up the charge, and at the 1955 state convention, they repudiated his leadership. Although it was traditional for the retiring president to be elected as a delegate to the national convention, Breakstone was defeated. The convention also decided to quit using materials from the American Heritage Council, and it returned several thousand copies of the U.S. and Illinois Constitutions. Finally, the convention voted against the report clearing UNESCO and in favor of withdrawing from the United Nations.[20]

A similar controversy affected the Indiana Legion, but here the "positives" won. In 1955, state Legion leaders began to stress community service and education. The Legion merged the Un-American Activities Committee with the Americanism Committee. State officials urged their members to refrain from accusing a person of Communist sympathies or activities "without first establishing a safe legal basis." This condition could be met by getting governmental documentation, consulting legal counsel, and obtaining approval by a state Legion officer, the judge advocate. Some of the anti-Communist activists were angry at these developments. The

convention of the tenth district censured the state commander for "impair-
ing" the work of anti-Communists. The new regulations nevertheless
remained in force.[21]

Liberal organizations did not respond to the Communist issue as conservative ones did, but in their own way. Rather than working "externally"
to promote loyalty or to restrict leftist activity, liberal groups had "internal"
disputes. Particularly in the early years of the postwar decade, liberals
debated their policy toward Communists and leftists as members. Such
membership controversies occurred in the following voluntary groups: the
Congress of Racial Equality, Independent Voters of Illinois, Chicago Civil
Liberties Committee, Wisconsin Farmers Union, and the National Lawyers
Guild. In all but the latter case, the groups expelled the Communists and
their allies.

The Congress of Racial Equality (CORE) had to confront the loyalty
issue in the postwar decade, even though its initial policy rejected Communism. Supporting integration and pacifism, CORE was founded in
Chicago in 1941 and had its greatest strength in the Midwest. Its anti-
Communist policy was caused by its fear of public resistance if it supported
Communist positions and by its belief that Communists might focus on
issues other than segregation and non-violence. Each CORE chapter
nevertheless was allowed to accept or reject individual Communists as
members. The Columbus, Ohio, group accepted Communists, but by 1947
had an internal struggle over the issue. The chapter at first invited Benjamin
J. Davis, Jr., an avowed CP leader, to speak, but soon, anti-Communists
called another meeting and withdrew the invitation. The national organization became concerned about this incident, and the 1948 Convention
unanimously issued a "Statement on Communism." It rejected affiliation
with Communist front groups, established procedures for ousting any
chapter that became Communist-dominated, and declared that Communists
used "violence, treachery, and political maneuvering without principle."
Four years later, the organization reaffirmed the policy. Despite its stance,
CORE's strength declined during the Red Scare because of its independent
radical nature.[22]

Liberal organizations with a white, middle-class base, such as the
Independent Voters of Illinois (IVI), also wrestled with the Communist
issue. The IVI, founded in 1942 by liberals in the Chicago area, was officially
nonpartisan, but it usually supported liberal Democrats. In the 1946
campaign, conservative Republicans attacked Democrats who had been
endorsed by the IVI. According to one GOP leader, the IVI's program
paralleled Communism "almost 100%." Conservatives repeated the charges
in the 1947 Chicago mayoral campaign. According to an American Legion
official, the Democratic candidate would appoint the IVI president as the
president of the Board of Education. This would cause more socialistic

indoctrination in the schools, he concluded. Although the Democratic candidate won the mayoral election, the charges in these two campaigns had an immediate impact on an upcoming IVI election. Liberals who wanted the IVI to adopt a harder anti-Communist policy were opposed by those who wanted to affiliate with the Progressive Citizens of America (PCA), a leftist group. This latter faction was supported by critics of the IVI's closed system of voting. The Board of Governors, composed of 108 members, selected the Board of Directors, which had twenty-three members and which in turn approved the governors. After a decision to allow proxy voting, the anti-Communist liberals won easily. Some of their critics resigned, and privately the victors rejoiced at the defeat of the "fellow travelers." Soon thereafter, the IVI affiliated with the Americans for Democratic Action (ADA), which prohibited Communists as members.[23]

Another liberal organization in Chicago experienced a similar crisis at the same time, but it swung farther to the right. The Chicago Civil Liberties Committee (CCLC), organized in 1929, had liberal and radical origins. For a time, it affiliated with the ACLU, but in 1945 it broke with the national organization over the defense of fascists and racists. The CCLC should not help "to pave the way to the gates of the torture chambers," declared one board member. This position was followed by a decision in June 1946 to affiliate with the Civil Rights Congress (CRC), a leftist group. The CCLC's magazine soon began to run left-wing articles, such as "U.S. Missed Fascism by Five Votes" and "Is Tom Clark a Fascist Influence?"[24]

The CCLC's new policies did not command total support among membership, and during the next few months, the group began a shift back toward a conservative position. In late 1946, the CRC's effort to establish a second chapter in Evanston, a Chicago suburb, antagonized the CCLC. The result was the formal break between the two groups. In April 1947, the CRC made a final attempt to win over the CCLC, but after a heated debate, the Chicago group declined the offer by a vote of ten to four. The CCLC began promoting itself as rejecting "any anti-American or un-democratic" policies. The conservative shift was finalized at the 1949 convention, which adopted two constitutional amendments. One barred knowing Communists and Fascists as members, and the other required board members to sign a non-Communist oath. This shift in policy was led by the CCLC's executive secretary who broke with the CP during this period. He moved increasingly to the right, and by the late 1950s had joined the Illinois Right to Work Committee and the Anti-Communist League of North America.[25]

The Communist issue touched not only urban but also rural liberal groups. The Wisconsin Farmers Union (WFU), a branch of the National Farmers Union, had been organized in the 1930s, and allowed Communists and leftists as members. Between 1945 and 1948, the WFU redefined its policies. Kenneth W. Hones, the WFU president since 1933, symbolized and led these changes. In his 1945 presidential message, Hones condemned red-baiters as supporters of war against "our great ally, Russia." Such attitudes brought conservative criticism, and several months later, the *Milwaukee Sentinel*, a Hearst newspaper, charged that the WFU was Communist-dominated and that Hones was a CP sympathizer. The tensions boiled up first at the local level because the president of the chapter at Hoard, Rolland Barrett, was an avowed Communist. In 1946, an opposition movement against Barrett was formed, and the county board of directors proposed his expulsion. Allegedly, any CP member was more loyal to the party than to the union. Despite the state board's endorsement of the county board's suggestion, Barrett fought back and won the presidency on the issue of local control. Hones became more antagonistic toward Communists during the Wallace-Truman fight of 1947–1948. Hones, a Truman supporter, decided to retain Communists as WFU members only if they remained quiet. If they tried to "use our union as a vehicle through which they can accomplish their ends," they would not be tolerated. Soon, Hones abandoned that policy and led the ouster of several WFU leaders, even though they were "very enthusiastic workers and on the surface loyal members." By the end of 1948, Hones had become convinced of a Communist effort to infiltrate and control the union. At the 1949 convention, the WFU by an overwhelming vote amended the constitution to bar Communists and fascists as members. Hones led the loyalty fight throughout the national organization, and later admitted that he was considered the "number one red-baiter in the Farmers' Union."[26]

Another liberal organization, the National Lawyers Guild (NLG), did not shed its radical members and policies, but in Detroit it experienced an internal dispute over the loyalty issue. The NLG's civil libertarian policies, which included defense of Communists, caused HUAC to label it "the legal bulwark of the Communist party." This September 1950 report energized the moderates in the Detroit chapter, who recommended that all members take a non-Communist oath. Declaring that the CP was a criminal conspiracy, these members felt the preservation of the guild's reputation required such an oath. Their critics charged that the oath would not convince their detractors, but would undermine the guild's civil liberties' policies. They proposed retention of the constitution which admitted members without regard to "political beliefs or affiliations." The national guild was greatly concerned over the Detroit proposal since it might set a precedent for other chapters. It sent a representative to the city, and he argued that the chapter should delay its decision until the national organization had time to reply to the HUAC report. After much debate, the chapter voted to accept this suggestion. The delay angered the moderates, and about twenty members quit the guild. The chapter thus lost most of its prominent members, but it never required a loyalty oath. Throughout the country, the NLG lost about one-half of its membership because of the HUAC report.[27]

Summary

Throughout the Midwest, conservative and liberal organizations had to define their position on the loyalty issue. Both types of voluntary organizations exhibited anti-Communism, but this similarity masks differences in the expression of that attitude.

Conservative organizations initiated many restrictive actions and held a much more limited view of freedom of speech and assembly. Groups, such as the American Legion, attempted to deny Communists any political expression, even when that expression was performed indirectly through entertainment. The Legion also attempted to block liberal groups, such as the ACLU, which had ousted its Communists several years before. The Legion was frequently successful in these efforts, and this effectiveness had several causes. It was a veterans' organization in a time when veterans were respected. Its local posts were already institutionalized in the community prior to the postwar decade, and its non-partisan conservatism had widespread legitimacy. The posts benefitted from a centralized information service, usually run by a state or national antisubversive official. Finally, while it had its detractors, no counter-organization came anywhere near to matching its strength. The wonder is not its successes but the limitations on its effectiveness. This resulted from the Legion's decentralized nature and its nonpartisan character. The Legion has been discussed in this chapter as a local organization because the activities occurred on that level. To be sure, the Legion operated as a lobbying force on the state and national levels, but it depended on the local officials to put its stated policies into actions against leftists. The commitment to the loyalty crusade by the local post determined whether or not it tried to ban a leftist meeting or boycott a Charlie Chaplin film. The variation in the local character of the Legion was partially caused by the nonpartisan nature of the veterans' group. Many posts were fraternal in orientation, and did not become involved in the conservative effort. Indeed, the Legion's activities point out the limitations of the Scare. The conservative movement never organized its own chapters; it never had its own formal structure. Without this, it lacked a certain consistency and uniformity, and thus effectiveness.

Liberal organizations became more openly anti-Communist during the postwar decade, but their expression of that attitude differed from conservative groups, such as the American Legion. Some historians exaggerate the non-Communist aspects of the liberal movement, and criticize the lack of a pure civil libertarian policy. Other scholars overly praise liberals for their opposition to the more blatant excesses of the Red Scare. In actuality, however, liberals neither "lost sight of vital civil liberties" nor moved "civil liberties to the forefront of their interests."[28]

Liberal organizations responded to the Scare in two different ways. First, liberals expelled Communists from their organizations. Unlike conservatives, though, liberals did not always proceed to persecute radicals. Liberals differentiated between leftists and Communists, and often fought against conservative attempts to enact general antisubversive laws or to prohibit specific meetings. Rejecting the Communist position, liberals nevertheless were less inclined to inflict "extreme and gratuitous humiliations" on leftists.[29] A few liberal organizations, such as the ACLU, extended this policy toward Communists.

Liberals also used the Scare in a way not fully examined in this study. They used the Communist issue to urge reform efforts. Communism could be defeated, they argued, by enacting measures to alleviate poverty and injustice. Throughout the Midwest on the state and local levels, liberals actively supported reforms, such as a fair employment practices commission. In Wisconsin and Michigan, liberals made the Democratic party into an avowedly reformist force. Liberal anti-Communism existed; without a doubt, it formed part of the Scare. Yet liberal anticommunism was not merely an effort to purge membership rolls of Communists. It was a broader and more ambivalent reaction. The essence of the Red Scare—the attacks on Communists and radicals as disloyal—came not from liberals but from the conservative movement. With a momentum and a strength of its own, it acted independently of the liberal response.

These three chapters on the local level have clearly shown the activity of the conservative movement: in city government, schools, and voluntary organizations. These incidents occurred in different cities at different times; they involved different people. In isolation, they seem to have no overt connection with one another. If an historian uses a snapshot approach, the result is a clear picture of the sporadic nature of the Scare. Yet by using the comparative approach, by using a movie camera, we can see connections, the existence of a movement. We can see that the Scare, while sporadic, was also pervasive. The loyalty crusade occurred in all areas, affected different types of institutions and groups, and often imposed its values on political nonconformists. This pervasiveness does not mean that the Scare flowed directly from the activities of a national leader or the federal government. HUAC did succeed in forcing the dismissal of several teachers and city workers, but Robert Griffith overstates his case when he argues that "the politics of anti-Communism originated at the national level and then spread to the states."[30] It should now be obvious that the conservative movement acted on all levels, and gained strength from the interactions. This complex mechanism, not a simple one, powered the Scare to its effectiveness.

6

Universities: Students

The conservative movement, as noted in previous chapters, was concerned about education. This was especially true about higher education. When Senator Joseph McCarthy wrote about his *Fight for America*, he asserted that loyal Americans could best help his cause by exposing radical teachers. "Countless times I have heard parents throughout the country complain that their sons and daughters were sent to college as good Americans and returned four years later as wild-eyed radicals."[1] Such conservatives were convinced that whoever controlled the education of the young would dictate the future of the country. They were thus prepared to investigate political nonconformity on campus and to impose limits on freedom of expression. These aspects will be examined in the following two chapters, the first examining the loyalty issue as it affected students and the next considering faculty members.

Throughout the Midwest, the Red Scare directly and indirectly affected students. Leftist student organizations found it difficult to receive and maintain recognition or university approval. Attempts to bring radical speakers on campus were rejected at times. The editorial direction of student newspapers was scrutinized. Legislative investigative committees questioned a few students because of their radical political activity. These controversies also had an inhibiting effect on the many students who were not involved in these activities.

These numerous incidents seem to confirm the severity of the Scare. According to Philip Altbach, "the pervasiveness of such repression can hardly be exaggerated."[2] Yet this chapter will assert that the effect can be overestimated. When a student political organization was banned, its members were not disciplined and usually entered other groups to continue their activity. When speakers were restricted from campus, they often went a few feet away from university property to address students. The publicity surrounding the banning, moreover, often caused a larger group to attend such rallies. Of the eight "unfriendly" students, only one was expelled. This criticism of Altbach's thesis does not deny that administrative policies toward leftist student activity were restrictive. It attempts to place these restrictions in a broader perspective. It points to paternalism as the basic university policy toward students and points out the ambivalent effects of such paternalism.[3] Thus, it questions the severity of the repression and the total conformity of the students.

Although the Red Scare arose at many colleges, this analysis focuses on seven institutions. The University of Illinois, Ohio State University, Michigan State College, the University of Michigan, and the University of Wisconsin are state universities. Wayne University, which was governed by the Detroit Board of Education, and the University of Chicago, a private institution, are both located in large metropolitan areas. The following chart summarizes the issues at the seven institutions.

	Recognition policy	Speaker policy	Newspapers' independence	Rights before legislative committees
Ohio State Univ.	X	X		X
Michigan State C.	X	X	X	X
Wayne University	X	X		X
Univ. of Michigan	X	X		X
Univ. of Chicago	X	X	X	X
Univ. of Wisconsin	X	X		
Univ. of Illinois	X			

Controversies about recognition and speaker policy first arose over the American Youth for Democracy (AYD), a leftist student group which allowed Communists to become members. This national organization had chapters at each of the seven colleges, but the development of each AYD controversy differed. Ohio State University and Michigan State College refused to even recognize an AYD chapter. Wayne University, the University of Michigan, and the University of Illinois initially recognized the group, but later banned it. The University of Chicago and the University of Wisconsin, on the other hand, continued to accept the group despite conservatives' protests. At the latter five institutions, the recognition dispute included a "speaker policy" controversy as the AYD attempted to schedule leftist speakers.

At Ohio State University, the administration successfully resisted an attempt to organize an AYD chapter. In November 1943, it had given recognition to the Ohio State Youth for Democracy (OSYD), which was aligned but not formally affiliated with the AYD. On April 4, 1946, the OSYD voted thirty to seven to affiliate with the national organization. Five days later, the *Columbus Citizen* reported that the national AYD had been accused of being a Communist front. The next day, President Howard Bevis appointed the vice-president and the dean of men to investigate the campus AYD. The AYD's faculty advisor attempted to reverse the vote to affiliate, but his motion failed by an overwhelming vote. He then resigned in protest. The campus AYD president denied that Communists dominated the local or national organization. The state AYD executive director, Frank Hashmall, admitted that some individual Communists might be members, but he praised the AYD policy of not screening its members' political beliefs and affiliations. Attacks on the student group, Hashmall concluded, were red-baiting techniques, patented by Hitler, to weaken progressive forces. Some students agreed that the AYD was a Communist front and favored its ban. Others suggested that it should remain on campus but should call itself Communist, while a few supported the AYD's right to exist whatever its affiliations. In late April, the administration's investigation concluded that the group did have Communist influences, and on the same day, President Bevis withdrew the OSYD's recognition.[4]

A few months later at Michigan State College in East Lansing, an AYD group also had a hard time in getting off the ground. This time, fellow students rather than the administration blocked the formation of an AYD chapter. In the fall of 1946, the AYD and the Spartan Citizens Committee (SCC), which was affiliated with the leftist National Citizens Political Action Committee, petitioned the Student Council for recognition. In the debate, some students accused the groups of being "Communist inspired," but others defended them on the basis of freedom of speech and association. On November 13, the Student Council approved the SCC by a vote of sixteen to three, but vetoed, twelve to seven, the AYD's bid for recognition.[5]

The AYD members did not stop their political activity, and this brought them into a confrontation with the administration. After meeting secretly off campus for a few months, the AYD members distributed pamphlets signed "Spartan AYD" at a rally in support of a Fair Employment Practices Commission. The Michigan State College president, John A. Hannah, asserted that the pamphlet implied university recognition of the group. He decided to expel any student who tried to establish or perpetuate the AYD either on or off campus. The next day, the Student Council debated the issue and recommended, nine to six, that the faculty discipline the AYD students. The Faculty Committee on Student Organizations questioned the students and proposed that six be placed on "continuous disciplinary probation." This barred them from holding any student office and participating in any extracurricular activity. If they committed further violations during their probation, they would be expelled. On February 6, 1947, President Hannah approved this recommendation. He maintained that the college imposed the sanctions because of the students' violation of university regulations and not because of their political beliefs. This assertion must be balanced with the original Student Council decision denying recognition to the AYD because of its political sympathies.[6]

One student on probation, James Zarichny, nevertheless continued his political activities and encountered further trouble. In December 1948, a year and a half after the probation, Zarichny helped to organize a meeting, held off campus, where the chairman of the Michigan Communist party made a speech. Less than two weeks later, President Hannah expelled him, claiming that Zarichny had violated his probation. The Student Council and the student newspaper both supported Hannah's decision. Zarichny filed suit to be reinstated, but the courts rejected his appeal.[7]

In contrast to Ohio State and Michigan State, Wayne University granted recognition to an AYD chapter and, more importantly, defended its right to exist when it was attacked initially. The controversy escalated dramatically over two months as conservative legislators tried to force the administration into taking restrictive action. When the AYD controversy at Michigan State erupted in early 1947, the governor quickly ordered Wayne University to investigate its AYD chapter. Formed three years earlier, the Wayne AYD had thirty active members and had been involved in desegregating a few Detroit restaurants in the fall of 1946. On February 10, 1947, the university president, David Dodds Henry, reported that the chapter had "not been subversive in action or intent." Although the national organization had been accused of Communist ties, the president indicated that he had received no proof. If such evidence was provided, Henry declared that he would ask the group to break its affiliation with the national AYD. This did not satisfy the state senate which formed its own commission, chaired by Matthew Callahan (R, Detroit), to probe for subversive influences.[8]

While the AYD controversy continued unresolved, the Wayne administration acted swiftly against another student group, the Marxian Study Society (MSS). A small group, the MSS received probationary recognition on January 20, 1947, and held three meetings in February. As its name suggests, the MSS proposed to study Marxism and to refrain from actively participating in politics. At its last February meeting, Marty Mitchnik, a local Communist official, discussed the *Communist Manifesto.* At the end of the meeting, Mitchnik announced that he would discuss the CP with anyone who wanted to stay. The next day, the Recognition Committee, composed of four faculty members and four students, unanimously recommended suspending the MSS. The Mitchnik meeting, the committee charged, had been intended not for objective study but for political discussion. The MSS, moreover, had not consulted its faculty advisor about scheduling Mitchnik, and had allowed non-members to attend. The proposed suspension would last for the remainder of the spring term. On March 3, President Henry went beyond this recommendation and made the ban permanent.[9]

Henry's action on the MSS did not satisfy the senate investigators, known as the Callahan Commission, who still wanted a ban of the AYD. Repeating his earlier arguments, President Henry defended the campus chapter to the commission. Senator Callahan protested that the AYD's efforts in integration—sit-ins and picketing—violated the rights of private property and the state's criminal syndicalism law. Another senator called the activities "mob rule and mob authority." The senators remained unconvinced even when the Department of Justice publicly refused to make any negative conclusions on the loyalty of the national AYD. Senator Callahan vowed to oppose the university's appropriation in the legislature, and the senate Republican caucus, a majority of the upper chamber, agreed to uphold his threat. In rebuttal, the Detroit Board of Education, which governed the university, supported Henry's position, and the president condemned the senators' threat.[10]

On April 3, the Department of Justice sent a second letter to President Henry. It again refused to release any specific information on the national AYD, but attached "for your information" testimony by J. Edgar Hoover, who condemned the group as a Communist front. This convinced the Wayne administration. The dean of student affairs met with the Student Activities Committee, which voted six to two to ask the campus AYD to disaffiliate. The students on the SAC split two to two, but the four faculty members sided with the dean. Although this occurred during spring break, the dean summoned the AYD executive committee to his office. They refused to break their ties with the national organization. On the next day, President Henry withdrew the AYD's recognition. He asserted that the group was influenced by outside political forces and that therefore it accepted goals and methods not listed in its local constitution. The administration's reliance on Hoover's testimony reveals its desire to end the two-month confrontation with the state senate. Almost two years later, an administrator remembered that "the situation was very tense. . . . The fate of the university for a number of years was wrapped up in the university's handling of the whole episode."[11]

Reaction on campus was divided. The faculty realized the danger of confronting powerful politicians and supported Henry's decision. The student newspaper criticized both the Senators and the AYD ban. Some students agreed, but others blamed the AYD for causing the commotion. Most worried that the administration might adopt other regulations and become more paternalistic. Members of the AYD, naturally upset at the ban, simply formed an off-campus AYD chapter, sometimes called the Collegian Club. It continued to participate in leftist political activity and to sponsor leftist speakers, such as Gerhardt Eisler and Carl Marzani, two Communists who had been convicted of contempt of Congress. In renting the hall for that meeting, the AYD got into a minor controversy. Its president seemed to represent the group as having recognition. This prompted the dean of student affairs to recommend suspending the student. Although the city newspapers sensationalized the Eisler speech, President Henry rejected the dean's proposal. Instead, the administration issued new guidelines on student political activity. If students linked an unrecognized group to the university, they would be subject to disciplinary action. Objectivity and neutrality must be preserved, the administration concluded.[12]

The University of Michigan, which also had a recognized AYD chapter, avoided a confrontation with the Callahan Commission by banning the group. This action brought sharp student criticism for its paternalistic basis. The Michigan Youth for Democratic Action (MYDA), which had more than forty members, affiliated with the AYD in 1946 and received recognition. After the AYD dispute at Michigan State College in January 1947, Governor Kim Sigler directed U.M. President Alexander Ruthven to investigate the MYDA in Ann Arbor. Some students supported the MYDA's right to exist, even though they disagreed with its policies. They formed the Michigan Committee for Academic Freedom, an ad hoc group that would last for several years. President Ruthven delayed action on the MYDA while the Wayne controversy was developing. A few days after President Henry banned the Wayne AYD, President Ruthven withdrew the MYDA's recognition. He asserted that it performed "a disservice to the educational and other interests" of the university since it was affiliated with a Communist front organization. This quick action averted a confrontation with the Callahan Committee. The Student Legislature protested Ruthven's ruling because he had not consulted with the Student Affairs Committee, which was formally responsible for ruling on recognition. In a poll, students also criticized Ruthven's ban 2,267–1,486, but this had no effect.[13]

The MYDA continued to meet off campus, just as the Wayne AYD did. In December 1947, it petitioned to bring Gerhardt Eisler as a speaker to campus. The University Lecture Committee, composed of five faculty members, denied the request. The committee pointed out that not only did the MYDA have no status at the university, but that Eisler had been convicted of criminal activity. The MYDA tried to have Eisler speak at a public park, but when 2,500 jeering students appeared, Eisler moved to a private home where he addressed a small group.[14]

In the spring of 1948, the MYDA attempted to gain recognition again. Supporters argued that the group had been banned without a hearing, had not violated any laws, and if given recognition would serve the best interests of education based on the free exchange of ideas. Almost 500 students signed a petition supporting their effort, and endorsements came from other student groups such as the Americans for Democratic Action, American Veterans Committee, National Lawyers Guild, and Inter-racial Association. On March 17, 1948, the Student Legislature voted to give recognition to the MYDA if it would either disaffiliate from the AYD or openly call itself a Communist organization. Before the MYDA acted, President Ruthven vetoed the Student Legislature's proposal. He maintained that his reasons for the ban a year earlier remained valid, and this effectively ended the AYD's life.[15]

At the University of Illinois, the state took an even more direct role in forcing the ban of the AYD chapter. The administration, just like at Wayne University, opposed the state's interference, but student conservatives encouraged the ban. The campus AYD chapter, which in 1947 had thirty members, had been given recognition. Dean of Students Fred Turner admitted that the group might be a Communist front, but accepted its status for two reasons. Recognition made the group operate in public where the administration could watch its activities more closely. Moreover, the administration should "permit a recognized Communist organization to operate on campus . . . as long as this is a free country we believe in."[16]

The attacks on the AYD by J. Edgar Hoover and others had been heard on campus during January and February of 1947, but the controversy became significantly enflamed when on March 20, the student newspaper launched a campaign against the AYD chapter. Although the *Daily Illini* did not characterize any student as a Communist, it accused the national AYD of being a Communist-front group, and demanded an end to the local's recognition. The AYD chapter denied the charge, and claimed that the newspaper hurt academic freedom with its red-baiting. For the next several weeks, the debate continued on campus with letters to the editor, editorials, and meetings in both support and opposition to the AYD.[17]

The controversy exploded into the state legislature in May. The AYD petitioned to bring an acknowledged Communist, Mollie Lieber, as a speaker to a closed meeting. Dean Turner permitted this, but the AYD allowed nonmembers into the meeting. Although the administration did not discipline the group, the presence of a Communist speaker outraged State Representative Charles Clabaugh, a Republican from the university's district. On the day after Lieber's speech, Clabaugh praised the *Daily Illini's* reports on the AYD, and introduced a bill specifically directed against the AYD chapter at the university. It proposed to deny the use of University of Illinois facilities to any "subversive, seditious, or un-American organization." Reflecting conservative suspicions of higher education, the preamble declared that "the universities of America have been the breeding ground of a series of invidious Communist inspired organizations." The house and senate quickly passed the bill with only one dissenting vote in each chamber. President George Stoddard urged the governor to veto the bill because the AYD chapter was not "subversive or dangerous." Stoddard also maintained that the administration could observe the group more closely if it operated openly. The governor nevertheless signed the "Clabaugh Act," and in August 1947 the administration withdrew recognition from the AYD.[18]

In contrast to the other five universities, the University of Wisconsin did not revoke the recognition of its AYD chapter. Yet the AYD and the administration did not always have a friendly relationship. In one case, the AYD petitioned to bring Gerhardt Eisler and Carl Marzani to campus. The

Administrative Council denied these requests because of "the moral impli-
cations involved in sponsoring a man of Eisler's known record." His
"record" was not his political affiliation, the Council declared, but his
conviction. The AYD protested that the two issues were not separate but
intertwined, and that the conviction came from the legitimate use of the First
and Fifth amendments. The AYD noted that others who had been arrested,
such as Norman Thomas, had been allowed to speak on campus. The
Student Board also condemned the ban on the basis of freedom of speech,
but to no avail. Eisler and Marzani spoke off campus.[19]

Like the University of Wisconsin, the University of Chicago did not ban
its local AYD chapter. The administrators were aware of the restrictive
actions of other colleges, and some suggested an investigation of the AYD
and another student group, the Communist Club. This proposal was rejected
by President E. C. Colwell, who restated the university policy of allowing all
organizations except those that supported the violent overthrowing of the
government. The AYD continued to meet and sponsor rallies, including one
featuring Gerhardt Eisler and Carl Marzani. Unique among these midwestern colleges, the administration allowed this meeting on the basis of free
speech, a desire to avoid martyrs, and a belief that such activities should
occur openly. Almost 400, not all sympathetic, attended.[20]

Although a few AYD chapters survived, basically it was broken as a
national student organization by the summer of 1947. This constituted
neither a great victory for Americanism nor severe repression, depending on
one's persuasion, because no significant decrease of leftist student activity
occurred. The AYD members continued their activities by simply moving
into local groups or other national groups, such as the Young Progressives
of America (YPA). Controversies over recognition and speaker policy thus
did not end with the AYD, but continued during the next several years at six
midwestern universities.

University of Illinois—recognition, 1948–1950
Ohio State University—recognition, speaker, 1948; speaker 1951
Wayne University—speaker 1950
University of Michigan—speaker 1950, 1952
University of Chicago—recognition 1950–1952
University of Wisconsin—recognition 1953

At the University of Illinois, the recognition controversy occurred a
year and a half after the AYD dispute, but the two were linked. Campus
conservatives tried to block the formation of a chapter of the Young
Progressives of America (YPA), a leftist group associated with the presidential campaign of Henry Wallace. After the election of 1948, a YPA
chapter petitioned for recognition. The Committee of Student Affairs (CSA)
refused to approve the petition until the YPA signed a loyalty oath denying

it was a front for the AYD, affiliated with the CP, or planning subversive activities. The YPA found the charges absurd, but refused to sign the oath on principle. Supporting the proposed oath, the student newspaper noted that three former AYD members now belonged to the YPA and that the group's connection with the Progressive party aroused suspicions about its loyalty. In January 1949, the CSA suddenly reversed itself, deciding that the oath wrongly presumed guilt, and granted recognition to the YPA. This action was supported, and perhaps initiated, by President George Stoddard. Taking a dimmer view, the University's security officer suspected that the YPA was "sponsored and controlled by the Illinois Communist party."[21]

The campus YPA lasted for only a year and a half. Its demise was caused by public resistance and administrative regulations. On August 9, 1950, a few weeks after the outbreak of the Korean War, YPA members went to Mattoon, a small town south of Champaign, in an effort to get signatures to put the Progressive party on the November ballot. Their efforts were unsuccessful as the local police harassed them. A few days later, the YPA tried to schedule a meeting in an Urbana park, but the park commissioners voted to ban "objectionable or subversive groups" from using the facilities. On August 20, the administration withdrew recognition from the group officially because it lacked a current membership list and sufficient undergraduate members. The administration reviewed the YPA's roster because of the complaints about the group's political activities. During the fall semester, the group tried to organize again, but soon gave up the effort. The administration required an open membership list, and students were afraid that their association with a leftist group would become known by future employers. Similarly, faculty members were reluctant to sponsor the YPA. This case reveals the manner in which general administrative regulations, based on a paternalistic approach, could be activated by public opinion for political reasons.[22]

At Ohio State University, two major controversies over recognition and speaker policy were also caused by community pressure, especially from newspapers. Yet at Ohio State, the administration sided with this conservative movement more quickly and forcefully. The first incident, which directly affected two student organizations, arose out of a community disturbance in the spring of 1948. Leftists and Communists distributed pamphlets critical of the Truman Doctrine and the Marshall Plan at factory gates in Columbus. A few minor fights broke out, and the CP asked for police protection. The police chief refused the request because "Columbus is a peace-loving and church-going community, and the city administration is not going to tolerate any Communists . . . interfering with our way of life." As the press sensationalized these incidents, people began to picket the home of Frank Hashmall, the county CP chairman. Three days in late March saw increasing violence at his house: a brief fight, the throwing of rocks at his house, and finally the ransacking of the house by about thirty people while a crowd outside cheered. Hashmall had moved his family away by this time, and no one was injured. The police, who were not at the house, made no arrests.[23]

These tensions touched Ohio State University when the press reported that a student, Arthur V. Rappeport, had distributed the CP pamphlets and later one of his own admitting his affiliation. The student Progressive Citizens Committee (PCC) quickly came under fire because Rappeport was a prominent leader.[24] Some conservatives wanted to ban the group, and the PCC debated its response to the controversy. Its chairman, James M. Early, favored the ouster of Communists from the group, but the constitution specifically admitted any person "regardless of his political beliefs and affiliations." On April 11, after much debate, the PCC voted thirty to eight to uphold the constitution. Early and four other executive committee members resigned in protest. The PCC then decided to invite Paul Robeson to campus to help publicize its cause and to help the presidential campaign of Henry Wallace. President Bevis denied the petition because of a regulation prohibiting "candidates for public office" as speakers on campus. Robeson, who was not a candidate, came anyway. He spoke a few feet from campus to almost 2,000 people, mostly students. According to the singer, Fascists created the hysteria in the country and in Columbus, and loyal Americans should ignore these efforts to incite fear.[25]

The PCC's vote to uphold its constitution and Robeson's speech alienated many of the group's original supporters. The student newspaper now condemned the PCC as "dominated by Communist followers" who brought "great discredit" on the university. Three of the PCC's faculty advisors resigned shortly before Robeson's speech. Later that same day, President Bevis banned the group. The university had no place for Communist propaganda, he asserted, although individual Communist students might remain if they behaved properly. The PCC criticized the lack of a hearing and specific charges. It suggested that Bevis appoint a committee to determine if Communists controlled the PCC. The President refused, and the ban remained. These events culminated when, four days after Bevis' ban, the Board of Trustees announced a more restrictive speaker policy. The university would now not allow any meeting in behalf of political candidates.[26]

OSU's desire for pure objectivity met a severe challenge beginning in the summer of 1951. The Board of Trustees reacted to restrict speaker policy even further, creating a "gag rule." The controversy arose over a speaker at the Boyd H. Bode Lecture in July 1951. Graduate students in the College of Education, who annually sponsored the lecture, invited Harold O. Rugg as the main speaker. The leftist professor cited the many world problems and emphasized the duty of education to shape a more just social order. Despite the speech's mildness, the *Columbus Dispatch* and the *Ohio State Journal* immediately criticized the conference for sponsoring a radical socialist. The newspapers tied socialism to communism, and proclaimed that the administration should investigate the conference's sponsors. Initially, President Bevis defended the conference, but the governor and some trustees requested an inquiry. On September 4, the Board of Trustees formally censured Rugg's lecture because "the function of the university is teaching, not indoctrination. The university must not be used as an agency for un-American propaganda." The board then ruled that all future speakers for any group must be cleared by the president.[27]

The board's ruling establishing a "gag rule" raised a new furor. On campus, criticism came from the College of Education, Student Senate, Faculty Council, and the AAUP chapter. Off campus, opposition arose from the Ohio Education Association, Council of Churches, CIO, Cleveland ACLU branch, and various newspapers. Students voted 2,986–637 to oppose the new rule. In the first three weeks of school, President Bevis received 137 requests for clearance of speakers, but he did not have an investigator to process the petitions. Tensions grew higher after Bevis denied a request by the Fellowship of Reconciliation (FOR), a pacifist group, to hear Cecil E. Hinshaw, a Quaker minister. The opposition was incensed because Hinshaw was not a Communist and because the president refused to give any reasons for his action. Several months later, a trustee announced that Hinshaw had been banned because he advised men to evade the draft. Hinshaw challenged this claim, and pointed out that he had only given advice about conscientious objection, a legal activity.[28]

The trustees initially defended their position by announcing their support for academic freedom "consistent with national security," but soon they began to modify their ruling because of the strong opposition. In November, the board announced that clearance was not required for speakers addressing classes, professional organizations, and off-campus groups, as long as the sponsor accepted responsibility. Since student political groups did not fit into any of these categories, the new policy required them to petition the administration for their speakers. In effect, the ruling pacified the faculty and put student groups where they had been before the controversy.[29]

After the "gag rule" furor died down, the administration began to act quietly rather than openly and bluntly to enforce its preference in speakers. In 1953, the Boyd H. Bode Conference planned to sponsor Harry N. Wieman, professor emeritus of Christian theology at the University of Chicago. The Ohio Un-American Activities Committee (OUAC) heard about the proposal and sent its file on Wieman to President Bevis. According to the OUAC's counsel, the president then pressured the conference's sponsors "very quietly, without any fanfare" to cancel the speaker, which they did.[30]

Wayne University also adopted a more restrictive policy during several speaker controversies, especially between 1948 and 1950. The administration, which had shown some leniency, initiated a new "speaker" policy when students petitioned to hear Herbert Phillips, an avowed Communist who had been dismissed from the University of Washington. In March 1950, the Student Council and the Program Planning Committee (PPC) approved a debate between Phillips and an unnamed instructor on whether a CP member should be allowed to teach at a university. On March 28, President David Dodds Henry vetoed the meeting. He declared that communism was "an enemy of our national welfare, dedicated to violence, disruption, and discord. . . . The university is under no obligation, in the name of education, to give him [Phillips] an audience." Henry's ban against Communist speakers constituted a new policy for Wayne, and it would last ten years. Yet freedom of speech was not curtailed completely. Students circulated petitions critical of Henry's action. Phillips came to Detroit and spoke across the street from the campus. The publicity gave him a crowd of almost 1,000, mostly students. Two days later on campus, students heard a debate on Phillips' original topic between a Wayne professor and Irving Howe, a radical.[31]

A few days later, the administration went even further by banning a non-Communist speaker. The Student League for Industrial Democracy wanted to sponsor the national chairman of the Socialist Workers Party (SWP), Farrell Dobbs. The Program Planning Committee (PPC) unanimously approved the meeting, but the dean of student affairs requested that it reconsider its action. He cited Dobbs' conviction of subversion in 1941 and the listing of the SWP on the attorney general's subversive list. The PPC ignored the dean's recommendation by a vote of six to four. The dean then vetoed the PPC decision. Dobbs, just like Phillips, spoke just outside university property to a crowd of at least 300 students.[32]

The University of Michigan showed its paternalism in two controversies over speaker policy in 1950 and 1952. In the first case, students requested that Herbert Phillips, the former University of Washington professor, debate a faculty member. The University Lecture Committee (ULC), composed of five faculty members, rejected the petition of the Michigan Forum because Phillips was a Communist. Although the Michigan Forum withdrew its sponsorship, some students formed an ad hoc group which arranged for Phillips to speak at an off-campus restaurant. The publicity over the ban brought more than 2,000 students to the meeting, even though only a few hundred could squeeze themselves inside the restaurant. Phillips defended the CP as a peaceful political organization, and ridiculed the idea that it favored the overthrow of the government or the restriction of freedom. His opponent in the debate noted the lack of freedom of speech and assembly in the Soviet Union, and doubted the promises of Communist propaganda. The debate generated many questions and lasted for three hours.[33]

In 1952, the University of Michigan experienced a much sharper confrontation over speaker policy. In February, the Young Progressives (YP) invited Arthur McPhaul, the chairman of the state's Civil Rights Congress (CRC). The CRC had been frequently accused of being a Communist-front organization. The ULC rejected the petition under a regental by-law that required meetings to be in the "spirit and expression worthy of the university." Despite the ruling, a "Henry Girard" then reserved a room at the Michigan Union for an unspecified meeting. About thirty people, including one reporter, attended the dinner, whose speaker turned out to be McPhaul. He discussed the CRC and his recent "unfriendly" testimony before HUAC in Detroit.[34]

The "Henry Girard" affair intensified the confrontation because McPhaul had spoken on campus. President Harlan Hatcher appointed an investigative commission composed of three deans, three students, and one faculty member. After questioning several people about the dinner, the committee recommended that fourteen students be charged with violating the regental by-law on holding a meeting after the ULC had barred it. The students responded that the dinner was a private gathering and that they had the right to attend. The investigative commission had indulged in guilt by association and political discrimination, the students concluded.[35]

The committee's findings were referred to the Joint Judiciary Council (JJC), a student group. The JJC questioned all of the students again before issuing its report. It decided to drop the charge of violating the regental by-law, but recommended that five students be placed on probation for their refusal to testify fully before the JJC and for misrepresenting the dinner as private when a reporter had been invited. Astonished at this ruling, the five students declared that the JJC had never advised them that their testimony might come under scrutiny. The punishment therefore was completely unjust. The Faculty Subcommittee on Discipline sustained the JJC ruling, and the five students were forced to abandon all extracurricular activities for one full semester.[36]

Whether viewed as dangerous leftist subversives or as "seriously maladjusted late adolescents, . . . a pathetic group of social and emotional misfits . . . [who] cling together from weaknesses," these students found little support among their peers. During the "Henry Girard" controversy, the student Civil Liberties Committee changed its policy to bar anyone who supported totalitarianism. The effort to oust the supposed Communists was initiated by the faculty advisor, who threatened to resign if the change was not made. The Young Progressives (YP) survived the "Henry Girard" affair, but the next year it was unable to get ten students to sign as members and became ineligible for recognition. Later, another leftist group, the Labor Youth League (LYL), organized an off-campus chapter, but it never attempted to gain recognition from the university.[37]

The University of Chicago, which had allowed Eisler and Marzani to speak, did not have "speaker" controversies but a "recognition" debate involving the Labor Youth League. Although the LYL received recognition, its three-year existence remained shaky because of its leftist sympathies. After eleven Communists were convicted of violating the Smith Act, the LYL faculty advisor, Malcolm Sharp, indicated that he did not want to remain in the post. Although the LYL served a "useful purpose" on campus and never advocated the violent overthrow of the government, Sharp worried that the Smith Act case might outlaw mere membership in an organization sympathetic to the CP. Sharp's objections caused some alarm among LYL members and the administration, but his worries were eased when the Internal Security Act, passed in the fall of 1950, did not make CP membership per se a criminal violation.[38]

The next summer, the LYL again suffered a setback when Sharp raised another concern. The Supreme Court upheld a local loyalty oath which made a crime of unknowing membership in a subversive organization. Sharp refused to be the LYL advisor when it applied for recognition in the fall of 1951. Not only did this force the group to find a new advisor, but it also raised the possibility of the group's ban because of its apparent CP ties. The LYL denied any illegal actions and any affiliation with the CP. The student group argued that its ban would curtail freedom of speech and assembly. The administration went cautiously, seeking legal opinions from other sources. One lawyer argued that the LYL was illegal because of its CP sympathies, while another found the LYL only in potential legal jeopardy because of its uncertain relationship with the CP. Suggestions on the LYL's future included the group's ban, a one-year probation, and disaffiliation from its national organization.[39]

The restrictive tide turned when the chairman of the Board of Trustees, Laird Bell, argued that the administration should assume the innocence and good faith of the students, rather than treating them "as if they were children." Criticizing the red-baiters, Bell concluded that revoking the group's recognition would not change the members' beliefs, but would only give them publicity and create unnecessary martyrs. While the administration had been examining this issue, the Student Legislature had engaged in a similar debate. On January 17, 1952, it voted thirty-four to two to grant recognition to the LYL. Unable to discover any illegal activities by the chapter, the Student Legislature decided to presume the LYL's innocence. Dean Robert Strozier initially doubted this decision and asked the group to disaffiliate from the national organization. He soon dropped his demand, and approved recognition in February 1952 ending the five-month dispute. The LYL continued to sponsor meetings where Communists spoke, but the next year fewer than ten students signed as members and the group could not obtain recognition.[40]

At the University of Wisconsin, a "recognition" controversy also involved the Labor Youth League. The chapter, after receiving recognition, sponsored many leftist and Communist speakers, including Abner Berry, the Negro affairs' editor of the *Daily Worker*, on January 15, 1953. To a crowd swelled by the publicity, Berry asserted that "concentration camps" existed in America and that freedom was gradually being eroded. Conservatives criticized the administration's acceptance of Berry as an on-campus speaker, but President E. B. Fred defended the university's policy. "The people of this state . . . [reject] the censorship of ideas." The president noted that Berry, while following the CP policy on domestic affairs, had not advocated the overthrow of the government.[41]

Conservatives continued their criticisms, and the Wisconsin Legislative Council recommended that the University re-evaluate its policy on recognition. According to a Republican senator, it was time "to get rid of the subversive organizations on campus." President Fred directed the Student Life and Interests Committee (SLIC) to review its procedures on granting recognition. After several weeks of study, the SLIC proposed no changes in the policy. Although the LYL had been put on the attorney general's subversive list, the SLIC noted that had no legal meaning or consequence. Quoting the regents' policy, the committee affirmed that "an opportunity critically to study the proposals and claims of systems alien to our own is the intellectual right of every student." No further investigations occurred, and the LYL chapter continued to exist until its voluntary dissolution in October 1956.[42]

In general, recognition and speaker policy became more restrictive at various midwestern universities. Student activities had long been subject to administrative approval; this paternalism was not new. What changed was the ease in obtaining approval. The new restrictions are even more striking when contrasted to the open activities of leftist groups in the 1930s.

In addition to recognition and speaker policy, students encountered the Red Scare in another area: freedom of expression for student newspapers. Administrations scrutinized the papers for loyalty and objectivity. Controversies over editorial content and direction occurred at Michigan State College and the University of Chicago. In both instances, censorship occurred.

The student newspaper at Michigan State College, the *Michigan State News*, found itself under attack for just one editorial: its report of the 1950 Boys State Convention sponsored by the American Legion. At the convention, a mock trial of an alleged Communist for perjury was designed to prove that "anyone in America has the right to a fair trial by jury regardless of his political or social affiliations." The jury, composed of the boy delegates, split evenly and could not reach a verdict. The *State News* editorially criticized the entire convention and especially the mock trial. The convention had an aura of military discipline rather than freedom and democracy, the paper argued. For example, the audience at the mock trial had booed and hissed the defendant. The convention in short was "an experiment shot through with narrow principles, bald-faced fascism, and militaristic ideas." The American Legion, the editorial concluded, needed to face the loyalty and security issue with less of a closed mind and more awareness of its complexity.[43]

The criticism caused a swift reaction from both the Legion and the college administration. The Legion charged that the editorial followed the "Russian Communist pattern and form," and demanded a retraction as well as an investigation by state officials. The next day, President John Hannah met with the deans of the college and the *State News'* editor, Ron Linton. The student denied that the editorial showed any Communist bias. He indicated that the writer of the piece, Russell McKee, had first-hand knowledge of the convention because the Legion had hired him to supervise a newspaper put out by the boy delegates. Linton, moreover, had just finished R.O.T.C., while McKee was a veteran; neither was a Communist. Despite Linton's defense, the president and the deans voted to suspend the newspaper for the remainder of the summer term. As a result, the *State News* did not report on the outbreak of the Korean War, which happened on the day of its suspension.[44]

The newspaper controversy at the University of Chicago did not involve a single editorial but the general conduct of the editor. The result was the same: firmer administrative control. On October 3, 1951, Dean of Students Robert M. Strozier suddenly fired Alan Kimmel as the editor of the student newspaper, the *Maroon*. Kimmel had been elected by the paper's staff in the spring of 1951 to serve during the next academic year. In the summer, he had taken a leave of absence to travel in Europe and in fact was still in Moscow at the time of his dismissal. While in Europe, Kimmel had attended the East Berlin Youth Festival. Dean Strozier objected to the student's attendance of the alleged Communist gathering and to his alleged use of his title as the *Maroon*'s editor in sponsoring the event. For Strozier, this made Kimmel unfit to edit a "free and independent newspaper." Strozier, furthermore, did not want the paper's staff to select another editor. He thus suspended the publication of the *Maroon* until a new method of selecting an editor was established.[45]

The campus erupted into a heated debate after Strozier's ruling. The Executive Council of the student government, after meeting for several hours, voted six to three to demand Kimmel's reinstatement and the resumption of publication. Strozier erred "on both legal and moral grounds," the council asserted. Similar criticism came from the All Campus Committee to Defend Student Rights. Its challenger, the Committee for a Free and Representative *Maroon*, was supported by several well-known faculty members including David Riesman and Milton Friedman. They argued that the *Maroon* must accept regulation since it was a monopoly. "The rights of students *as students* must always be qualified by the ultimate authority of the University," the faculty members concluded. On October 8, the student legislature debated the recommendation of its Executive Council opposing Strozier's ruling, but after four hours of discussion, could reach no conclusion. Finally after two days of intensive debate, the student legislature voted to support the dean's action. Some members of the *Maroon* wanted to fight back by publishing an underground paper, but the day after the student legislature's decision, they also accepted a new editor. The weekly *Maroon* resumed publication, having missed one issue.[46]

When Kimmel returned from Europe later that month, he was met with a fait accompli, but he still tried to clear himself and regain his position. He declared that he neither had sponsored the East Berlin Festival nor had spoken of himself as representing the university or the *Maroon*. The International Union of Students, not Communists, had sponsored the festival, he proclaimed. Kimmel's protests were ineffective. The Council of the University Faculty Senate voted twenty-seven to four to support Dean Strozier. The ACLU examined the case, and found that the dean had not violated any regulation or freedom of the press, although he had interpreted his power over student publications broadly. The National Student Association's investigation criticized both Strozier's action and Kimmel's irresponsibility at the Youth Festival.[47]

Just as the controversies involving speaker policy, recognition, and press independence concerned freedom of expression, so the final Red Scare cases involving students dealt with this issue. Students at five universities refused to testify about their political affiliations and associations when questioned by a legislative investigative commission. The five administrations did not react in the same way to these "Fifth Amendment" incidents. Michigan State, the University of Chicago, and the University of Michigan took no disciplinary action against the "unfriendly" witnesses, but Ohio State University made a partially restrictive decision and Wayne University took the harshest action.

At Michigan State College, the "Fifth Amendment" case, which touched a student who had been active in the AYD, involved a state legislative committee. In 1947, the state senate established a committee to investigate subversives—the Callahan Commission, named after its chairman, Senator Matthew Callahan. After its successful attack on the AYD, it continued to probe the educational system. In April 1948, the commission quizzed officials of Michigan State College. President John Hannah admitted that one MSC student was a Communist. Soon thereafter, the commission summoned James Zarichny, who had been one of the six AYD members placed on probation in February 1947. In his testimony, Zarichny, a veteran, asserted that he was a loyal American who would fight to defend the country in case of war against the Soviet Union. He acknowledged that he had belonged to the AYD, but he refused to testify if he was a CP member. The commission then cited him for contempt, and a week later, he was brought before the senate for his "trial."[48]

The senate, which had never considered contempt proceedings before, went slowly. An early attempt to dismiss the charge as an invasion of freedom of speech and association was defeated twenty-two to three. The next day, Zarichny's supporters argued that the student could legitimately refuse to testify on the basis of the Fifth Amendment. This motion to close the case also failed by a vote of fourteen to eleven. After a three-week delay, Zarichny presented his defense. The commission operated illegally, he argued, because it was neither a joint legislative committee nor directed to produce any legislative proposals. Questions about his political affiliations violated the First Amendment, the student concluded. Support came from 1,500 MSC students who signed a petition asking for the abolition of the Callahan Commission and from two officials of the Michigan Committee for Academic Freedom who testified on the case's potential damage to freedom. The senate, meeting in private session, found him guilty of contempt, reportedly by a vote of twenty-one to seven. It gave the student a suspended sentence for the remainder of the legislative session, which ended that night. The college administration did not discipline the student even though he was on probation from the AYD incident.[49]

The University of Chicago had students appear before legislative committees on two different occasions, but they were not punished either time. In the first instance, student political activity helped to create the legislature's decision to investigate. In March 1949, a group of students from the University of Chicago and Roosevelt College went to the state capital to lobby against antisubversive proposals. Their activities angered the legislature, which formed the Seditious Activities Investigation Commission (SAIC) to probe the two institutions. The SAIC, however, virtually ignored student groups during its investigations. It only questioned one student, Elias Snitzer, the chairman of the Communist Club. He testified about the club, but refused to answer questions about his affiliation with the CP. Unlike the Callahan Commission, the SAIC did not try to cite Snitzer for contempt. The university administration resisted the SAIC investigation and did not discipline the student or restrict any student organizations.[50]

Four years later, two other Chicago students were questioned by a legislative committee, this time federal. On June 8 and 9, 1953, the Senate Internal Security Subcommittee (SISS) questioned several university personnel, including two students. Samuel Friedman, a part-time history student who also worked at the University Press, took the Fifth Amendment on questions about his membership in the CP and AYD. Ira A. Kipnis, a law student, also refused to answer questions about his affiliation with the National Council for the Arts, Sciences, and Professions, the International Workers Order, and the CP. The hearings created little stir on campus. The university provided counsel for both students, and took no action against either.[51]

The University of Michigan also had a "Fifth Amendment" case, but it featured HUAC. In May 1954, the committee questioned Edward H. Shaffer, a veteran working toward his doctoral degree in economics, and Myron E. Sharpe, a graduate student in political science. Both invoked the Fifth Amendment when questioned about their affiliations. President Harlan Hatcher appointed a four-member student advisory committee to study the two cases. Two years earlier, both had been placed on probation after the "Henry Girard" incident in which they had brought an unscheduled speaker to campus. This time, the student committee recommended that no disciplinary action be taken, and on May 19, the president agreed.[52]

At Ohio State University, the administration acted more harshly toward its "Fifth Amendment" student. In May 1952, the Ohio Un-American Activities Committee (OUAC) questioned George D. Pappas, a graduate assistant in zoology and entomology, who refused to answer if he belonged to the CP. Although the graduate student had signed the University's loyalty oath denying sympathies toward the violent overthrow of the government, President Howard Bevis at first suspended and later withdrew his assistantship. The administration allowed Pappas to remain at the university to finish his graduate work.[53]

Wayne University rendered the harshest judgment against an undergraduate who gave "unfriendly" testimony. In February 1952, HUAC interrogated Lorraine F. Meisner, who took the Fifth Amendment about her attendance at the East Berlin Youth Festival in the summer of 1951 and about her membership in the CP. President David Dodds Henry immediately suspended her. Her refusal to testify was "either an unreasonable refusal to cooperate or a prima facie admission of criminal guilt. . . . In either case, it is inconsistent with the obligations of responsible university citizenship," the president concluded.[54]

The Student Council by a vote of eleven to two condemned the suspension. Meisner only used her constitutional rights, the council affirmed, while "responsible university citizenship" constituted a new, unformulated policy. In a hearing before the Committee on Non-Academic Discipline, composed of three deans, Meisner's attorney reiterated the argument that the use of the Fifth Amendment was legal and legitimate. There existed "only one citizenship, that of state and country, not a separate brand for university students," he declared. The committee was convinced otherwise by the university's counsel, who argued that negative inferences could be derived from the use of the Fifth Amendment. The committee suggested that Meisner testify fully before HUAC. When she refused, it recommended her expulsion, asserting that the issue was not political discrimination but "good citizenship." President Henry agreed to her expulsion.[55]

The university's paternalism became evident in this matter because of the uproar caused by the HUAC hearings. Before she had appeared before the committee, she was just another insignificant leftist. The university had allowed her to attend classes even though a year earlier a former Communist had identified her as a Party member, and even after she had attended the East Berlin Youth Festival. The administration moreover took no disciplinary action against two other students, one being her husband of three weeks, who attended the festival. President Henry nevertheless expressed a full-blown paternalism. "Any conduct of a student . . . which is detrimental to the welfare of the university, even though it may be no violation of the law, is subject to university appraisal and approval."[56] Administration policy, under this wide-ranging paternalism, could thus by-pass sensitive political issues and rely on either university regulations or the power of the university president to determine such issues.

To characterize students of the 1950s as the Silent Generation is only partially true. Throughout the Midwest, leftists on campus tried to organize groups, schedule controversial speakers, and engage in political activity. Although weaker than comparable groups in the 1930s and 1960s, leftists were active. As a result, administrations imposed more restrictions on recognition, speaker policy, freedom of the press, and freedom to use constitutional guarantees. There can be no doubt that university officials, with the assent of the faculty, curtailed student rights in the postwar decade. Michigan State and Ohio State adopted the toughest policies because of their respective presidents' influence. Wayne University, the University of Michigan, and the University of Illinois showed some tolerance initially but became more restrictive. The University of Chicago and the University of Wisconsin allowed students the greatest amount of freedom, but even here there were exceptions. Chicago fired Alan Kimmel as editor of the *Maroon*, and Wisconsin banned Gerhardt Eisler from speaking on campus.

Despite these excessive restrictions, this chapter has also pointed out the lack of systematic repression, or in other words the limitations of these restrictions. Administrative policy did not cause leftist students to abandon their beliefs. If anything, it confirmed to them the conservatism of the educational system and the necessity of change. Indeed, student radicals created incidents just to test the administration on its commitment to academic freedom. Yet when a university withdrew recognition from a student group, the leftists could join other recognized groups or off-campus groups. When radical speakers were banned, they often spoke a few feet off campus, and students attended in large numbers. Student activists who invoked the Fifth Amendment were usually not disciplined. Finally, although the Red Scare destroyed nationally organized groups—the AYD, YPA, and LYL—this might not have been crucial to the failure of radicalism on campus.[57] Students can be mobilized by local ad hoc groups as events in the 1960s show. In short, the Scare's overt repression—its effect on particular students—was limited.

The reason for this ambivalence—for both the restrictions and the limitations—is found in the policy of paternalism. Administrative policies were based not only on the emotional politics of the Scare, but also on the established policy of *in loco parentis*. Regulations concerning recognition, speaker policy, and newspapers did not originate in the postwar decade. Instead, they came from the long-standing parental role taken by administrators and faculty. The Red Scare reached its effectiveness among students because it did not arise out of a vacuum. It merely energized the prevailing administrative policy toward students: paternalism.

Yet this same policy caused the restrictions to be limited. If the parental belief accepted the need for discipline because students were young and immature, it at the same time held that students should not be judged as severely as adults. They needed their education and they still had time to see the errors of their ways—or so university officials believed.

A more difficult historical question involves the subtle effects of the Scare. How did the confrontations between leftists and the administration affect students generally? Some observers have viewed students as "a sterile assemblage of prisoners of orthodoxy . . . a group hungry for a rut to cower in,"[58] but actually students were a mixed group with different responses to the Red Scare. Students both criticized and accepted administrative policy. At the University of Michigan, a student referendum condemned the banning of the AYD. At Wayne University, the Student Council protested the suspension of Lorraine Meisner after her "unfriendly" testimony before HUAC. At various colleges, students turned out in large numbers to hear banned speakers. On the other hand, the Michigan State Student Council supported the expulsion of James Zarichny, and the Ohio State student newspaper supported the banning of the Progressive Citizens' Committee. This mixed response was caused by the students' position in the university structure, a subordinate position with almost no control over policy. Most students disagreed with the radicals, but seemed to feel little concern about their existence. Left to themselves, it is doubtful that students would have initiated as many or as restrictive rules. They accepted both the leftists' right to organize and hear speakers and the administration's right to ban such groups and speakers. Forced to choose, students usually supported the administration, the paternalistic donor which gave them football, fraternities, and a degree. The general student attitude was not ardent conservatism; pro-McCarthy groups, such as Students for America, fizzled quicker than the LYL.[59] Students, in conclusion, were passive politically with a mild touch of tolerance.[60] The Red Scare was thus limited in that it did not create conservatives who were mobilized or even terribly worried about the danger of the internal Communist threat.

7

Universities: Faculty Members

Just as students were subject to administrative control, so to a lesser extent were faculty members. Throughout the Midwest, conservatives questioned the loyalty and objectivity of liberal and leftist instructors. The issue in these incidents rarely involved classroom behavior or scholarship but rather political associations, affiliations, and activity. This conservative pressure originated from federal, state, and local sources.

At times, the university invoked academic freedom and defended the accused. More often, the institution, having a public nature, treated non-conformity harshly. These incidents had overtones of town-versus-gown disputes, but they were more than that. The controversies involved politics in a broader sense. This sword then cut into the unity of the academic community. No "gown," no single academic voice, existed.

According to some scholars, these incidents caused severe repression. They cite the dismissals of individual teachers, which further caused fear and conformity in the academic ranks.[1] This chapter will confirm repressive actions, but will also note some limitations of the Red Scare. Even when a single factor, such as the use of the Fifth Amendment, caused incidents at several universities, the controversy at each institution developed differently. Neither dismissal nor retention was automatic. More broadly, neither fear nor conformity was automatic.

This chapter examines several different midwestern universities. This regional perspective reveals four different types of controversies involving faculty members. First, legislative investigative committees interrogated instructors, who used the Fifth Amendment on political questions. Second, the committees confronted a few faculty members who denied the accusation of Communist involvement. I have termed these "active defense" cases. Third, activity supporting the Progressive party or labor unions brought controversy to some teachers. Finally, some administrations initiated their own local or internal purge.

"Fifth Amendment" cases are the most well known. These occurred after 1950 when governmental committees, such as HUAC and SISS, began to scrutinize higher education. In the Midwest, the committees questioned only a few instructors, most of whom did not teach politically oriented fields such as history, political science, or economics. Indeed, the inquisitors never made allegations that the witnesses indoctrinated their students. Instead, they relied on testimony from former Communists, who asserted that any Communist instructor lacked objectivity and always served the party's cause. Since the investigative committees did not directly challenge the competence and integrity of the witnesses, they avoided overt anti-intellectual accusations. Seemingly, they focused on the individual rather than on intellectuals or the university. Many faculty members therefore did not view the committees as a threat to academic freedom. They criticized the use of the Fifth Amendment and supported disciplinary proceedings against the "unfriendly" witnesses. Yet the committees did not focus on the witness as it seemed, but on the university. By exposing the individual and then withdrawing from making the final judgment on the case, the committees put the university in a position where its decision imbued the individual case with a larger meaning for both the public and the academic community. The actions of the committees and the various results of the cases point to the significance of both national and local factors in the development of these controversies. Such Fifth Amendment incidents occurred at the following institutions:[2]

> Ohio State University, 1952, 1953: dismissals
> Wayne University, 1953: dismissals
> University of Michigan, 1954: dismissals and retention
> University of Chicago, 1953: retention
> Antioch College, 1954: retention

Ohio State University (OSU) encountered two separate cases in which instructors invoked the Fifth Amendment. Both times, the OSU president, Howard Bevis, acted with little or no consultation with the faculty before quickly dismissing the instructors, one of whom had tenure.

In May 1952, the Ohio Un-American Activities Committee (OUAC) questioned Marston A. Hamlin, an OSU fine arts instructor. He had already signed the university loyalty oath in which he denied advocating or belonging to an organization that advocated the violent overthrow of the government. In his testimony, he reiterated his opposition to violent actions, but used the Fifth Amendment when questioned about his political affiliations. President Bevis immediately suspended him, and soon held an informal conference with the instructor. Hamlin again refused to answer questions about his politics, and the president dismissed him. The OSU chapter of the AAUP criticized the lack of specific charges against Hamlin, but failed to find any violation of academic freedom in the case.[3]

A year later, OSU experienced a much greater furor when HUAC twice interrogated Byron T. Darling, a tenured professor of molecular physics. On

March 3, 1953, in Washington, D.C., the professor, who had been at the university for six years, invoked the Fifth Amendment more than 100 times. His case aroused special interest because he refused to answer questions about his possession and unauthorized transfer of classified government documents. Although Darling had not been identified as a Communist by another witness, and although he had signed the OSU loyalty oath, President Bevis immediately suspended him.[4]

The administration followed the same procedure in Darling's case as in Hamlin's. The local AAUP chapter proposed that Darling be presented with written charges against him, heard before a faculty committee, and allowed to have an attorney at the hearing. President Bevis rejected these suggestions and scheduled an administrative hearing at which three faculty members, chosen by him, could act only as observers. Several faculty members and graduate students signed a statement that they had never heard Darling engaged in political debate or advocate disloyal activities, and President Bevis did not accuse the professor of subversion. Instead, the charges were "gross insubordination" and a lack of "moral integrity." Public opinion strongly supported Bevis' actions. When the AAUP chapter debated its response to these developments, it feared that Darling's supporters might also become targets of criticism so it voted 200 to 1 to bar the press from the meeting.[5]

Darling made his defense in an almost three-hour meeting with the president. He denied that he had ever belonged to the CP or any front organization, and claimed his ability to deny all of HUAC's allegations. He refused to testify because he feared that the committee might hold information, which if wrongly interpreted, could leave him liable for prosecution for perjury. The use of the Fifth Amendment was neither immoral nor insubordinate, but entirely legal and constitutional. The professor concluded that he was a loyal citizen, good scholar, and in no way deserving of termination.[6]

President Bevis, unconvinced, recommended Darling's dismissal two days later. Acknowledging that no evidence existed showing Darling's Communist sympathies or bias as a teacher or scholar, the president declared that the professor was "a competent and devoted man of science." The issue in the controversy, however, was Darling's failure in "his duty to the university." The president concluded that refusal to answer HUAC's questions had hurt the reputation of the university. The AAUP chapter urged the Board of Trustees to delay final action on the case until its national organization had issued a report, but on April 20, the board unanimously approved Darling's dismissal.[7]

The drama had not yet ended, for two months later HUAC came to Columbus to question Darling again. On June 17, 1953, the Committee interrogated his wife, who had recently resigned as a secretary in the

Romance Language Department. She used the Fifth Amendment twenty-two times when questioned about her associations, CP membership, and attendance at Communist meetings. Berniece Baldwin, a former CP official, testified that Darling's wife had attended a party convention in 1944, but this did not directly implicate the professor because the Darlings were not married until 1946. Another witness associated Darling with a leftist political group and the Young Communist League in 1939 and 1940. Darling himself again invoked the Fifth Amendment sixty-six times. Thus, HUAC's most damaging testimony against the professor was his possible affiliation with a radical youth group thirteen years earlier and his wife's attendance at a Communist convention seven years earlier. Whatever the actual evidence, President Bevis had rejected the validity of the use of the Fifth Amendment. This action later had its own consequence when the national AAUP censured OSU for violating academic freedom in the case.[8]

Wayne University also had two instructors who were "unfriendly" witnesses, but in determining their fate, the administration adopted a more deliberate process and gave faculty members a more active role than at Ohio State. As a result of these different procedures, retention became a serious option.

When HUAC held hearings in Detroit in May 1954, Gerald I. Harrison and Irving Stein used the Fifth Amendment on questions about leftist and CP affiliations. Although no witness had identified either man as a Communist, President Clarence B. Hilberry suspended them without pay a few hours later. Under Michigan law, a public employee's refusal to testify about Communist or Communist-front activities before a legislative committee was considered "prima facie evidence" of the truth of the accusation. This 1952 law, known as the Trucks Act, had been incorporated into the regulations of the university. The defiant witness "has a prima facie case against him. He will be expected to clear himself."[9]

Harrison, a tenured professor of mathematics, had relied on the First Amendment until HUAC had warned him of contempt. He then reverted to the Fifth Amendment on questions about the Progressive party, American Federation of Teachers (AFT), and the CP. Several faculty members came to his defense by declaring that he had never engaged in political discussion in the classroom, and some AFT members indicated that he had not supported any Communist policies. President Hilberry appointed an Advisory Committee on Loyalty (ACL), composed of two administrators and two faculty members, to hold hearings on the case. Harrison's attorney pointed out that while the courts were considering the constitutionality of the 1952 Trucks Act, the state attorney general had stipulated that he would not enforce its provisions. Thus, the use of the Fifth Amendment could not be considered "prima facie evidence" under that law. Harrison denied CP membership, admitted participation but not membership in the Progressive party and the Civil Rights Congress (CRC), and acknowledged belonging to the International Workers Order (IWO) from 1947 to 1950. He also denied being knowingly affiliated with any organization designed to overthrow the government. Harrison indicated his willingness to sign an affidavit on this testimony. The ACL privately and tentatively concluded that the professor was "innocent of any real disloyalty" and proposed his reinstatement. Before making this recommendation public, the ACL investigated further the CRC and IWO, both of which were on the attorney general's subversive list. On July 2, the ACL asked Harrison to fulfill his earlier promise and sign an affidavit on his testimony. He refused because he feared being charged with perjury in his HUAC testimony. The ACL found this prosecution a remote possibility, and felt shaken that it had no assurances of the truthfulness of his statements. It then reversed its tentative report, and by a vote of three to one concluded that Harrison had not met the burden of proof and thus should be dismissed.[10]

Harrison appealed to the Committee on Rights and Responsibilities (CRR), composed of five faculty members and two deans. In November, six months after the HUAC hearings, the CRR reluctantly concluded that it had "no option except to proceed" under the university regulation based on the 1952 Trucks Act. Without Harrison's affidavit, the CRR approved his dismissal by a vote of five to two. Later, the CRR sent a separate report to President Hilberry that indicated its uneasiness with its reliance on the Trucks Act. It admitted that "no substantial evidence . . . [only] presumptive evidence" existed against the professor, but felt that the committee had to rely on the Trucks Act since it had been enacted to deal with such presumptions. President Hilberry accepted the recommendation, and in January 1955, the Detroit Board of Education dismissed Harrison.[11]

Stein's case, although it also originated from the use of the Fifth Amendment, developed somewhat differently because of his nontenured status. After his "unfriendly" testimony, the Wayne administration decided not to renew the physics instructor's yearly contract, even though he had received good recommendations from students and faculty members. His appeal to the Advisory Committee on Loyalty (ACL) thus directly concerned only his suspended pay, although indirectly it dealt with his termination. Before the ACL, Stein admitted activity in the Progressive party, but denied belonging to the Young Communist League or the CP. More belligerent to the ACL than Harrison, Stein also refused to sign an affidavit on his statements. On that basis, the ACL unanimously recommended that he should neither receive any salary for his suspended term nor be reinstated. The Committee on Rights and Responsibilities, President Hilberry, and the Board of Education upheld this course of action.[12]

The University of Michigan had three "unfriendly" witnesses who, a few days after the Wayne University instructors, appeared before HUAC. The university did not rely specifically on the 1952 Trucks Act, but its policy followed the spirit of the law. The administration consulted with faculty committees, and one case ended in a sharp difference of opinion. In another case, the university decided to retain the professor. On the same day as their testimony, President Harlan H. Hatcher suspended "without prejudice" and with pay H. Chandler Davis, a mathematics instructor; Mark Nickerson, a tenured professor of pharmacology; and Clement L. Markert, a zoology professor. Each had signed a loyalty oath at the university denying membership in any organization which favored the violent overthrow of the government.[13]

The three cases were first examined by the President's Special Advisory Committee (PSAC), composed of five faculty members. Addressing the PSAC, President Hatcher did not specifically refer to the 1952 Trucks Act, but he argued that the three men had to answer many questions in order to demonstrate their honesty and integrity. "Respect for the law . . . [does not] conflict with freedom of the mind," he declared. The inquiry should not be concerned with the instructors' competence, the president maintained, but their relationship with the Communist party. On June 2, the PSAC met with the chief investigator for HUAC, who refused to name the committee's sources of information but vouched for their reliability. On June 14, 1954, the PSAC began to interview the three men.[14]

Chandler Davis' case was unique in that he had relied only on the First Amendment. The nontenured instructor received support before the PSAC from the Executive Committee of the College of Literature, Science and the Arts. It declared that Davis not only had been a competent and objective teacher, but also had the right to use the First Amendment. Before the PSAC, Davis refused to answer any questions about his current affiliation with the CP. Disputing that the party was a criminal conspiracy, he maintained that such questions dealt with private political beliefs. Judgment should rest solely on "competence and integrity," he argued. Later, Davis attacked a popular syllogism: Communists are enemies of the country; the government and the university have the right to know if you are an enemy; thus, they have the right to determine if you are a Communist. According to Davis, he could refute all evidence that he was disloyal. This then would destroy the syllogism: either he was not a Communist or not all Communists were enemies of the country. Davis' arguments that he should be retained did not convince the PSAC. On July 13, it pointed to his "lack of candor" and "deviousness" in his testimony, and recommended two alternatives: either immediate dismissal, or termination after the final year of his contract. Two weeks later, President Hatcher chose the first alternative, and implied that Davis belonged to the CP. His "inexcusable" conduct had hurt the "mission and trust" of the university and had rendered him unfit for future service. Davis appealed Hatcher's ruling to the Subcommittee on Intellectual

Freedom and Integrity (SIFI), a faculty group, on the basis that his "sole fault was silence" before HUAC. SIFI examined all of the testimony before HUAC and PSAC, and questioned Davis again. He again refused to answer questions about his alleged Communist affiliation. SIFI unanimously recommended his dismissal, and on August 26, the Board of Regents approved this.[15]

Mark Nickerson's case provoked a greater dispute between the faculty committees and the administration. Before the PSAC convened, the Executive Committee of the Medical School questioned the tenured professor and recommended his dismissal. In the PSAC hearing, he admitted his former Communist affiliation, but asserted that he had not been active in the party since 1948 because of lack of time. Although he acknowledged that Marxism had influenced some of his economic and political ideas, he denied that he was still a Communist. On July 13, the PSAC voted three to two to retain the professor, although with censure. Two weeks later, President Hatcher sided with the PSAC minority report, and recommended dismissal. Hatcher did not believe Nickerson's departure from the Party was complete, and implied that he could have gone underground. The burden of proof, the president concluded, rested with the accused to dispel the inferences resulting from his reliance on the Fifth Amendment. Nickerson appealed to the Subcommittee on Intellectual Freedom and Integrity (SIFI). After reviewing both the PSAC report and the president's recommendation, the SIFI on August 11 unanimously supported Nickerson's reinstatement, though with censure. The SIFI found him an "arrogant . . . perhaps also a foolish man" who had used "bad judgment," but he was neither a present CP member nor a biased teacher or researcher. The president remained unconvinced, and echoing his earlier arguments, proposed Nickerson's dismissal. On August 26, the Board of Regents by a vote of six to one agreed with the president and dismissed Nickerson without severance pay.[16]

The case of Clement Markert developed much more smoothly. Like Davis, he got the support of other faculty members in his department and the Executive Committee of the College of Literature, Science, and the Arts. Before the PSAC, Markert admitted his former membership in the CP, but declared that he had left the party in 1948 because of its insistence on dogma and its ties to the Soviet Union. The PSAC found that Markert was an "unregenerate intellectual Marxist," but denied that such political beliefs, since not tied to the CP, justified dismissal. It therefore supported Markert's reinstatement with censure by a vote of four to one. President Hatcher approved the PSAC report, and on August 26, the Board of Regents with only one dissenting vote lifted his suspension, though imposing censure.[17]

For Davis and Markert, all of the official inquirers—PSAC, SIFI, the president, and the regents—agreed, but on the Nickerson case, the two faculty groups opposed the final administrative judgment. While each of the cases caused debate and division among the faculty as a whole, the Faculty Senate specifically expressed its regret at Nickerson's dismissal, 314 to 274. Several months later, the senate swung a bit to the other side, and defeated a general policy report critical of the concept of placing the burden of proof on the witness, 353 to 317. Both votes indicated the divisions within the faculty.[18]

As indicated by the Markert case, an instructor's refusal to testify did not mean automatic dismissal for the "unfriendly" witness. Both the University of Chicago and Antioch College retained "Fifth Amendment" instructors. At Chicago, the administration acted a bit less forthrightly than at Antioch.

The University of Chicago reacted ambivalently to the investigation of the Senate Internal Security Subcommittee (SISS) in June 1953. Before the hearings, administrators privately conferred with some who had been subpoenaed, and tried to convince them to cooperate with the SISS, as another faculty member, Daniel Boorstin, had done a few months earlier. The SISS first questioned several persons in executive session, and then opened a public hearing for the "unfriendly" ones. In a relatively brief session, eight persons including five instructors refused to answer questions on leftist associates and affiliations.[19] Although the university had provided counsel for the witnesses, it soon formed a joint trustee-faculty-administration committee to interview the defiant witnesses. The university neither defended the witnesses to the public nor dismissed them. The joint committee's report never became public because, according to the student newspaper, the administration feared further publicity and controversy. In the only public statement on the investigation, Chancellor Lawrence A. Kimpton merely referred to two professors who, after denying CP membership in executive session, had been refused the opportunity to repeat their denials in an open hearing. Praising them, Kimpton concluded that "this challenge to integrity and loyalty of our university was met with foresight, and with honor." The university's response thus successfully avoided a confrontation with both the general community which supported such investigations and the portion of its own constituency which was antagonistic to such probes.[20]

Antioch College also refused to discipline an "unfriendly" witness, but it went further in defending the accused instructor. The college had come under fire from the *Yellow Springs American* and the district's GOP senator for having leftists and Communists on the faculty. In September 1954, HUAC came to Dayton, twenty miles from the college, where it questioned Robert M. Metcalf, a native of the area who had been an art instructor at Antioch since 1945. He admitted that he had belonged to a "Marxist discussion group" for a few months in 1945, but pointed out that he had withdrawn when it began to affiliate formally with the CP. Metcalf refused to answer on a "purely moral" basis all other questions about his acquaintances at the time since none were subversive or dangerous. He did not rely on either the First or Fifth amendments. On the next day, the Antioch president praised Metcalf's loyalty and integrity, and indicated that he would be retained on the faculty. Metcalf's tenuous connection with communism, his well-established reputation in the area, and his avoidance of the Fifth Amendment, had protected his position.[21]

The issue of professors' loyalty also arose in a slightly different manner, what I have called "active defense" cases. As in the Fifth Amendment cases, official committees questioned instructors on their affiliations and actions, but now they met active resistance. In other words, the faculty members refused to use the Fifth Amendment and refused to recant. Yet these incidents at Indiana University and the University of Chicago also reveal the power of the loyalty issue since the suspected instructors publicly proclaimed their anticommunism.

The "active defense" case at Indiana University involved an American Legion-initiated investigation of three law professors. In the summer of 1946, the professors and several other prominent liberals asked the State Election Board to approve the CP's petition to qualify for the November ballot. Although all asserted their anticommunism, the state American Legion urged the governor to investigate the situation. "The personnel of our institutions of learning . . . should not aid or abet such un-American activities in any manner," the Legion declared. The governor referred this to the trustees, who launched an investigation in December. All the witnesses, which included administrators, faculty members, and students, denied that any Communist or Communist sympathizer held a position at the university. The particular faculty members did not confess to any sin in signing the petition supporting the CP's right to appear on the ballot. The trustees' report cleared them of all disloyalty charges.[22]

At the University of Chicago, the "active defense" case saw a fiery confrontation between university personnel and conservative state legislators. In the spring of 1949, the state legislature created the Seditious Activities Investigating Commission (SAIC) to probe the University of Chicago and Roosevelt College. The SAIC, chaired by Senator Paul Broyles, believed that leftist professors indoctrinated students. The committee focused on the political affiliations of a few professors from the university. Chancellor Robert M. Hutchins testified in defense of the Chicago faculty. While the university opposed communism, he argued that "thought control" constituted the "greatest menace to the United States since Hitler." When confronted with accusations that over sixty faculty members had associated with alleged Communist-front organizations, Hutchins denied that the charge alarmed him. He further acknowledged that the administration made no effort to discourage political activities by faculty members. Several professors filed affidavits denying their communist affiliations but defending their right to participate politically. The SAIC questioned five instructors who reiterated this argument. Harold C. Urey, a chemistry professor, declared that "I cannot help it if the Communists fellow-traveled with me on the Spanish situation [the Civil War]. I didn't fellow-travel with them. It was the reverse. Since then, they have not seen fit to fellow-travel with me." None of this testimony convinced the SAIC about the loyalty of the Chicago faculty. Its report urged the dismissal of anyone who held membership in a subversive organization. The administration and trustees presented a united front in rejecting the SAIC's proposals.[23]

While outside agencies, usually HUAC or SISS, generated Fifth Amendment and "active defense" incidents, controversy could also be created by community or internal forces. Local conservative groups or administrators reflecting such conservatism objected to the open involvement of instructors in leftist political activity, such as the 1948 Progressive party (PP) campaign. Henry Wallace, the PP presidental candidate, attracted Communist backing but primarily had a non-Communist base. Conservatives nevertheless saw this effort as "pink" at least, and exerted pressure to oust Progressive instructors. They usually succeeded, especially when the instructor did not have tenure. Such incidents occurred at Bradley University, Eastern Illinois State Teachers College, Evansville College, Northwestern University, and Western Reserve University.

At two small colleges in Illinois, the administration terminated instructors who became involved in the Progressive campaign. At Bradley University in Peoria, the president suggested that faculty members refrain from becoming too involved with the Progressive party (PP). Although one professor did introduce Wallace to a Peoria audience, others found it advisable to act cautiously. When a PP state candidate came to Peoria, about a dozen faculty members went outside of the city limits to meet him. One instructor involved in the campaign did not get a renewal of his contract for the next year.[24] At Eastern Illinois State Teachers College in Charleston, a faculty member chaired the local Progressive group. In the early fall, the president asked him to stop his political activities. Although the instructor soon resigned his chairmanship, the administration decided not to renew his contract for the next year. In both of these cases, the instructors' political activities can only be partially linked to the termination.[25]

The "Progressive party" incident at Evansville College in Evansville, Indiana, reveals a much more overt connection between the instructor's political actions and his termination. In January 1948, George Parker, an instructor in philosophy and religion, became the chairman of the county Citizens for Wallace, a group of about thirty members. The college's president, Lincoln B. Hale, summoned Parker for a conference and advised him of the dangers of his political activity. Some involvement was permissible, Hale declared, but Parker's official position was too visible. The town's conservatism might force the administration to take stern measures, the president concluded. The men reached no decision on Parker's activities, and in the next few weeks, protests continued to come to the administration and trustees. A few persons threatened to withhold further financial contributions unless Parker ceased his activities. President Hale asked some other faculty members to caution Parker again. Although the instructor did not agree to quit his political post, the president interpreted the absence of Parker's name in the press for a few weeks as signifying his acceptance. Otherwise pleased with Parker's performance as a teacher, the administration gave him another one-year contract, which he signed.[26]

Trouble started brewing again when Wallace announced his plan to speak in Evansville on April 6, 1948. The Council of Veterans Organizations charged that Wallace accepted the support of "groups dedicated to the overthrow" of freedom and that his foreign policy followed the Soviet Union's. An independent veterans' group, the Spirit of Kilroy, decided to picket the Wallace meeting. More than 1,000 protestors came to the auditorium, carrying signs "Stalin, Tito, Wallace" and "Unfair to the U.S.A.," and heckling those who entered the Coliseum with jeers of "pink," "Communist," and "I don't want him; you can have him; he's too red for me." Parker gave the invocation as well as a short speech on the need to overcome fear in America. During Wallace's speech, the crowd outside beat against the doors and windows, breaking one of them, and soon tried to force their way into the auditorium. Three Progressive supporters were injured as they resisted the onslaught and barricaded the doors. The police finally dispersed the crowd, and no incidents occurred as the Wallaceites left the building.[27]

President Hale decided that Parker had harmed the College's prestige, and two days later, the Board of Trustees demanded that Parker resign. According to Hale, the administration could not "subject students directly or indirectly to his influence." When Parker refused to resign, Hale immediately dismissed him. Two days later, the administration raised a new charge against the instructor, alleging that he had distributed Wallace literature to his classes. No trustee, administration official, or newspaper ever called Parker a Communist. According to the president, Parker had ignored "his obligation and duty" to the college in favor of expressing his political beliefs, and this ended "his usefulness." The administration did not give Parker a chance to defend himself at a hearing, but he publicly denied any wrongdoing. He defended his right to express himself politically, and claimed that he had used the Wallace material in his classes as topical references, and not as propaganda. His students were not subjected to indoctrination, he concluded.[28]

The community supported the college's action. According to the *Evansville Courier*, Parker was a "badly misguided" person who had to take responsibility for his actions. The town had an active role in running the college; twenty-three of the thirty-six trustees lived in the city and nine were directly elected by the Chamber of Commerce. Naturally, financial contributions also came from the town. The student body and the faculty, on the other hand, showed some criticism of the dismissal. The students finally voted to support the administration by a vote of 324 to 235. While most faculty members also supported the administration, the national AAUP formally censured the college for abridging academic freedom.[29]

Not every faculty member involved in the Progressive campaign met Parker's fate, even though they might have been the target of pressure. Curtis D. MacDougall, a journalism professor at Northwestern University in Evanston, Illinois, was the PP's nominee for the U.S. Senate. After the administration received letters accusing MacDougall of being sympathetic to Communism, the university president referred the matter to the dean of the journalism college, Kenneth E. Olson. Although Dean Olson declared that he spoke only as a friend rather than as a university official, he publicly warned the instructor against inadvertently tainting the college "with a red brush," and suggested that MacDougall withdraw from the campaign. Several days later, MacDougall decided to quit the race, but after further thought, he again changed his mind and campaigned until the November election. The administration refrained from exerting any further pressure, and responded to continued criticism of MacDougall's activities by scorning the Communist method of thought control and praising the American system of free political expression.[30]

A similar "Progressive party" controversy touched Western Reserve University near Cleveland, Ohio. Calvin S. Hall, a psychology professor, became the chairman of the state Wallace for President Committee. In the summer of 1948, the secretary of state, Edward J. Hummel, denied the Wallace committee's petition to get on the Ohio ballot, and he accused Hall of having Communist associations and affiliations. Hall allegedly had been a sponsor of the American Slav Congress and active in a Lenin Memorial meeting. Hall denied both accusations, and the PP won a court fight to get on the ballot. Hall resigned his position in the PP soon thereafter in a dispute over campaign tactics. Although the university President had expressed his displeasure with the PP and Hall's activities, he did not discipline the professor.[31]

Just as support for the Progressive party aroused conservative suspicions, so did support for labor unions. Cases at the University of Illinois and the University of Michigan reveal these attempts to purge the university of outspoken union sympathizers. These two incidents, just as importantly, illustrate administration efforts to refute the loyalty charges and yet to pacify the conservative critics. As a result, officials relied on a bureaucratic solution which achieved a restrictive result without being based on the loyalty issue.

At the University of Illinois, conservatives attacked two professors in the Institute of Labor and Industrial Relations (ILIR), and for a while threatened the Institute's existence. On May 17, 1949, the controversy erupted at a state senate hearing on the university's appropriation. A Republican senator questioned President George Stoddard if any ILIR professors were Communists. Stoddard denied this, although he admitted that a few might be sympathetic to labor. Another GOP senator attacked ILIR because of its prejudice against management, specifically in the Rockford area. Stoddard promised to investigate that situation, but the senator was not appeased. The next day he offered an amendment to cut out the ILIR appropriation, but it was defeated on a voice vote. On May 23, the senate passed the full budget.[32]

The ILIR controversy became enflamed again when the bill went to the house. An official of the Rockford Chamber of Commerce sent a letter to the legislators accusing the ILIR director, Phillips Bradley, of subversive affiliations. These included the Society for Cultural Relations with Russia, the League for Industrial Democracy, World Peaceways, and the Fellowship of Reconciliation. Representative John Lewis (R, Marshall) made these charges public on June 7 at a House Appropriation Committee hearing. President Stoddard denied that Bradley was subversive or disloyal. Representative Lewis also condemned another ILIR professor, Herman Erickson, who had recently argued for the superiority of socialism to the student Socialist Study Club. In Erickson's defense, Stoddard declared that the democratic system permitted peaceful efforts in support of socialism. He further maintained that Erickson did not advocate those beliefs in the classroom. Stoddard concluded that the ILIR could not be considered socialistic or communistic since only Erickson held leftist views. The president's defense received support from another representative, who denied that any leftist activity had occurred while she had belonged to the ILIR advisory committee. Unconvinced, Lewis urged the abolition of ILIR. He got significant support the next day from two Republican legislators who represented the university's district. Charles Clabaugh endorsed Lewis' proposal, while Ora Dillavou felt that slashing ILIR's budget by one-half would be sufficient to force the dismissal of some faculty members. The *Champaign-Urbana News-Gazette* supported Dillavou's proposal because the institute was "pro-labor." Since Dillavou sponsored the UI appropriation in the house, his proposed amendment commanded much support.[33]

Attempting to defuse the ILIR controversy, Phillips Bradley and another professor hurriedly went to the capital. In a private meeting with fifteen legislators, Bradley denied the subversive charges. He pointed out that his participation in three of the allegedly subversive organizations occurred many years earlier and only for a short time. He admitted still belonging to the Fellowship of Reconciliation, but he denied that the pacifist group was disloyal. Defending Herman Erickson, Bradley emphasized academic freedom and the right of instructors to express their political views outside of the classroom. Erickson remained an objective teacher, Bradley argued, while a Communist could not be objective and should be dismissed. Some of the legislators doubted the validity of Bradley's distinction between a socialist and a communist. Neither could be objective, they explained, and thus Erickson should be dismissed. Bradley rejected this demand, but agreed to consult more often with management's representatives on the "usefulness" of faculty members. Dillavou accepted this compromise and dropped his amendment to cut the ILIR budget. Two weeks later, the house passed the full budget.[34]

The ILIR controversy nevertheless lingered on for another month. On July 22, Bradley and Erickson went to an informal conference with eleven businessmen in Rockford. The professors again defended themselves against charges of radicalism, but the businessmen were not convinced. They urged President Stoddard to fire Erickson and to establish a committee of trustees to investigate Bradley and the entire staff and activities of ILIR. Two weeks earlier, Bradley had quietly submitted his resignation as ILIR director, deciding to return to being a political science professor. When this became public, the state labor councils rallied to his defense, but on July 28, President Stoddard accepted the resignation. The trustees did not investigate Erickson or ILIR, and in fact the institute was not attacked again in the postwar decade.[35]

A similar "union" controversy affected the Worker Education Service (WES) of the University of Michigan. This case found the attacker being backed by a conservative corporation and the governor. In the spring of 1948, General Motors economist Adam K. Stricker attended two WES classes. Stricker felt that the instructor was too sympathetic toward labor and relayed his complaints to Governor Kim Sigler, a Republican. Soon after, General Motors paid for Stricker's trip to Washington, D.C., where he testified before a house labor subcommittee. He charged that the WES classes had an antimanagement bias and "Marxist ideas of class economy."[36]

The university initially fought the accusation. President Alexander Ruthven indicated that the testimony was only "hearsay and unverified assertions." Stricker's WES instructor, Samual Jacobs, denied that he held any Marxist beliefs. He had distributed to the class a CIO-PAC pamphlet which pointed to profits as the primary cause of inflation, but he considered its use to be legitimate since the discussion topic was inflation. The instructor also noted that neither Stricker nor any of the other twenty students had ever complained about the classes to him. The head of WES, Arthur Elder, defended the program as being free from subversive influences. Governor Sigler, however, announced that he had received other complaints against the WES, summoned the regents to the capital, and urged an investigation of the program. The regents then suspended the WES and directed President Ruthven to examine the charges.[37]

Ruthven made his report to the board on September 21, 1948. WES had done "much good work" without any subversive indoctrination. Jacobs had erred in distributing the CIO-PAC pamphlet, but no other mistake could be found. The WES director, Arthur Elder, had shown integrity, enthusiasm, and dedication, but had used bad judgment in selecting Jacobs as an instructor. No changes in the program were planned until the complaint was made public, but now Ruthven declared that the WES should be controlled more directly by the university. The board should re-examine the role of Arthur Elder.[38]

Three days later, the regents asked Elder to resign. When he refused, they abolished his position as supervisor. On October 16, the board reinstituted the WES and put the program in the extension division. In January 1949, the new WES began its spring semester, but the CIO, which criticized Elder's dismissal, urged a boycott of the classes. By the first of February when only one student had appeared, in comparison with the previous year's total of 6,000, the regents decided to cancel the entire program. The delicate balance of the WES under Elder had been broken, partly by Governor Sigler and partly by the university's decision to exercise more bureaucratic control over the program.[39]

Throughout this chapter, divisions within the university have been pointed out. When conservative pressure and attacks came from the outside, the university rarely responded with a unified voice. The final three controversies illustrate these divisions even more forcefully. These "local" incidents occurred at the University of Illinois, Antioch College, and Olivet College. In other words, these divisions affected both public and private institutions.

At the University of Illinois, the longest and most intense controversy affecting faculty members erupted in the College of Commerce and particularly in the Department of Economics. Bitter intrafaculty divisions caused the dispute, but conservatives injected the loyalty issue into the squabble. These charges of radicalism and indoctrination were fueled by sensationalism in the press, particularly the *Champaign-Urbana News-Gazette*.

The tensions between faculty members in the Department of Economics broke into public view on May 9, 1950. The *News-Gazette* reported that Ralph Blodgett, an economics professor for many years, had decided to take a position at the University of Florida. According to the newspaper, Blodgett, a believer in free market economics, had been restricted from teaching his regular courses by the department's chairman, Everett E. Hagen. This discrimination had occurred because of Hagen's liberal economic biases, the paper concluded. Sensationalizing the story for the next few weeks, the *News-Gazette* asserted Hagen's partiality not only in editorials but also in news stories. "There is a definite trend toward indoctrinating students with [Keynesian theories] ... Objectivity, and impartial presentation of divergent economic viewpoints, is gradually diverted to a one-sided ideological pattern."[40]

Hagen, in fact, had been hiring many new instructors because of the dramatic increase in student population since the end of the war. Some courses had been rearranged to accommodate the new professors, but this had not occurred because of political favoritism. As the accusations against Hagen continued, the dean of the College of Commerce, Howard R. Bowen, requested an investigation by the administration. On May 18, in the absence of President George Stoddard, the provost appointed a three-member investigative group, chaired by Albert J. Harno, the dean of the College of Law.[41]

As the Harno Committee conducted its inquiry, the controversy escalated. The attacks soon shifted from Hagen to Dean Bowen and President Stoddard. According to the conservatives, the administration had hired new leftist instructors, who had overthrown the older, more conservative professors, not only in the economics department but throughout the university. The *News-Gazette's* editor saw "a planned heavy infiltration of New Deal followers," while Representative Charles Clabaugh feared socialist instructors teaching students. "A socialist is like a typhoid carrier. He can't rid himself of socialism in the classroom if he advocates it outside the classroom," Clabaugh proclaimed. Such charges continued every day with the terms "outsiders," "liberals," "Keynesians," "socialists," "New Dealers," and "pinks" being used as synonyms. The critics demanded that Dean Bowen and President Stoddard stop this dangerous trend. According to the *News-Gazette's* editor, the citizens of Illinois "don't want a Harvard or [a University of] Chicago down here in the black dirt country. Let the east and the big cities espouse those kinds of universities."[42]

The controversy became widely known throughout the state. The *Chicago Tribune* warned that even if Blodgett retained his position, the issue would not be settled because the faculty would still contain Keynesians. Just as quacks should not teach medicine, so Keynesians should not be allowed to indoctrinate "quack economics," the paper concluded. When an economics professor, Donald Kemmerer, supported Blodgett before the Champaign Rotary Club, the Associated Press and United Press reported the speech, and the *Chicago Tribune* ran its own version on the front page.[43]

The charges against Bowen and Hagen were blunted by the Harno Committee report of June 12, issued slightly over a month after the controversy began. The report acknowledged that the hiring of new instructors had caused the rearrangement of some courses, and that some "direct statements" supported the charges against Bowen and Hagen. Yet, the dispute was not caused by political or ideological favoritism but by "inadequate consultation" by Bowen and Hagen with the veteran professors. This was an administrative problem, the report concluded. Echoing these points, Bowen admitted that a morale problem existed among the "Old Guard." This could not be caused by political discrimination because, according to Bowen, he was not "a socialist . . . an advocate of the 'welfare state' . . . a follower of Lord Keynes . . . [or] a Washington bureaucrat."

President Stoddard attempted to end the furor in a report to the Board of Trustees on June 22. Reaffirming the Harno report, Stoddard promised that the administrative problem could be solved with more consultation.[44]

These arguments did not convince the critics. The *Peoria Star* felt that Stoddard's report was "unsatisfactory," and urged a further investigation. The *News-Gazette* insisted that the trustees acknowledge that the Blodgett case was not an aberration, but part of a general pattern throughout the university. If the trustees did not take action, the newspaper predicted that the legislature would. According to the *Chicago Tribune*, Bowen favored socialism and should be dismissed.[45]

The dispute became an issue in the fight over the nomination for university trustees at the Republican State Convention in August. Under the traditional procedure, the Alumni Association (AA) suggested three candidates to each of the two political parties, which accepted them as the nominees. As the 1950 GOP candidates, the AA proposed Wayne A. Johnston, N. B. Megran, and Chester Davis, the latter of whom was a current member of the board. The conservatives found Johnston and Megran acceptable, but they balked at Davis. He had chaired the trustees' search committee that had recommended the hiring of Stoddard in 1946. As a result, they saw Davis as a supporter of the president's policies. Led by the Champaign County delegation, the conservatives found their own candidate, Harold "Red" Grange, the famous ex-football player.[46]

At the convention, a fierce fight between the Grange and Davis factions occurred. The nominating committee voted nineteen to seven for Davis, largely due to the support of the delegation from Cook County, his home. Grange's supporters—Grange himself did not attend the convention—took the issue to the floor. Reed Cutler, the GOP minority leader in the house, charged that "some of the professors over there are so pink you can't tell them from reds." According to Representative Ora Dillavou from Champaign, "fifty reds, pinks, and socialists" were faculty members. Others claimed that Grange would not be a rubber-stamp for Stoddard. The nomination went to Grange 869 to 798. Praise for the action came from the conservative press. The *News-Gazette* predicted an end to the "disturbing trends" at the university.[47]

Trying to defuse the situation and defend his faculty, President Stoddard asked Dillavou to name the fifty radical faculty members. The tone of Stoddard's reply was not demanding but conciliatory, requesting Dillavou's help in controlling subversion. Like Senator McCarthy, Dillavou did not provide the names, but declared that the president could find the subversives if he only tried. Implying Stoddard's negligence or complicity, Dillavou reiterated his belief that "our university is being used to indoctrinate youth with radical political philosophies." Stoddard's second denial of the charge did not ease the conservatives' fears.[48]

Since so many accusations of disloyalty and indoctrination had been thrown against the university, the Board of Trustees asked the security officer, Joseph Ewers, to give a report on the situation. At the Board's September meeting, Ewers declared that the faculty contained no Communists but "ten or fifteen persons with 'will-of-the-wisp' subversive ideas." Ewers did not define his terminology, and President Stoddard added to the confusion two weeks later when he declared that the faculty contained "a few misguided persons." To his critics, the admission that some instructors did not accept political orthodoxy only confirmed their worst fears. To Stoddard's supporters, the controversy was illusory because no faculty members were Communists. In short, polarization continued.[49]

In November, the Republicans swept the state elections including the race for trustees. The election of three GOP candidates gave control of the board to the Republicans. Ora Dillavou, who won reelection to the state house, promised "to continue to fight for a still greater university, dedicated to true Americanism."[50]

The controversy in the College of Commerce continued unresolved. On October 15, 1950, the Executive Committee of the college, an "Old Guard" group, issued a report which agreed with the Harno report that the dispute was not based on political biases. This conservative shift was overlooked because the committee also released an informal poll which indicated that most faculty members, seventy-four to twenty-six, wanted Bowen to leave his position as dean. Senator Everett Peters from Champaign County urged the trustees to end the dispute by conducting its own hearing into the case. On November 24, the trustees—with the three trustees elected two weeks earlier not yet sworn in—held a long and heated hearing. Several professors testified against Bowen, but none asserted that he was a socialist or a subversive. Bowen angrily jumped on this point, arguing that the *News-Gazette* had stirred up the controversy and that the only issue was "resistance to change." He also disputed the Executive Committee's poll, although he admitted that the college was split fairly evenly. The trustees deferred any action on the dispute until their next meeting. On December 28, Stoddard presented a review of the entire controversy to the board. Again, he rejected all charges of favoritism, radicalism, and indoctrination. He praised Bowen for his innovations and improvements in the academic quality of the college. Yet, because of the "revolt," Stoddard felt that he could not recommend that Bowen be reappointed as dean when his contract expired in June. When the trustees accepted this, Bowen resigned immediately as dean.[51]

Although by this time all admitted that the basic issue in the dispute was not ideological, the strains and resentments continued. Due to statements made by a few of the "Old Guard" and their supporters in the press, many conservatives throughout the state still believed that the dispute concerned radicalism. They could remember statements that the Blodgett case was not unusual and that there were "fifty" radical staff members. Many wondered why Stoddard had not acted sooner. On the other hand, the supporters of Bowen also felt worried and uneasy. In July 1951, Hagen resigned as chairman of the economics department and seven other instructors also resigned. Hagen asserted that the University had been unable to protect him from "highly questionable outside pressure." According to another instructor, "freedom of teaching and research is no longer possible in terms of outside pressures—business, political, and journalistic." A year later, three more resigned, citing continued pressure and dissension. Thus while the controversy officially ended, the antagonisms between both camps remained.[52]

A much less intense dispute occurred at Antioch College, a small private college in Yellow Springs, Ohio. This case involved only one instructor, whose leftist activities and personality created divisions at the college. On December 4, 1952, President Douglas McGregor unofficially informed Robert Rempfer, a mathematics instructor who had been at the college for two years, that the administration would not issue another yearly contract to him. According to McGregor, Rempfer's political activities raised doubts about his honesty and independence. While Rempfer at present was not being considered for tenure, the president indicated that the instructor's activities would cause several faculty members to oppose any tenure proposal in the future. Upset at the president's decision and inferences, Rempfer decided to fight the action as an infringement of academic freedom. On January 20, 1953, Rempfer issued two statements on his political and educational attitudes: "On Democratic Living" and "To Have and to Hold." He condemned the political screening of teachers and the general anti-intellectual climate in the nation. Implicitly referring to Antioch, the latter statement even criticized "liberal" educational efforts. "Homogeneity may lead to congeniality, or even to 'one happy family.' But is this necessarily the best road to education?"[53]

Rempfer's action not only failed to convince the administration, but it also hardened his critics' resolve to terminate him. On February 9, the president officially announced the decision to terminate the instructor, and listed three reasons: poor teaching ability with beginning students, little productive scholarship, and doubts about his "independence of judgment and . . . responsibility as a faculty citizen and leader." The Antioch program did not distinguish between education in or out of the classroom, McGregor maintained. "Behavior associated with activities of whatever nature could be considered relevant [in decisions on employment]. We would not consider behavior exempt from criticism simply because it was exhibited in the name of political activity." Later, the administration cited several specific incidents showing Rempfer's dishonesty and lack of judgment, though not necessarily his disloyalty. For example, in Rempfer's initial job interview, he did not mention the Progressive party in his list of leftist affiliations. Later, when he distributed a petition for clemency for the Rosenbergs, he did not discuss the possible ramifications with students before they signed it. Finally, he held secret meetings in his house during which he supported Communist party positions. The administration concluded that it should terminate Rempfer.[54]

Rempfer appealed this decision, with the specific criticisms still publicly unknown, to the Administration Council (Adcil). For the next three months, Rempfer and the Adcil debated procedural questions, and the former wrote frequent letters to the faculty while the administration remained quiet. Ultimately, a Committee of Inquiry (CI), composed of three faculty members, was formed. In June, it issued its report listing several anonymous complaints against the instructor and including a letter by another faculty member pointing out ambiguities in Rempfer's actions and statements. The CI asserted that Rempfer's scholarship and administrative responsibilities had suffered because of his political activities. It also declared that his organization of pressure groups only increased the tensions in the small community. Rempfer responded in two ways: by declaring his honesty and political independence, and by rejecting the use of political activities as a factor in an academic case. The instructor preferred to focus on purely scholarly issues. On June 22, the CI recommended to not renew his contract but to pay him the yearly salary since notification had not been given in time. Two days later, the Adcil agreed.[55]

This dispute occurred during a stormy period at Antioch. A former Communist, Harvey Matusow, had charged that the administration had allowed the Young Progressives of America to sponsor radical and Communist speakers on campus, and his accusations had received considerable publicity. Moreover, the Ohio Un-American Activities Committee had questioned President McGregor about Communist influences at the college. Yet the college did not sacrifice Rempfer solely to calm these waters. The termination was caused by both his ideology and his problems in interpersonal relationships. Even one of Rempfer's supporters acknowledged his "peculiar shyness at his age, lack of sophistication, minority complex, [and] gullibility." Because of his aloof personality, many faculty members did not like to associate with him. This also had political overtones since some thought him arrogant in showing the fault in their politics while ignoring their complaints about his politics. Rempfer incorrectly interpreted his termination as a purely academic freedom case, but politics did play its part. The controversy on campus was reduced by the administration-faculty consultation.[56]

At Olivet College in Olivet, Michigan, internal strains were much more severe. The administration-faculty struggle lasted for a relatively long period of time and ultimately caused the departure of several instructors. In the 1930s, the college, which was affiliated with the Congregational Church, adopted a tutorial program and began to attract a wide range of students to the small town. Conservative alumni became disenchanted with the changes and attempted to reverse the liberal policies. In 1944, they helped to ease out the president who had inaugurated the tutorial program, and installed Malcolm Dana as the new president. Although initially pleased with Dana's actions, the conservatives soon came to believe that he would not make significant changes in the direction of the college. In February 1947, they decided to directly approach the Board of Trustees about terminating four leaders of the liberal faction of the faculty. President Dana beat the conservatives to the punch by condemning such outside pressures in a chapel speech. Students also voted to support academic freedom. The trustees were forced to dismiss the conservatives' complaints.[57]

The controversy continued to smolder for the next year. On campus, students formed a Young Progressives' Club and viewed *Ten Days that Shook the World*, a movie sympathetically describing the Russian Revolution. The liberal faculty members formed the Olivet College Teachers Union, OCTU (AFT), with sixteen of the thirty-five instructors as members. Since all faculty members received only yearly contracts, the union began pressing for the establishment of a tenure system. Such actions prompted the conservatives to take more drastic action. In the spring of 1948, the trustees decided to exclude the four liberal leaders from any tenure consideration. This decision was not made public, however. At about the same time, President Dana and Dean Robert G. Ramsay resigned. On July 21, 1948, the board hired as its new president, Aubrey L. Ashby, an alumnus who had been vice-president of the National Broadcasting Company. With J. F. Mathias as the new dean, Ashby would oversee an uncompromising purge of both faculty and students.[58]

It is unclear whether Ashby demanded the first termination as a requirement for his own employment, or if the trustees acted on their own. In any case, at the same meeting at which the trustees formally hired Ashby, they also decided that the end had come to the academic "usefulness" of T. Barton Akeley, a political science instructor and liberal leader, and his wife Margaret, the librarian. This shocked the liberal faculty members because Barton not only had been on the faculty since 1936 but also had signed a yearly contract in April. His wife had signed one in June. The board promised to pay the Akeleys' salaries which ran until June 1949, but it also began eviction proceedings against them. Although Akeley was somewhat of a nonconformist in the small town, a man who wore a goatee, beret, and at one time shorts in public, his dismissal resulted basically from political differences with the conservatives. One leading conservative trustee privately pointed to a 1941 teachers' strike in which Akeley revealed his "capacity for intrigue and undue influence . . . his philosophy of agitation . . . and his method of organized action." One unnamed administrator indicated that

Akeley was an "ultraliberal" whose presence was drying up financial contributions from the alumni. This sentiment was echoed by the chairman of the trustees and by a prominent banker in the small town, who called Akeley a "pink."[59]

The Akeleys' dismissal began the public phase of the controversy, which lasted for five months and split the college bitterly. Out of a student body of 300, almost 60 formed the Student Action Committee (SAC). They urged the reinstatement of the Akeleys, retroactive tenure, and an investigation by an impartial educational agency. They picketed the administration building and refused to register for the fall term. President Ashby denied the students' right to protest, and threatened the loss of the pre-registration fee of seventy-five dollars. At one time, he announced that the protestors could register only if they would quit picketing, release no more statements to the press, and accept probationary status. Ashby declared that "a college is like a business. . . . When you defy constituted authority, all you have left is anarchy." He refused to rehire the Akeleys, and characterized them as "termites" who bored from within to weaken the structure of the college. The town's only newspaper, the *Olivet Optic*, viewed the student boycott as a subversive action which occurred because they had been taught "radical notions." The boycott only proved that the trustees had acted correctly on the Akeleys' case, the paper concluded. The boycott lasted beyond three administration deadlines, including the beginning of classes. The liberal faculty members affiliated with the Olivet College Teachers Union (OCTU-AFT) generally wanted the students to register since their departure would only ensure conservative control. Ultimately, most of the students did agree to register for classes; only nine left the college.[60]

Determined to push ahead with the purge, President Ashby and the trustees viewed the liberal faculty members as the cause of all the unrest. Conservatives were especially angry at the OCTU and its president, Tucker P. Smith, who at this time was also the vice-presidential nominee of the Socialist party. The administration saw itself as besieged. The president believed that he was only exercising the prerogatives of a governing body. He received support from the town newspaper which continued to editorialize on the limitations of academic freedom. The administration, however, received more critical than congratulatory letters, and dissenting alumni formed a pressure group, the Federation of Olivet Alumni. In October, more than 100 students signed a petition asking the administration to reconsider the Akeleys' dismissals. Rallies supporting the liberal cause occurred even during Homecoming. Several faculty members and students asked for an investigation from both the AAUP and the Congregational Church. At the same time, though, the liberal faculty members saw themselves as the minority in the dispute. The trustees had dismissed one of their leaders without consulting the faculty as required by the college constitution, and no one had the protection of tenure.[61]

In November, the trustees granted tenure to six instructors, but rumors about other dismissals still floated around the campus. The OCTU urged President Ashby to convene the Faculty Cabinet and determine a tenure policy so that those who might be terminated could search for other employment at academic conventions over the Christmas break. Two weeks later, the union again pointed to the need for increased communication on the issue, though at the same time it revealed its lack of sympathy toward the administration. According to the OCTU, a college needed four assets: an ideal; dedicated teachers; students; and, least in importance, administrators. Tensions grew higher when three instructors announced their resignations at the end of the academic year. On December 7, faculty representatives met with President Ashby and Dean Mathias in a stormy session. Both sides felt that the other was trying to exercise total control, and no compromise was reached.

Although the Faculty Council met to consider tenure, the trustees soon overruled its recommendations. While they gave tenure to two instructors, the trustees refused to renew the contracts of four faculty members who had led the defense of the Akeleys and the OCTU: Tucker P. Smith, economics; Arthur Moore, fine arts; Julian Fahy, political science; Herbert Hyde, music. The board also gave one-year contracts to three other instructors. It gave no official reason for its action, but its chairman cited financial difficulties. Some trustees indicated that Smith, the OCTU president, had weak "academic qualifications." The *Olivet Optic* boiled the issue down to ideology and praised the board for ousting the "leftist elements." In a speech to the town's Chamber of Commerce, President Ashby acknowledged that he had accepted the presidency in order to end "subversive indoctrination." In a later speech, he accused the OCTU of plotting to turn Olivet into a labor college, and he repeated a rumor that the liberals wanted Henry Wallace as the president. Ashby concluded that "the issue at Olivet is not personalities but ideologies. . . . Our challenge is to promote the American way of life."[62]

Although President Ashby and the trustees were firmly in control, their actions not only shocked the college but also many alumni and supporters. After an investigation, the Congregational Church denied that the administration had violated academic freedom, but it also urged compromise and reconciliation. "The functions of the president should be redefined; a new dean should be appointed; and a faculty-trustee committee should temporarily run the college," the report concluded. An editorial in the student newspaper called the administration "morally bankrupt," and urged Ashby to resign. Needless to say, nothing came of these proposals. Soon, some students, three trustees, and seven faculty members, including two who had been given tenure, resigned in protest. This group tried to form a new college, but failed for lack of funds. The controversy seriously weakened the college for several years.

	1948–49	*1949–50*	*1950–51*	*1951–52*
students	284	167	150	140
faculty	35	25	24	24
				(3 part-time)
expenses	$324,996	$227,697	$244,287	
income	$282,955	$160,228	$153,366	

While the college experienced serious financial difficulties before President Ashby arrived, and while donations increased during his administration, the basic reason for the controversy was not financial, but political differences. In 1950, Ashby left the presidency, claiming that his job was finished.[63]

Throughout the Midwest, the Red Scare affected individual faculty members. This regional perspective has enlarged the analysis from individual universities, and has revealed that instructors were dismissed because of their use of the Fifth Amendment, their involvement in the Progressive party, their avowed sympathy for unions, and their nonconformity in a particular community. These cases of repression would be increased if we knew about all of the terminations that were done privately and did not cause public controversy. For example, in early 1947 the president of Ohio State University admitted that he had already dismissed two faculty members with "Communist leanings." The president of Western Illinois State Teachers College privately disclosed that one "liberalist" had been terminated and that another had resigned. The University of Illinois also quietly refused to renew the contracts of two leftists.[64] These incidents were not publicly known at the time, and they remain difficult to uncover partially because, as has been noted, administrations often relied on bureaucratic language ("usefulness," "duty to the University," etc.) to solve loyalty cases. Stated differently, these incidents reveal that the Scare tended to affect younger, less-established professors rather than their tenured colleagues whose contracts could not be privately cut.

This chapter nevertheless has also pointed to some limitations in the effectiveness of the Communist issue. Some universities retained professors despite their use of the Fifth Amendment, involvement in the Progressive party or unions, and nonconformity. The number of retentions would be greatly increased if this chapter had included all of the "nuisance incidents" that occurred in the postwar decade. These types of incidents featured conservatives accusing faculty members of radicalism, but ended with no effect. For example, no reaction occurred after J. B. Matthews, a prominent conservative, wrote a magazine article accusing professors at ten midwestern universities of having Communist sympathies. Furthermore, loyalty crusaders on the local level often attacked leftists, such as John J. DeBoer at the University of Illinois or Oliver Loud at Antioch College, without success.[65] In conclusion, therefore, the degree of repression cannot be answered in any absolute terms. The unjust dismissal of any person should be condemned, but repression touched only a minority of instructors.

The Scare's effect nevertheless involves not only the actual victims but also all professors. While some historians have criticized the academic community as "cautious and conformist careerists,"[66] this study reveals a varied and mixed response. At the University of Michigan, faculty members wanted to retain Nickerson and Markert but to terminate Davis. The chancellor of the University of Chicago, Robert M. Hutchins, castigated J. B. Matthews and State Senator Paul Broyles for their acceptance of guilt by association, but promised to dismiss any Communist party members from the faculty. At Antioch College, faculty members supported Robert Metcalf against HUAC, but did not back Robert Rempfer in his termination dispute. In each of these cases, the academic community cannot be neatly labelled as either challengers of popular norms or as fearful conformists. Adopting an abstract formulation of conformity only obscures the historical record, which in this case means an uneven and uncertain response.

These responses can be understood only by examining the particular incidents. Response varied according to the factors in the development of a particular case: the degree of direct administrative consultation with the faculty, personal knowledge of the accused, amount and type of evidence on the charges, and the nature of the "attacker" (perhaps acting as a negative reference point).[67] Naturally, these controversies featured similar debates over the relationship of political activity and academic freedom, debates which borrowed heavily from Sidney Hook and others. Yet the theory did not invariably become translated into particular policy.

This mixed response by faculty members finds some confirmation in a 1955 poll of social scientists. Almost eighty percent denied that their own academic freedom had been threatened in the postwar decade, but almost two-thirds felt that a general threat to "intellectual activity" was more pronounced than a generation before. Over a wide range of issues relating to political expression and academic freedom, the authors found that fifty-one percent were neither worried nor cautious, thirty-one percent were worried but not cautious, and eighteen percent were worried and cautious.[68] It is impossible to conclude precisely the degree of fear and caution because no similar testing was taken at periodic intervals over the years. Moreover, no testing of faculty in other disciplines was done. Yet at the least, it points out that professors responded differently to the Scare.

The Red Scare was pervasive since it affected both public and private colleges throughout the Midwest. Yet it did not exert a uniform effect on either its specific targets or on the general academic body. The university as an institution therefore cannot be characterized as a repressive environment. The mixed response—the divisions within the university—reveal that the university reflected the divisions within the society, but the basic response, unlike the society's, associated with the liberal movement. The liberal response included both partial acceptance of the Communist issue and partial rejection of the conservative crusaders. In these battles with the loyalty supporters, the liberals often lost. Yet they did not lose the war. The liberal direction in the university did not so much prevail during these years as persist.

8

Conclusion

The Second Red Scare operated on the state and local level just as much as on the national level. In the Midwest, the Communist issue affected state legislatures, city governments, schools, voluntary organizations, and universities. Although it featured conservative and liberal movements, there were limits to the Scare's pervasiveness and its repression.

The conservative movement, along with a weaker and reactive liberal movement, generated the Second Red Scare. The conservative crusade did not have a formal structure with affiliated chapters, elected representatives, and a constitution. Nevertheless, its loose organization—its operation within the political structure—does not contradict its status as a movement.[1] Its leadership and the core of its strength came primarily from the Republican party.[2] Conservative Republicans perceived the New Deal as revolutionary, and passionately wanted to reverse the liberal trend. Although the New Deal began to end after 1938, the conservatives' alienation was only partially eased because Franklin Roosevelt remained president. His death brought them new hope to save the country. These conservatives formed the basis for the Red Scare activities.[3]

This conservative movement functioned on the national, state, and local levels, and it gained strength through these interactions. Neither the Cold War nor the loyalty efforts of the federal government solely caused the Scare. Rather, the Scare arose from a series of developments as the conservative movement effectively pursued the loyalty issue on all levels. International tensions accelerated this drive, but the viability of this issue did not originate with Truman's loyalty activities.

In the Midwest, conservatives won many victories in the early postwar years, prior to the 1948 Progressive campaign, the Alger Hiss case, and the emergence of Senator McCarthy. In 1945, the Communist issue dominated the mayoral campaign in Detroit. In 1946, Ohio State University and Michigan State College banned the American Youth for Democracy (AYD), and the Indiana American Legion prompted a probe of three Indiana University professors. The school board in Dayton, Ohio, refused to accept Rev. Harold Marley as a member because of his leftist activities.[4] That same year, newspapers such as the *Ann Arbor News* printed long series of articles on the dangers of the Communist party inside the U.S.[5] In the 1946 fall campaign, GOP politicians successfully used the Communist issue in several congressional campaigns. In 1947, the Scare became even more heated. The Illinois legislature created the Seditious Activities Investigating Commission under Senator Paul Broyles, and the Michigan senate established its own un-American activities committee led by Senator Matthew Callahan. AYD chapters were banned at the University of Illinois, Wayne University, and the University of Michigan. That same year, the Communist issue arose in the Chicago mayoral campaign and in a referendum on proportional representation in Cincinnati. The *Chicago Tribune* launched an exposé on "subversive" textbooks, and the school board in Delavan, Wisconsin, banned a book because of its favorable view of the Soviet Union. Various liberal groups began purging themselves of leftist and Communist members, and the American Legion pressured the city council of Peoria, Illinois, to ban Paul Robeson. The successes of the conservative movement were not inevitable; at times, it met defeat. Nevertheless, there can be no doubt that its strength in the first years of the postwar decade was considerable.

The Second Red Scare was thus created by a conservative movement that operated on state and local levels at the same time it acted on the national level. Contrary to the thesis of Robert Griffith and Robert Goldstein, the Communist issue did not originate on the national level and then spread to the states and localities. Contrary to the thesis of Athan Theoharis, the Scare was not legitimized by a national leader. This study does not argue that the Scare originated at the local level.[6] Instead, it stresses connection, interraction, complexity.[7]

In contrast to the relatively unified effort of the conservatives, the liberal movement had a more mixed response to the Scare. Liberals became more overtly anti-Communist during the postwar decade, but they were often alienated by the conservatives' wild, partisan use of the Communist issue. As a result, they only occasionally united with the conservatives. Liberals led the opposition to loyalty proposals in state legislatures, city governments, and universities. Although they purified their own organizations, they did not support the American Legion's attempts to deny political expression to all leftists.

Because of this mixed response, the liberal movement found itself in a defensive position throughout the Scare. The public consistently revealed negative attitudes about American Communists and about all leftists and nonconformists. In three Gallup polls taken in 1946 and 1947, only twenty-three percent, eighteen percent, and nineteen percent thought that Communists were loyal to the U.S. Twice in 1947, polls found that over sixty percent wanted CP membership forbidden by law. Even as early as July 1946, almost eighty percent believed that Russian spies operated in the country. In 1953, over two-thirds would deny Communists the right to speak in their city.[8] This points out the public pressure on liberals to become more outspokenly anti-Communist. The public tended to support the conservative position on the Communist issue even in the early postwar years. Contrary to Athan Theoharis' argument, the public was concerned about internal security matters between 1945 and 1948.[9]

This consideration of public attitudes raises the pervasiveness issue and the role of the "elite" and the "masses." In criticizing the pluralist theory of the masses being energized by status anxiety, some historians have seemed to deny the extent of the Scare. Michael Paul Rogin has argued that "McCarthyism made little impact on the mass level."[10] According to Donald Crosby, who examined the Catholic response, "the masses of lay Catholics participated sporadically or watched in a largely passive manner."[11]

This problem is largely semantic, however; many historians have not clearly defined "mass" and "elite." Rogin, for example, gives a broad definition to "elite": the conservative elite constituting "precinct workers to national politicians."[12] Other historians give a narrower definition. Thomas Holmes points to "an economic and political oligarchy" in Hawaii who exploited the Communist issue, and Don Carleton has argued that the elite of Houston—seven people identified by the reputational approach—sustained and legitimized the Scare.[13]

This study relies on the broader definition. Suzanne Keller, in a theoretical analysis of American society, concludes that there is "no single comprehensive elite" but "numerous and varied" elites.[14] In a political phenomenon such as the Scare, elites would constitute the politically active. This study has confirmed the importance of such elites as they coalesced into voluntary organizations. Whether the American Legion or the CIO, such voluntary groups played a significant role in forming the Scare: its extent, and its limitations. Yet in American politics, this influence is not unusual.[15] Voluntary organizations have a significant impact because of the diffused and nonideological character of the two political parties. In short, the Red Scare did not deviate from traditional political channels. It can be considered an elite phenomenon only in the sense that all political efforts are elite phenomena. As a result, I would suggest that historians drop the use of such terms; they do not explain anything.

The pervasive quality of the Red Scare was limited because it remained in these traditional channels. It did not energize the "masses," who shall be defined as the apolitical and the apathetic. Moreover, the Scare received only the usual degree of response from the group which can be called the "middle group," the politically aware, the occasional participant, the average voter. This middle group acted in two ways: in opinion polls and in voting. As we have seen, polls tended to support restrictions on Communists and leftists. The "middles" also tended to support loyalty crusaders in elections. In Michigan, where three loyalty measures were on the ballot at different times, the voters endorsed these proposals by comfortable margins.

Another way of measuring the limited yet pervasive quality of the Scare is to examine the degree of repression. There is no need to repeat all the incidents in this study in order to conclude that the Scare claimed victims in an overt sense and scored symbolic victories over leftists. Yet at the same time, the effectiveness of the Communist issue had its limits.[16] Two Illinois governors vetoed antisubversive proposals; Wisconsin enacted no loyalty laws; and no state created a permanent "little HUAC." Some state laws were not enforced or were ruled unconstitutional. The Communist issue did not succeed in several city elections in Chicago and Cincinnati; even the Detroit loyalty program granted significant rights to the "defendant." The public schools did not create blind believers in the status quo, and at universities, students had opportunities to hear leftist speakers and form political groups. Organizations like the American Legion did not always succeed in preventing meetings where leftists entertained or spoke. This list of limitations could be greatly expanded by including numerous minor incidents, "nuisance incidents," which had no effect on the community.[17]

The Scare's limits are revealed in the different responses by government and by voluntary organizations. Not only was overt repression limited, but the subtle pressures to conform never reached their full expression. This argument does not deny that the postwar decade was characterized by a conservative climate. It only suggests that the conservative movement did not achieve its total objective: mobilization against internal "subversives." The conservative mood had force, but it was also limited in its intensity and in its duration. The country was not evolving toward a fascist state, as some Communists then claimed, or toward a "nonterroristic totalitarian society."[18] Perhaps this mixed character of the Scare can be better understood by referring to the impact of the New Deal on the state and local levels:

> [It] produced neither federal dictation, a completely cooperative federalism, nor a new state progressivism. Instead, it helped create a rather flat mixture of achievement, mediocrity, and confusion. For all the supposed power of the New Deal, it was unable to impose all its guidelines on the autonomous forty-eight states.[19]

Thus it was with the Red Scare: a mixture of conservative effort, noticeable achievements, but at the same time not total success. The conservative movement had limitations.

Yet just as no one would deny that the 1930s were characterized by the New Deal, so the postwar decade must still be characterized by the Second Red Scare. The Scare can be considered pervasive since the conservative movement forced government and voluntary organizations to confront the issue. No place in the Midwest—no one either on the national, state, or local level—was immune. The limitations of the conservative movement occurred within the context of the Scare. The limitations should be seen as a secondary characteristic; the conservative effort, which simultaneously occurred on national, state, and local levels, set the dominant mood for the era.[20]

Notes

Introduction

1. Earl Latham, *The Communist Conspiracy in Washington: From the New Deal to McCarthy* (Cambridge: Harvard University Press, 1960), pp. 28–44. Robert Goldstein, *Political Repression in Modern America* (Cambridge: Schenkman Publishing Co., 1978), pp. 202–58.

2. Ralph B. Levering, *American Opinion and the Russian Alliance, 1939–1945* (Chapel Hill: University of North Carolina Press, 1976), pp. 53, 76–77, 172–73. John Lewis Gaddis, *The United States and the Origins of the Cold War, 1941–1947* (New York: Columbia University Press, 1972), pp. 42–44, 52, 56–61. Richard Polenberg, *War and Society: The United States, 1941–1945* (Philadelphia: J.B. Lippincott, 1972), pp. 74–77, 208–9. *Chicago Tribune,* 9 August 1944, p. 1.

3. There have been many books written on these subjects. A recent review article is Geoffrey S. Smith, "Harry, We Hardly Know You: Revisionism, Politics, and Diplomacy, 1945–1954," *American Political Science Review* 70 (June 1976): 560–82.

4. Illinois, Michigan, California, New York, Maryland, and Washington were examined in Walter Gellhorn, ed., *The States and Subversion* (Ithaca: Cornell University Press, 1952).

5. Ronald Johnson, "The Communist Issue in Missouri, 1946–1956" (Ph.D. dissertation, University of Missouri, 1973). Thomas Holmes, "The Specter of Communism in Hawaii, 1947–1953" (Ph.D. dissertation, University of Hawaii, 1975). Don E. Carleton, "A Crisis of Rapid Change: The Red Scare in Houston" (Ph.D. dissertation, University of Houston, 1978). Dale Sorenson, "The Anti-Communist Impulse in Indiana" (Ph.D. dissertation, Indiana University, 1980).

6. Robert Griffith, "American Politics and the Origins of 'McCarthyism,'" *The Specter: Original Essays on the Cold War and the Origins of 'McCarthyism'* ed. Robert Griffith and Athan Theoharis (New York: Franklin Watts, 1974), pp. 14–16.

7. Goldstein, *Political Repression,* pp. 348–49.

8. Athan Theoharis, "The Rhetoric of Politics," in *Politics and Policies of the Truman Administration,* ed. Barton J. Bernstein (Chicago: Quadrangle Books, 1972), pp. 196–241. See also Richard Freeland, *The Truman Doctrine and the Origins of McCarthyism* (New York: A.A. Knopf, 1973), pp. 359–60.

9. My definition and use of the term "movement" is derived from current theory. See the *International Encyclopedia of the Social Sciences,* s.v. "Social Movements: The Study of Social Movements," by Joseph Gusfield. I have used the term "persuasion" rather than attitude or ideology. This is borrowed from Robert Griffith who borrowed it from Marvin

Meyers. See Robert Griffith, *Politics of Fear: Joseph McCarthy and the Senate* (Lexington: University of Kentucky Press, 1970), p. 31.

10. A number of historians have effectively criticized the "status anxiety" theory of Richard Hofstadter. Nelson Polsby, "Towards an Explanation of McCarthyism," *Political Studies* 8 (October 1960): 250–71. Latham, *Communist Conspiracy*. Michael Paul Rogin, *The Intellectuals and McCarthy: The Radical Specter* (Cambridge: MIT Press, 1967).

    For the intellectual aspect of the loyalty crusade, see George N. Nash, *The Conservative Intellectual Movement in America since 1945* (New York: Basic Books, 1976), pp. ix, 104–7, 151.

11. It is true that both the conservative and liberal movements were anti-Communist. This similarity in goals should not be used to deny their separate existence, based on the method or expression of anticommunism.

    Indeed, anticommunism does not even have to coincide with sentiments favoring the restrictions of "subversives." Persons can believe that the Soviet Union curtails their citizens' freedoms and thus support a pure civil libertarian policy in the U.S. One example of this type of anticommunism can be found in Michael Harrington, *Fragments of the Century: A Personal and Social Retrospective of the 50's and 60's* (New York: Simon and Schuster, 1972), pp. 60–93. Although this belief system might be rare, its existence suggests that using anticommunism in a general sense as a working definition is a poor choice.

12. The phrase is borrowed from Richard Hofstadter's discussion of a "moral consensus" and a "policy consensus." The former term suggests that opponents accept conflict on policy matters, while the latter term suggests general agreement on policy. In a moral consensus situation, "one party or interest seeks the defeat of an opposing interest on matters of policy, but at the same time seeks to avoid crushing the opposition, denying the legitimacy of its existence or its values, or inflicting upon it extreme and gratuitous humiliations." Richard Hofstadter, *The Progressive Historians* (New York: A.A. Knopf, 1968), p. 454. Liberals did not have a moral consensus with their Communist opponents, but their repudiation of the Left was narrower than the conservative position.

13. These terms are partially derived from William Spinrad, *Civil Liberties* (Chicago: Quadrangle Books, 1970), p. 310 n.9. I do not use his exact terminology because I do not accept fully his definition. My study examines "significant controversies" rather than "nuisance incidents" or attitudes.

14. John Gunther, *Inside the U.S.A.* (New York: Harper and Brothers, 1947), p. 274.

15. Ira Sharkansky, *Regionalism in American Politics* (Indianapolis: Bobbs-Merrill Co., 1970), p. 62.

16. Theoharis, "Rhetoric of Politics," p. 235 f.1.

17. The histories of unions and the Progressive party during this period have been dealt with only briefly because other historians have examined them in detail.

18. The conservative literature is dominated by the biographies and memoirs of ex-Communists, such as Whittaker Chambers. Senator Joseph McCarthy was defended in William F. Buckley and L. Brent Bozell, *McCarthy and His Enemies* (Chicago: Regnery, 1954). No avowedly conservative historian is currently writing on the subject to my knowledge.

Chapter 1

1. Griffith, "American Politics," pp. 14–16.

2. On the federal level, there was little opposition to the Red Scare. The House approved the

HUAC by overwhelming margins every year. For example, in 1949 the vote was 353–29. Congress enacted the Internal Security Act in 1950 and the Communist Control Act in 1954 by similar margins. It is beneficial then to measure the degree of opposition on the state and local levels for it gives a quantifiable means of checking the deviation from the national pattern. In other words, it helps determine the power of local factors.

3. See chap. 6 concerning students for a full discussion of the AYD controversy at Michigan State College. See nn. 7 and 8 in that chapter.

4. The United Public Workers (UPW) was formally named the United Public Office Workers of America. *Detroit Free Press*, 2, 3, 4, 9, 10, 17, 18 February 1947. *Lansing State Journal*, 6, 9, 10 February 1947. Various citizens' letters to the governor are in Papers of Governor Kim Sigler, Correspondence of the Legal Advisor Relating to Communism. The file on Foss Baker is in the Papers of Governor Kim Sigler, Administrative Records, State Police. Both are located at the Michigan Historical Division, Department of State, State Archives, Lansing (hereafter referred to as the Michigan Historical Division).

5. Donald S. Leonard to Governor Kim Sigler, 24 February 1947, in the Papers of Governor Kim Sigler, Correspondence of the Legal Advisor Relating to Communism, Michigan Historical Division. U.S., Congress, House, Committee on Un-American Activities, *Investigation of Un-American Propaganda Activities in the United States*, 80th Congress, 1st session, pp. 390–26.

6. *Lansing State Journal*, 29, 31 March 1947. *Detroit Free Press*, 29 March 1947. *Detroit News*, 28 February 1947. The file on Stanley Nowak and the memo from Victor C. Anderson to Governor Sigler on the Fellowship of Reconciliation are in the Papers of Governor Kim Sigler, Correspondence of the Legal Advisor Relating to Communism, Michigan Historical Division. For a description of the more general disenchantment with Kim Sigler, see Frank B. Woodford, *Alex J. Groesbeck: Portrait of a Public Man* (Detroit: Wayne University Press, 1962), pp. 306–18.

7. *Lansing State Journal*, 13 February; 12 March 1947. *Detroit Free Press*, 12, 14 February; 19 March 1947. *Ann Arbor News*, 6 February 1947. Senate Resolution 24 in *Journal of the Senate of the State of Michigan, 1947 Regular Session* (Lansing: Franklin de Kleine Co., 1947), pp. 182, 207, 212.

8. *Journal of the Senate of the State of Michigan, 2nd Extra Session of 1948* (Lansing: Franklin de Kleine Co., 1948), p. 23. *Lansing State Journal*, 2 April 1947. *Ann Arbor News*, 5, 22 April 1947. *Detroit Free Press*, 7, 16 February; 19, 21, 23 March; 3, 5, 9 April 1947. Robert Mowitz, "Michigan: State and Local Attacks on Subversion," in *The States and Subversion*, ed. Walter Gellhorn (Ithaca: Cornell University Press, 1952), p. 193 n. 21.

9. One minor bill that was debated in the 1947 legislative session was designed to keep the CP off the ballot. Sponsored by Representative Edward Hutchinson, it required every political party to get one hundred signatures on petitions in each county of the state in order to quality for the ballot. The measure sailed through the house without a dissenting vote, but the Senate Elections Committee killed it after a number of small political parties, such as the Prohibition party, condemned the bill as discriminatory. See House Bill 151 in *Michigan Senate Journal of 1947*, p. 346; and in the *Journal of the House of Representatives of the State of Michigan, 1947 Regular Session* (Lansing: Franklin de Kleine Co., 1947), pp. 279, 407, 414.

10. Senate Resolution 44 in *Michigan Senate Journal of 1947*, pp. 1247, 1398. *Ann Arbor News*, 18 February; 7, 12, 31 March 1947. *Lansing State Journal*, 4 April; 27 May 1947. The Callahan Bill (Senate Bill 332) was passed on a party line vote. The senate passed it: aye 27R; nay 1R, 3D. The house passed it: aye 69R, 1D; nay 2R, 1D. *Michigan Senate Journal of 1947*, pp. 735, 822, 884, 936, 958, 1430, 1557, 1582; *Michigan House Journal of*

1947, p. 1197, 1405, 1542, 1726. *Detroit Free Press*, 1, 21, 29 May 1947. *Lansing State Journal*, 13, 18, 21, 27 May 1947. "Transcript, Hearing on the Callahan Bill, 18 June 1947," in the Papers of Governor Kim Sigler, special subjects, legislature, Michigan Historical Division.

11. Mowitz, "Michigan," pp. 191–95. *Detroit Free Press*, 15 September; 1 October 1947. *Detroit News*, 4 September 1947.

12. *Lansing State Journal*, 7, 16, 22 April 1948. By 1947, the Michigan State Police had files on 14,000 citizens; *Detroit Times*, 19 February 1947. House Bill 24 in *Journal of the House of the State of Michigan, 1948 Extra Session* (Lansing: Franklin de Kleine Co., 1948), pp. 69, 89, 120, 136, 147; and in *Journal of the Senate of the State of Michigan, 1948 Extra Session* (Lansing: Franklin de Kleine Co., 1948), p. 133. House Bill 6 in *Michigan House Journal of 1948*, pp. 66, 83, 227, 233; and in *Michigan Senate Journal of 1948*, pp. 78, 150, 178, 180.

13. House Concurrent Resolution 19 in *Journal of the House of Representatives of the State of Michigan, 1949 Regular Session* (Lansing: Franklin de Kleine Co., 1949), pp. 307, 398. Stephen Roth, attorney general, to the legislature in *Michigan House Journal of 1949*, pp. 437–38. *Detroit Free Press*, 17 February 1949.

14. Senate Bill 4 in *Michigan Senate Journal of 1948*, pp. 237, 250, 322; and in *Michigan House Journal of 1948*, pp. 224, 257, 277.

15. *Michigan Senate Journal of 1948*, pp. 208–11, 220–21, 250–51, 302–16, 332–66. *Lansing State Journal*, 23, 29 April 1948. *Detroit News*, 24 April 1948. *Michigan Senate Journal, Second Session of 1948*, pp. 21–36.

16. Senate Bill 315 in *Journal of the Senate of the State of Michigan, 1949 Regular Session* (Lansing: Franklin de Kleine Co., 1949), p. 117. *Michigan Daily*, 15, 16, 24 April 1949.

17. *Lansing State Journal*, 12 March; 14, 15, 16, 17, 21 April 1950. *Detroit Free Press*, 22 April 1950. Senate Joint Resolution 14 in *Journal of the Senate of the State of Michigan, 1950 Extra Session* (Lansing: Franklin de Kleine Co., 1950), p. 166.

18. *Detroit News*, 8, 9, 16, 27 July 1950. *Lansing State Journal*, 7, 8, 20, 26 July 1950. Colin L. Smith to Governor G. M. Williams, 25 July 1950, in the Papers of G. Mennen Williams, 1950, legislature, special session: subversion, in Michigan Historical Collections, Bentley Historical Library, The University of Michigan, Ann Arbor (hereafter referred to as Bentley, UM).

19. G. M. Williams to Colin L. Smith, 29 July 1950, in the Papers of G. Mennen Williams, 1950, legislature, special session: subversion, in Bentley, UM.

20. In the special session, Governor Williams also called for a massive civil defense program. "We cannot be blind to the great probability that Korea is only the beginning [of a larger war] . . . We have no choice except to act as if atomic attacks on Detroit and possibly other Michigan cities were a certainty sometime in the next five years." His full address is in *Journal of the House of Representatives of the State of Michigan, 1950 Extra Session* (Lansing: Franklin de Kleine Co., 1950), pp. 411–16. The Senate Loyalty Commissions's report is in *Michigan Senate Journal of 1950*, pp. 385–87. Senate Joint Resolution "G" is in *Michigan Senate Journal of 1950*, p. 430. *Detroit News*, 18 August 1950. *Lansing State Journal*, 17 August 1950.

21. House Bills 40 and 41, Senate Bills 43 and 44, and the governor's letter to the senate are in *Michigan House Journal of 1950*, pp. 406, 414, 416, 420, 429, 433, 446, 452, 457, 463, 474; and *Michigan Senate Journal of 1950*, pp. 423–25, 427, 430–32, 467, 472, 474. *Lansing*

State Journal, 31 August; 1 September 1950. *Detroit News*, 25 August 1950. National Lawyers Guild, Detroit chapter, "Statement on Recent 'Anti-Subversive Legislation' Passed by the Michigan Legislature," in the Papers of Harold Norris, box 1, September 1950, in Bentley, UM.

22. *Detroit Free Press*, 7, 31 October; 5 November 1950. *Detroit News*, 26, 31 October 1950.

23. *Detroit Free Press*, 12 August; 14 October 1950.

24. *Detroit Times*, 6, 12, 30 October; 2 November 1950. *Detroit Free Press*, 6, 11, 14, 16, 20 October; 1, 3, 5, November 1950. *Lansing State Journal*, 27 September 1950. Fay Calkins, *The CIO and the Democratic Party* (Chicago: University of Chicago Press, 1952), pp. 123–33.

25. House Bills 121, 131, 390, and 408, and Senate Bill 408, in *Journal of the House of Representatives of the State of Michigan, 1951 Regular Session* (Lansing: Franklin de Kleine Co., 1951), pp. 434, 447, 455, 501, 511, 516, 836, 843, 960, 1004, 1062, 1090, 1120, 1151, 1193, 1250, 1424; and in *Journal of the Senate of the State of Michigan, 1951 Regular Session* (Lansing: Franklin de Kleine Co., 1951), pp. 355, 393, 406, 504, 594, 709, 735, 749, 806, 815, 981, 1417.

26. *Detroit Times*, 4, 6 March 1952. *Detroit Free Press*, 2, 4 March 1952. *Detroit News*, 1 February; 2, 7 March 1952. *Lansing State Journal*, 4 March; 3 April 1952. House Bill 20 in *Journal of the House of Representatives of the State of Michigan, 1952 Extra Session* (Lansing: Franklin de Kleine Co., 1952), pp. 783, 893, 941. Other antisubversive proposals which did not pass include Senate Bills 96 and 97, Senate Resolutions 13 and 20, and Senate Joint Resolution "0."

    David Caute hopelessly confuses the two registration laws: the Callahan Act of 1947 which was not enforced by Attorneys General Black and Roth; and the Trucks Act of 1952 which was later ruled unconstitutional by the courts. See David Caute, *The Great Fear: The Anti-Communist Purges Under Truman and Eisenhower* (New York: Simon and Schuster, 1978), pp. 72–73.

27. Michigan State Police, "Communist Registration Form," in the Papers of the Attorney General (Frank Millard), case files, in Michigan Historical Division. See also the Papers of the Civil Rights Congress, box 53, Trucks Act, at Archives of Urban and Labor Affiars, Wayne State University, Detroit (hereafter referred to as Labor Affairs, Wayne). *Detroit Free Press*, 18, 20, 23 April 1952. *Flint Journal*, 10, 17, 23 April 1952. *Detroit News*, 18 April 1952.

28. *Flint Journal*, 17, 18, 19, 25, 28 March; 21, 26 April 1952. Two years later, HUAC came to Flint for an explosive series of hearings. This probably a case of the state giving information to federal authorities.

29. Donald S. Leonard to Frank Millard, 25 March 1952 and 31 March 1952, in Papers of Donald S. Leonard, Detroit Police Commisioner, box 20, Communism in Bentley, UM. *Detroit Free Press*, 26, 27 March; 1, 22 April; 9 May 1952.

30. House Bill 408 in *Journal of the House of Representatives of the State of Michigan, 1953 Regular Session* (Lansing: Franklin de Kleine Co., 1953), pp. 800, 829, 837, 1050, 1063; and in *Journal of the Senate of the State of Michigan, 1953 Regular Session* (Lansing: Franklin de Kleine Co., 1953), pp. 739, 762, 791. See also House Resolution 8 and Senate Resolution 11.

31. *Detroit Free Press*, 21 February; 6 May 1953. Albertson v. Millard, 345 US 242, 73 SCt 600 (1953). Albertson v. Attorney General of the State of Michigan, 345 Mich 519, 77 NW 2d 104 (1956). Alan R. Hunt, "Federal Supremacy and State Anti-Subversive Legislation,"

Michigan Law Review 53 (January 1955): 427–438. Daniel Pevos, "The Present Status of Michigan Anti-Subversive Legislation," *Wayne Law Review* 2 (Summer 1956):221–28.

32. See chap. 4 for the teachers who were dismissed and chap. 7 for the university professors who fell under the Trucks Act.

33. Senate Bill 44 in *Journal of the Proceedings of the 68th Session of the Wisconsin Legislature: Senate* (Madison: Democratic Printing Co., 1947), p. 127. *Madison Capital-Times*, 23 January; 9 February; 6 March 1947.

34. Senate Bill 429 in *Wisconsin Senate Journal, 68th Session*, pp. 424, 647. *Madison Capital-Times*, 20 February; 10, 11, 13, 16, 18, 21, 23 April; 4 June 1947. *Wisconsin State Journal*, 10, 11 April; 2, 9 May 1947.

35. Assembly Bill 123 in *Journal of the Proceedings of the 68th Session of the Wisconsin Legislature: Assembly* (Madison: Democratic Printing Co., 1947), pp. 886, 1005. The vote was not a party-line vote, and it shows divisions within the Republican ranks: aye 46R, 11D (to table); and nay 24R, 1D. *Madison Capital-Times*, 19 February; 1 May; 12 June 1947. *Wisconsin State Journal*, 19 February; 2, 9 May 1947.

36. Senate Bill 504 in *Journal of the Proceedings of the 69th Session of the Wisconsin Legislature: Senate* (Madison: Democratic Printing Co., 1949), p. 849. Other antisubversive bills that were proposed but were not passed included Assembly Bills 391 and 563 and Assembly Joint Resolution 49. *Wisconsin State Journal*, 21, 28, 30 April; 6 May 1949. *Madison Capital-Times*, 30 March; 21, 25, 28 April; 5 May 1949. See also the Papers of the American Legion, State of Wisconsin, boxes 49 and 50, in Wisconsin State Historical Society, Madison.

37. The 1951 legislature had only one loyalty bill, which would have required a class in Americanism in the public schools. It remained in committee: Senate Bill 790.

38. Assembly Bill 172 in *Journal of the Proceedings of the 71st Session of the Wisconsin Legislature: Assembly* (Madison: Democratic Printing Co., 1953), pp. 121, 1104, 1334, 1417, 1458; and in *Proceedings of the 71st Session of the Wisconsin Legislature: Senate* (Madison: Democratic Printing Co., 1953), pp. 1347, 1350, 1479. *Madison Capital-Times*, 21 May; 4, 9 June; 13 July 1953. *Wisconsin State Journal*, 26 February; 10 June 1953.

39. John H. Fenton, *Midwest Politics* (New York: Holt, Rinehart, and Winston, 1966), pp. 67–68. Leon Epstein, *Politics in Wisconsin* (Madison: University of Wisconsin Press, 1958), p. 4. Richard C. Haney, "A History of the Democratic Party of Wisconsin since World War II" (Ph.D. dissertation, University of Wisconsin, 1970), pp. 142, 147. Michael J. O'Brien, *McCarthy and McCarthyism in Wisconsin* (Columbia: University of Missouri Press, 1980), pp. viii, 197–202.

40. Epstein, *Politics in Wisconsin*, p. 12. Arnold A. Rogow, "The Loyalty Oath Issue in Iowa, 1951," *American Political Science Review* 55 (December 1961): 861–69.

Chapter 2

1. The conservative spirit of the 1947 session of the legislature was revealed in a resolution passed by the senate. We "proposed to take care of ourselves . . . to wrest control of our domestic affairs from the bureaucracy in Washington and bring it back within the boundaries of the State . . . to restore the American Republic and our forty-eight States to the foundations built by our fathers." Senate Joint Resolution 18 in *Journal of the Senate of the 65th General Assembly of the State of Illinois* (Springfield: State of Illinois, 1947), p. 186.

2. This incident is discussed in more detail in the chapter on students, chap. 6, especially nn. 18–20.

3. Senate Bill 313 in *Illinois Senate Journal, 65th Assembly*, pp. 441, 454, 586, 1593; and in *Journal of the House of Representatives of the 65th Assembly of the State of Illinois* (Springfield: State of Illinois, 1947), pp. 765, 1062, 1173, 1921, 1977.

   The other major antisubversive bill proposed in this session was a complicated registration measure. It would have required all groups with more than twenty members to register their members' names and their activities with the secretary of state. The senate passed the bill, but the house feared administrative chaos in trying to exclude loyal organizations from the requirement, and it defeated the bill. Senate Bill 330 in *Illinois Senate Journal, 65th Assembly*, pp. 834, 854; and *Illinois House Journal, 65th Assembly*, p. 1517. Two minor bills concerning loyalty were House Bill 171 and Senate Joint Resoution 37.

   During the 1947 session, the Communist party in the state proposed a United Front State Legislative Committee to oppose these restrictive bills. The Chicago chapter of the ACLU rejected the offer because of "wide areas of possible disagreement, especially as to tactics." Harvey Zeidenstein, "The ACLU and the Broyles Bills, 1949–1955" (master's thesis, University of Chicago, 1957), pp. 7–8.

4. Two persons in the 1950s examined the Broyles Commission. E. Houston Harsha, "Illinois: The Broyles Commission," in *The States and Subversion* (Ithaca: Cornell University Press, 1952), pp. 55–88; and Martin G. Pierce, "Red-Hunting in Illinois, 1947–1949: The Broyles Commission" (master's thesis, University of Wisconsin, 1959).

5. State of Illinois, Seditious Activities Investigating Commission (SAIC), *Report 1947–1948* (Springfield: n.p., 1949), p. 121. The report includes both summaries and transcripts of the meetings.

6. SAIC, *Report 1947–1948*, pp. 122, 125–28, 130, 134, 138, 144–49, 155–58, 164–75, 187, 191–93, 203–7, 368–78, 418–38.

7. SAIC, *Report 1947–1948*, pp. 140, 146–49, 164, 167, 173, 191, 197, 222.

8. SAIC, *Report 1947–1948*, pp. 121–23, 127–28, 130–33, 187, 225–29, 235–367, 384–412.

9. SAIC, *Report 1947–1948*, pp. 16–18.

10. Broyles also introduced two other bills which did not clear the senate because of their redundancy and complicated administration. Senate Bills 155, 152, 153, 154, and 156, respectively, in *Journal of the Senate of the 66th General Assembly of the State of Illinois* (Springfield: State of Illinois, 1949), pp. 224–26, 237, 249–50.

11. *Illinois State Journal*, 2, 3, 9, 10 March 1949. *Chicago Tribune*, 2, 3, 10 March 1949. *Chicago Sun-Times*, 10 March 1949. *Champaign-Urbana News-Gazette*, 16 March 1949. House Joint Resolution 21 in *Journal of the House of Representatives of the 66th General Assembly of the State of Illinois* (Springfield: State of Illinois, 1949), p. 249; and in *Illinois Senate Journal, 66th Assembly*, pp. 272, 293. The appropriation bills were House Bill 418 and Senate Bill 607. Governor Stevenson did not sign these. He considered vetoing them, but let them become law without his signature because he felt that the two colleges should have the forum to clear themselves. Walter Johnson, ed., *The Papers of Adlai E. Stevenson: Governor of Illinois 1949–1953* (Boston: Little, Brown, 1973), p. 69.

12. State of Illinois, Seditious Activities Investigating Commission (SAIC), *Report of Proceedings, Investigation of the University of Chicago and Roosevelt College* (Springfield: n.p., 1949). Harsha, "Broyles Commission," pp. 93–132.

13. Ibid.

14. Senate Bills 153, 154, and 156, in *Illinois House Journal, 66th Assembly*, pp. 673–674, 1943–1944, 1972. Senate Bill 270 in *Illinois Senate Journal, 66th Assembly*, pp. 647, 816. The liberals were able to expand their organizational base quickly because many held membership in more than one liberal organization. This was especially true in Chicago. Zeidenstein, "ACLU and Broyles," pp. 19, 106.

15. John Bartlow Martin, *Adlai Stevenson of Illinois* (Garden City, N.Y.: Doubleday Co., 1976), p. 396. Under cumulative voting, each district elects three representatives to the house. The voter has three votes. He can give all of his votes to one candidate, or he can divide them among two or three candidates. A minority party can usually elect one of their candidates by having their supporters give all their votes to just one nominee.

16. The Communist issue even affected reform efforts, such as Governor Stevenson's proposal for a constitutional convention. When the legislature defeated the measure, the *Chicago Tribune* went into ecstasy. "This was a victory for the republican form of government. . . . Governor Stevenson, who played his minor part in the evil conspiracy to conceal the guilt of the Roosevelt crooks, was found once again on the side of those seeking to overthrow republican government." *Chicago Tribune*, 16 June 1949.

17. In the 1951 session, legislators submitted fourteen bills and resolutions which dealt with loyalty: House Joint Resolutions 10, 24, 27, and 41; House Bills 92, 93, 96, 98, and 978; and Senate Bills 33, 34, 35, 36, and 102 (the Broyles' bill). Only the latter was passed by the legislature.

18. *Champaign-Urbana News-Gazette*, 3 April 1951.

19. *Illinois State Journal*, 7, 8 March 1951. *Chicago Tribune*, 7 March; 19 April 1951. During a house hearing, the executive secretary of the Illinois CP, Claude Lightfoot, testified against the bill. When asked if he would fight for the U.S. in a war against the Soviet Union, he responded that he would fight against lynchers in the South. He was held for contempt, but later explained that he did not mean any disrespect to the legislators, and he was released. Donna J. Preston, "Newspaper Influence on the Broyles Bill in the 1951 Illinois Legislature" (master's thesis, University of Illinois, 1952), p. 21.

20. *Chicago Tribune*, 30 June; 3 July 1951. Senate Bill 102 in *Journal of the House of Representatives of the 67th General Assembly of the State of Illinois* (Springfield: State of Illinois, 1951), pp. 705, 1214, 1448, 1592; and in *Journal of the Senate of the 67th General Assembly of the State of Illinois* (Springfield: State of Illinois, 1951), pp. 187, 214, 252, 296, 312, 428, 461, 596, 1919, 1946, 1949. Zeidenstein, "ACLU and Broyles," pp. 32–36. Preston, "Newspaper Influence," pp. 21–30.

    The definition of a party-line vote is based on William Keefe's study of the 1949 and 1951 Illinois' legislature. He has proposed that a party-line vote be defined as one in which 80% of each party was united. For the 1951 Broyles' bill, the Republicans met this test, but the Democrats did not. Thus I have used the term "partial party-line vote." The split in the senate was 94% R, 72% D unity; and in the house was 87% R, 62% D unity. William J. Keefe, "Party Government and Lawmaking in the Illinois General Assembly," *Northwestern University Law Review* 47 (March–April 1952):58–60.

    It is of course ironic that J. Edgar Hoover, who had so much to do with the creation of the scare on the national level, would help to deflate state antisubversive efforts. His motive was to protect his fiefdom and power-base, the FBI.

    Stevenson's veto attracted liberal support throughout the country, and was instrumental in building his coalition for the 1952 presidential race. Johnson, *Papers of Stevenson*, pp. 412–18. Martin, *Stevenson of Illinois*, pp. 419, 470–71, 482, 511, 514, 642.

21. Austin Ranney, *Illinois Politics* (New York: New York University Press, 1960), pp. 30–31.

Paul T. David et al., *Presidential Nominating Politics in 1952: The Midwest* (Baltimore, Johns Hopkins Press, 1954), p. 102.

22. *Illinois State Journal*, 29 April 1953. *Champaign-Urbana Courier*, 21 May 1953. Ryerson, Swift, and Bell were all connected with the University of Chicago, and had formed their opposition probably in the 1949 SAIC probe. The downstate opposition to the Broyles' bills is found in the Papers of John J. DeBoer, University Archives, University of Illinois, Urbana.

23. Senate Bills 101 and 102 in *Journal of the Senate of the 68th General Assembly of the State of Illinois* (Springfield: State of Illinois, 1953), pp. 242, 264, 281, 483, 534, 550; and in *Journal of the House of Representatives of the 68th General Assembly of the State of Illinois* (Springfield: State of Illinois, 1953), pp. 1031, 1047. *Chicago Tribune*, 17, 18, 19, 20, 21 May 1953. *Illinois State Journal*, 20, 21 May 1953. The vote to revive the Broyles' bills reveals a significant regional division as well: downstate 68 aye, 25 nay; Cook County 15 aye, 30 nay.

24. *Illinois House Journal*, 68th Assembly, pp. 1268, 1398, 1808, 1818, 1831, 1933, 2017, 2209. *Chicago Tribune*, 19 June; 2 July 1953. *Illinois State Journal*, 12, 19 June 1953. American Legion, Department of Illinois, *Report of the 35th Annual Convention*, August 6-9, 1953 (Chicago: n.p., 1953), pp. 64-65, 69. Latham Castle to Governor William Stratton, 29 June 1953, in the Papers of Governor William Stratton, Attorney General Opinions, Senate bills 1953, Illinois State Archives, Springfield. As in 1951, this was a partial party-line vote. In the house, there was 85% R, 67% D unity, and in the senate, 94% R, 75% D unity. Keefe, "Party Government," pp. 58-60. Contrary to Frank Fetter, the party aspect was more important than the regional divisions. Supporters of the bill came from Republican ranks (68-12) by a greater percentage than downstaters (69-21). Similarly, opponents of the bill came from Democratic ranks (39-19) more than from Cook County (30-18). I would agree with Fetter that the core of each group was downstate Republicans and Cook County Democrats, but a regional emphasis is incorrect. Frank W. Fetter, "Witch Hunt in the Lincoln Country," *AAUP Bulletin* 41 (Summer 1955):236-37.

25. Senate Bill 193 in *Illinois Senate Journal, 68th Assembly*, pp. 489, 535, 1329; and in *Illinois House Journal, 68th Assembly*, pp. 1746, 1904, 2237. The loyalty oath for tenants was later ruled unconstitutional by the state supreme court; Chicago Housing Authority v. Blackman, 4 Ill 2d 319, 122 NE 3d 522 (1954).

Senate Bill 195 (teachers) in *Illinois Senate Journal, 68th Assembly*, p. 1439; and in *Illinois House Journal*, 68th Assembly, p. 1816. Loyalty bills that were introduced but not passed include Senate Bills 78, 79, 382, and 448, and House Bills 159, 613, and 886. *Chicago Tribune*, 23 April 1953.

26. Senate Bills 58 and 59 in *Journal of the Senate of the 69th General Assembly of the State of Illinois* (Springfield: State of Illinois, 1955), not consecutively numbered, see 15, 22, 29 March; 28, 29 June; and in *Journal of the House of Representatives of the 69th General Assembly of the State of Illinois* (Springfield: State of Illinois, 1955), not consecutively numbered, see 10 May; 28, 29 June.

Latham Castle to William Stratton, 14 July 1955, in the Papers of Governor William Stratton, Attorney General Opinions, Senate Bills 1955, Illinois State Archives, Springfield.

Chicago Tribune, 9 February; 6, 8, 17 April; 27 June 1955. *Illinois State Journal*, 16, 30 March; 29 June 1955. *Chicago Sun-Times*, 15 February; 1, 15 April; 2 May; 19 July; 19 August 1955.

As in 1951 and 1953, this vote was a partial party-line vote. In the house, there was 84% R, 68% D unity, and in the senate, 93% R, 82% D unity. Keefe, "Party Government," pp. 58-60.

27. Lens v. Board of Education of Chicago, 9 Ill 2d 599, 138 NE 2d 532. *The Brief*, October 1955, November 1955, February 1956, April 1956, October 1956, December 1956. George K. Plochman, *The Ordeal of Southern Illinois University* (Carbondale: SIU Press, 1957), p. 240. *Daily Illini*, 20 September 1955.

28. Senate Resolutions 27 and 35. *Cleveland Plain Dealer*, 20, 26 March; 17, 30 April 1947. *Ohio State University Alumni Magazine*, 15 January 1947.

29. Curtis D. MacDougall, *Gideon's Army* (New York: Marzani and Munsell, 1965), pp. 437–40. *Ohio State Journal*, 21 June 1948. State v. Hummel, 150 OS 127, 37 00 435, 80 NE 2d 899 (1948).

30. House Bill 88 in *Journal of the House of Representatives of the 98th General Assembly of the State of Ohio* (Columbus: F. J. Heer, 1949), pp. 1116, 1238; and in *Journal of the Senate of the 98th General Assembly of the State of Ohio* (Columbus: F. J. Heer, 1949), pp. 771, 1127. *Ohio State Journal*, 3, 14 June; 21 July 1949. *Columbus Citizen*, 3, 14 June; 16 July 1949. *Cleveland Plain Dealer*, 14 June 1949. *Canton Repository*, 19, 26 May; 22 July 1949.

31. Senate Bill 142 in *Ohio House Journal, 98th Assembly*, p. 899; and *Ohio Senate Journal, 98th Assembly*, p. 531. The senate did not vote on the loyalty oath amendment separately from the other amendments. At least six people did not sign the oath. It was held constitutional in Dworken v. Collopy, 56 OLA 513, 91 NE 2d 564 (1950).

32. *Ohio State Journal*, 26 February; 1, 4, 5, 9, 16, 24 March; 19 April; 5, 18 May 1949. House Bill 106.

33. Peter B. Petrovich, "Taft and the Ohio Press," *The Reporter*, December 12, 1950, p. 36. Calkins, *The CIO*, pp. 26–50. James T. Patterson, *Mr. Republican: A Biography Of Robert A. Taft* (Boston: Houghton Mifflin, 1972), pp. 462–63. Fenton, *Midwest Politics*, pp. 137–41, 227. *Cincinnati Enquirer*, 1 September 1950.

34. This was sponsored by William Saxbe. House Joint Resolution 21 in *Journal of the House of Representatives of the 99th General Assembly of the State of Ohio* (Columbus: F. J. Heer, 1951), p. 335; and *Journal of the Senate of the 99th General Assembly of the State of Ohio* (Columbus: F. J. Heer, 1951), p. 241.

35. Testimony before the JASIC is found in the Papers of the Ohio Un-American Activities Committee, Ohio Historical Society, Columbus. *Columbus Citizen*, 4, 10, 23 April; 1, 4, May 1951.

36. *Ohio House Journal, 99th Assembly*, pp. 1022–1029. Senate Bill 358 in *Ohio Senate Journal, 99th Assembly*, p. 858; and *Ohio House Journal, 99th Assembly*, pp. 1437, 1546, 1567, 1572, 1643. Other loyalty bills which were not passed include House Bills 11, 20, and 351, and Senate Bill 11.

    At this time, a branch of the executive department also took antisubversive action. The Division of Film Censorship examined the film, *Native Son*, on July 23, August 9, and October 24, 1951. It rejected the film in part because it "presents racial frictions at a time when all groups should be united against everything subversive." The producers challenged the censorship in court, but the Ohio Supreme Court upheld the finding. The U.S. Supreme Court, however, reversed the decision and ruled the law unconstitutional. Patricia B. Gatherum, "Film Censorship in Ohio: A Study in Symbolism," (seminar paper, Ohio State University, n.d.), pp. 9–12.

37. The testimony (21 January; 11, 25 February; 17, 31 March 1952) is in the Papers of the OUAC, Ohio Historical Society. The OUAC hired Harvey Matusow as an investigator,

but found him unreliable and let him go. Frederick C. Thayer, Jr., "The Ohio Un-American Activities Committee," (master's thesis, Ohio State University, 1954), pp. 17–29, 37, 39, 44–46.

38. Those questioned in Columbus (April 1) were Robert E. L. Terrill, Anna H. Morgan, David Jackson, and Oscar Smilack. Those questioned in Dayton (April 21 and 22) were Harriston T. McGill, Melvin Hupman, Vassel Thamel, and Julia Pearl Hupman. Those questioned in Columbus (May 20) were George D. Pappas, Bernice Pappas, and Marston A. Hamlin. The testimony is found in the Papers of the OUAC, Ohio Historical Society. Warren P. Hill, "A Critique of Recent Ohio Anti-Subversive Legislation," *Ohio State Law Journal* 14 (Autumn 1953):445. State of Ohio ex. rel. Smilack v. Bushong, 159 OS 259, 93 OAR 201, 111 NE 2d 918 (1953).

39. Those questioned in Cincinnati (October 20) were Abraham Biderman, Talmadge Raley, Joseph Stern, Philip Paleschnitzki, Emmett Calvin Brown, and Reuel Stanfield. The testimony is found in the Papers of the OUAC, Ohio Historical Society. Thayer, "Ohio Committee," pp. 65–67. *Cincinnati Enquirer*, 21, 22, 23 October 1952.

   David Caute is wrong in stating that the OUAC released Scott's testimony, that only four persons demanded a hearing, and that it took nine months to get one; Caute, *Great Fear*, p. 80.

40. OUAC, *Report 1951–1952*, in the Papers of the OUAC, Ohio Historical Society. House Bill 6 in *Journal of the House of Representatives of the 100th General Assembly of the State of Ohio* (Columbus: F. J. Heer, 1953), pp. 85, 125, 146, 167, 184, 288; and *Journal of the Senate of the 100th General Assembly of the State of Ohio* (Columbus: F. J. Heer, 1952), p. 279.

41. For a full discussion of the Darling affair, see chap. 7, nn. 4–8.

42. Senate Bill 38 and House Bill 575 in *Ohio House Journal, 100th Assembly*, pp. 481, 546, 720, 1314, 1400, 1837, 1878; and *Ohio Senate Journal, 100th Assembly*, p. 284, 1024. *Ohio State Journal*, 11, 26 February; 1 April; 18 June 1953. *Columbus Citizen*, 25, 26 February; 13 March; 4, 7, 23 April 1953.

43. House Bill 308 in *Ohio House Journal, 100th Assembly*, pp. 320, 363, 628, 656, 1048, 1061; and in *Ohio Senate Journal, 100th Assembly*, pp. 1026, 1169. *Columbus Citizen*, 27 May; 18 June; 30, 31 July 1953. *Ohio State Journal*, 7, 29 May; 24 June; 15 July 1953. American Civil Liberties Union, *Annual Report January 1951–June 1953* (New York: n.p., 1953), p. 52.

44. Those questioned in Akron (September 2) were Mae Probst, Christian Probst, Vani Mitri, and Ralph Kern as "friendly" witnesses. Those who invoked the Fifth Amendment (October 6) included Thelma Furry, George E. Lyons, Benedict Gorday, Lloyd Arnold, Myron W. Thomas, Anna Glauser, Karl E. Carrigan, Amos B. Murphy. See testimony in the papers of the OUAC, Ohio Historical Society. *Akron Beacon-Journal*, 3 September; 7, 18 October, 1953.

45. Those questioned in Canton (October 21) were Olga D. Perry, Paul Bohus, Eula Ann Cooper, Rose Mladjan, and LaVerne Slagle. Those questioned in Cleveland (December 1 and 2) were Benjamin Gray, Sally W. Morillas, Edwin F. Broggini, Albert Young, Admiral Kilpatrick, Paul M. Abert, Leo Fenster, Edward Likover, and Joseph Kamen. Likover was a teacher who lost his job (see chap. 4), and Kilpatrick also lost his job. Kilpatrick tried to get unemployment compensation, but was refused. He appealed, and the Court of Common Pleas in August 1957 vacated the ruling, giving him compensation. Kilpatrick v. Bureau of Unemployment Compensation as noted in *Civil Liberties Docket*,

November 1958, p. 4, and February 1960, p. 34. *Canton Repository*, 22 October 1953. *Cleveland Plain Dealer*, 2, 3, 4, 8, 22, 23 December 1953.

46. OUAC, Report 1953–1954, in Papers of the OUAC, Ohio Historical Society. Morse Johnson to Jim Selcraig, January 1, 1980. State v. Morgan, 164 OS 529, 58 OLA 411. State v. Raley, 100 OA 75, 360 US 423. State v. Arnold, 69 OLA 148, 124 NE 2d 473. State v. Slagle, 170 OS 216, 366 US 259, 6 LEd 2d 277 (1961).

   David Chaute is wrong in calling the OUAC the Blackburn Commission and in stating that it only cited twenty witnesses for contempt. He also omits the court action in the contempt cases, thus leaving the impression that punishment was given. Caute, *Great Fear*, p. 80. An OUAC member wrote to me that the OUAC "produced neither momentous legislation nor any ground swell of response from the general public." I would agree that the effect was not overt, but I still maintain that the OUAC reinforced the conservative climate. John V. Corrigan to Jim Selcraig, March 10, 1980.

47. Thomas D. Clark, *Indiana University: Midwestern Pioneer, Years of Fulfillment* (Bloomington: Indiana University Press, 1977), pp. 294–302. Rihard M. Clutter, "The Indiana American Legion, 1919–1960" (Ph.D. dissertation, Indiana University, 1974), pp. 253–56.

48. Senate Concurrent Resolution 15 in *Journal of the Indiana Senate of the State of Indiana, 86th Session of the General Assembly* (Indianapolis: Bookwalter Co., 1949), p. 788; and *Journal of the Indiana House of Representatives of the State of Indiana, 86th Session of the General Assembly* (Indianapolis: Bookwalter Co., 1949), p. 1022, 1047. *Indianapolis Times*, 3, 5 March 1949. *Indianapolis Star*, 3, 4 March 1949.

49. *Indianapolis Star*, 8, 11, 12 July 1950. *Indianapolis News*, 11 July 1950. The press probably got the story from the police who had detained the petitioners temporarily. LaRue Spiker to Jim Selcraig, February 2, 1980.

50. *Indianapolis News*, 13, 18 July; 21, 23 August 1950. Papers of Governor Henry Schricker, box 163 and 165, in Indiana State Library, Archives, Indianapolis.

51. *Indianapolis Star*, 11, 12, 13, 14, 15, 16, 19, 20, 26 July; 17 August 1950. *Terre Haute Star*, 19, 21, 26 July 1950. LaRue Spiker to Jim Selcraig, February 2, 1980.

52. House Bill 72 in *Journal of the Indiana House of Representatives of the State of Indiana, 87th Session of the General Assembly* (Indianapolis: Bookwalter Co., 1951), pp. 598, 669, 736, 970; and *Journal of the Indiana Senate of the State of Indiana, 87th Session of the General Assembly* (Indianapolis: Bookwalter Co., 1951), pp. 540, 543, 663, 606, 726. Other loyalty proposals which were not passed were House Bills 183 and 507 and Senate Concurrent Resolution 16. *Indianapolis Star*, 18 January; 2, 16, 22 February; 1, 2 March 1951. *Indianapolis Times*, 21, 25, 26, 28 February; 2, 5, 6 March 1951.

53. House Bill 114 was the major bill. See also House Bills 176 and 427 and Senate Bills 15 and 64. *Indianapolis News*, 13, 23 January; 5 February 1953. *Indianapolis Times*, 6 March 1953.

54. *Indianapolis Star*, 9, 12 May 1953. *Chicago Sun-Times*, 17 May 1953.

55. House Bill 586 in *Journal of the Indiana House of Representatives of the State of Indiana, 89th Session of the General Assembly* (Indianapolis: Bookwalter Co., 1955), pp. 357, 548, 740, 837; and *Journal of the Indiana Senate of the State of Indiana, 89th Session of the General Assembly* (Indianapolis: Bookwalter Co., 1955), pp. 741, 749. *Indianapolis Star*, 2, 8 March 1955. *Indianapolis Times*, 2 March 1955.

56. House Bill 350 in *Journal of Indiana House, 89th Session*, pp. 270, 381, 721; and *Journal of Indiana Senate, 89th Session*, pp. 663, 784, 836–37. *Indianapolis Star*, 28 January; 2, 17

February; 5 March 1955. *Indianapolis Times*, 2 February 1955. UE's formal name was the United Electrical, Radio, and Machine Workers of America.

57. Clutter, "Indiana American Legion," pp. 270–71. Howard Peckham, *Indiana* (New York: W. W. Norton, 1978), pp. 190–91. Edwin K. Steers to Jim Selcraig, February 27, 1980.

58. This confirms the arguments of the antipluralists.

59. Griffith, "American Politics," pp. 348–49.

60. There was also interaction between states. The California and Washington legislative investigative committees sponsored a conference in 1948 which was attended by several other states. The "Ober" law, enacted in Maryland, was copied by a few other states. This study does not discuss local influences affecting federal policy because these are the traditional activities: public opinion (polls), elections, and the passage of antisubversive laws prior to congressional enactment. The latter refers to the fact that four states outlawed the CP prior to congressional action, thus refuting the theory that the states copied the federal government.

   This model emphasizes interaction. It does not try to determine which group or institution had the strongest influence. The key is the interaction, the complexity—not a single group, person, or governmental agency. "The interaction between government and opinion . . . cannot be broken into neat pieces and nicely tabulated to produce persuasive two-way tables indicative of the interconnections between mass opinion and public decision. . . . A complex interaction occurs with government (and other centers of influence as well) affecting the form and content of opinion; and in turn, public opinion may condition the manner, content, and timing of public action." V. O. Key, Jr., *Public Opinion and American Democracy* (New York: A. A. Knopf, 1964), pp. 409–10.

61. Samuel Patterson. "Political Cultures of American States," *Journal of Politics* 30 (February 1968):195. His argument is echoed by V. O. Key, Jr., *American State Politics: An Introduction* (New York: A. A. Knopf, 1965), pp. 18–19.

Chapter 3

1. The UPW was formally named the United Public Office Workers of America. Although some mention of police "red squads" will be made, it is quite difficult to study their activities and procedures because their records either remain closed or have been destroyed. Richard Gutman to Jim Selcraig, February 17, 1980.

2. *Saginaw News*, 11, 12, 18, 25 January 1949. *Ohio State Journal*, 14 June; 21 July 1949. *Columbus Citizen*, 13, 14, 15 June 1949. *Lorain Journal*, 6, 7 February 1950. *Wyandotte News-Herald*, 18 September 1950. *Terre Haute Star*, 14 October 1950. *Terre Haute Tribune*, 14 October 1950. *Chicago Sun-Times*, 23 January 1951. *Indianapolis Star*, 5, 6 June 1951. David Caute emphasizes registration laws in his discussion of municipal ordinances, but these were not as typical as loyalty oaths. Caute, *Great Fear*, pp. 70–73, 586 f.6.

3. *Peoria Star*, 16, 17, 18, 19, 22, 24, 25, 28, 29 April; 10 May 1947. *Peoria Journal and Transcript*, 16, 17, 18, 19, 20 April 1947. Robert Goldstein wrongly places this as an effect of the Korean War; *Political Repression*, p. 359.

4. *Indianapolis Star*, 3, 17 October 1950. *Indianapolis News*, 6 September 1950. *Indianapolis Times*, 28 September; 17 October 1950. Sorenson, "Anti-Communist Impulse," chapter five, pp. 8–20.

5. Carl O. Smith and Stephen B. Sarasohn, "Hate Propaganda in Detroit," *Public Opinion*

Quarterly 10 (Spring 1946):26, 47. Robert Conot, *American Odyssey* (New York: Morrow and Co., 1974), pp. 393–94.

6. James C. Foster, *The Union Politics: The CIO Political Action Committee* (Columbia: University of Missouri Press, 1975), p. 59. *Detroit News*, 18, 19, 22, 25 September 1945. *Detroit Free Press*, 20, 28 September; 2, 18, 19 October 1945.

7. Jeffries' campaign material is in the Papers of the Mayor, 1945, box 2, campaign, Burton Historical Collection, Detroit Public Library, Detroit (hereafter referred to as Burton, Detroit). *Detroit Free Press*, 17, 18, 19, 23, 24, 26, 27, 29 October; 2, 3, November 1945.

8. Smith, "Hate in Detroit," pp. 28, 44–45. *Detroit Free Press*, 28 September; 19, 27 October; 1, 3 November 1945. *Detroit Times*, 31 October; 4 November 1945.

9. Smith, "Hate in Detroit," pp. 35–37. Foster, *Union Politic*, pp. 59–60. *Detroit Free Press*, 28 September; 5, 23 October; 5 November 1945. Alan G. Clive, "The Society and Economy of Wartime Michigan, 1939–1945" (Ph.D. dissertation, University of Michigan, 1976), pp. 481–85.

10. Frankensteen's campaign material is in the Papers of Richard Frankensteen, Labor Affairs, Wayne. *Detroit Free Press*, 18, 19, 27, 31 October; 1, 2, 3, 4, 8 November 1945. *Detroit Times*, 20, 21, 29 October 1945.

11. Smith, "Hate in Detroit," pp. 48–50. Conot, *Odyssey*, p. 366. Samuel Lubell, *The Future of American Politics* (New York: Harper and Row, 1965), p. 188. "Memo on Detroit Mayoralty Situation," Mayor's Papers, 1945, box 5, campaign, in Burton, Detroit.

12. Mowitz, "Michigan," pp. 206–7. *Detroit Free Press*, 4, 6 July 1949. *Detroit Times*, 29 June 1949.

13. *Detroit Times*, 3, 6, 7 July 1949. *Detroit Free Press*, 6, 7, 10 July 1949. Mowitz, "Michigan," pp. 207–9. Executive Order No. 16 in Mayor's Papers, 1949, box 3, Mayor's Loyalty Commission, Burton, Detroit. David Caute refers to Donald Sublette as "Subletto;" *Great Fear*, pp. 339–40.

14. Mayor's Committee, Report, 11 July 1949, in Mayor's Papers, 1949, box 3, Burton, Detroit. Mowitz, "Michigan," pp. 210–13. *Detroit Times*, 13, 14, 16 July 1949. *Detroit Free Press*, 12, 14, 16 July 1949.

15. Mowitz, "Michigan" pp. 213–215. *Detroit Times*, 9, 10 August 1949. *Detroit Free Press*, 10, 11, 12, 13 August 1949.

16. Yale Stuart to Common Council, 11 July 1949, in Mayor's Papers, 1949, box 3, Mayor's Loyalty Commission, Burton, Detroit. Mowitz, "Michigan," pp. 222–25. *Detroit Times*, 8, 9, 11, 12, 13, 15 July 1949.

17. *Detroit Free Press*, 17 July; 13, 27 August 1949. *Detroit Times*, 31 July; 12 August 1949.

18. Yale Stuart to Common Council, 15 August 1949, in Papers of Yale Stuart, box 2, loyalty oath controversy, Labor Affiars, Wayne. *Detroit Times*, 13, 15, 19 August 1949. *Detroit Free Press*, 20 August; 6 December 1949; 16 February 1950. Mowitz, "Michigan," p. 224 f.92.

19. *Detroit Times*, 17 July; 20, 24, 27, 28 August; 8, 12 September 1949. *Detroit Free Press*, 16, 27 August; 10 September 1949.
      Conot indicates that Mayor Albert Cobo "established" the LIC, but this is misleading. Although Cobo did appoint the first members, the LIC was approved by the Common Council and ratified by the voters while Van Antwerp was mayor. Conot, *Odyssey*, p. 444.

At this same time, the county (Wayne) established its own investigative board. See *Detroit Free Press*, 12, 14, 26 July 1949.

20. Mowitz, "Michigan," pp. 228–30. *Detroit Free Press*, 10, 12 July 1949; 11, 16 January; 7 March 1950. *Detroit News*, 10, 17 January 1950.

21. *Detroit Free Press*, 26 January; 19 July 1950. *Detroit News*, 13, 19, 25, 26 July 1950. This controversy on the newspaper ban is in Mayor's Papers, 1954, box 2, Communist literature, Burton, Detroit.

    Dearborn, a suburb, enacted a similar ban on subversive literature. *Detroit Free Press*, 25 July 1950.

22. Wiggins v. City of Detroit; Green v. City of Detroit, no. 453, 757. *Detroit News*, 18, 20, 22 July; 3 September 1950. *Detroit Free Press*, 19 July; 3 September; 2 October 1950.

23. Mowitz, "Michigan," pp. 216–19. Charter Amendment No. 25 in Attorney General's Papers, lot 22, box 9, Michigan Historical Division.

24. "Condensation of Transcript: Thomas J. Coleman Hearing" and "Analysis of Proceedings before the Loyalty Commission: Re, Thomas J. Coleman" are both in Mayor's Papers 1951, box 6, Loyalty Commission, Burton, Detroit. *Detroit Free Press*, 7, 28 November; 21 December 1950; 4, 6 January; 21 March 1951. Coleman resigned the day after his victory. David Caute is wrong about the verdict; *Great Fear*, p. 340.

25. *Detroit Free Press*, 14 January; 4 February; 30 March; 3 April; 8 May 1951. *Detroit News*, 7 January; 25, 27 March; 22 May; 3 June 1951. The voters also changed the composition of the Loyalty Commission from elected officials to appointed citizens.

26. *Detroit Free Press*, 15 February 1952. *Detroit News*, 14 February 1952.

27. *Detroit Free Press*, 16, 19, 20, 21 February; 5 April; 6 May; 12 July; 12 December 1952. *Detroit News*, 19 February; 1, 4 March 1952. David Caute only mentions Jurist in his discussion of this incident; *Great Fear*, p. 583.

28. Walter Goodman, *The Committee: The Extraordinary Career of the House Un-American Activities Committee* (New York: Farrar, Strauss, and Giroux, 1964), p. 317. *Detroit Free Press*, 6, 7, 26, 29 March; 1, 22 April; 9 May 1952. *Detroit News*, 5 March; 18 April 1952.

29. U.S., Congress, House, Committee on Un-American Activities, *Communism in the Detroit Area*, 82nd Congress, 2nd session, p. 2840. *Detroit Free Press*, 30 January; 7 June 1953.

30. *Detroit Free Press*, 15, 26 March; 17 April 1952. *Detroit News*, 4 March; 3, 16 April 1952.

31. *Detroit Free Press*, 20 March 1952. *Detroit News*, 11 March 1952.

32. *Detroit Free Press*, 20, 21, 23, 25 March 1952. *Detroit News*, 20, 25 March 1952.

33. *Detroit Free Press*, 14 January; 29 April 1954; 20 April 1958. Alfred A. May to Albert Cobo, 25 February 1955; and Audit Report of Loyalty Investigating Committee in Mayor's Papers, box 6, Loyalty Commission, in Burton, Detroit. Report on Michigan Committee to Secure Justice for the Rosenbergs, 22 December 1952, in Papers of Donald S. Leonard, box 20, Communism, in Bentley, UM. In August 1952, Anne S. Crowe refused to sign the county loyalty oath. The bookkeeping operator was fired. Later, she challenged the constitutionality of the oath, and demanded compensation since she had been unable to find other employment after her dismissal. Her suit was dismissed. Crowe v. County of Wayne, State of Michigan 365 Michigan 656.

34. *Detroit News*, 12, 13, 14, 15 January; 1, 3, 6, February 1953. *Detroit Free Press*, 13, 14 January; 2, 3, 6, 7 February 1953.

35. *Chicago Tribune*, 3, 4, 18, 19, 22, 23, 24, 25, 26, 29 March 1947. Every day in March, the *Chicago Herald-American*, a Hearst newspaper, linked the mayoral election to a referendum on Truman's militarism.

36. *Chicago Tribune*, 17, 18, 24, 26, 27, 28, 30 March 1947. *Chicago Sun-Times*, 17, 18, 24, 27 March 1947.

37. Sol Dorfman et al., "Report to the Executive Committee of the ACLU," 25 October 1951, in the papers of the American Civil Liberties Union, Chicago chapter, Department of Special Collections, University of Chicago, Chicago (hereafter referred to as University of Chicago). *Chicago Tribune*, 26, 29 January; 25 February 1951.

38. Dorfman, "Report to ACLU." *Chicago Sun-Times*, 10 March 1951. *Chicago Tribune*, 22, 25 February; 2, 6, 10 March 1951.

39. House Joint Resolutions 10 and 41 in *Illinois House Journal, 67th Assembly*, pp. 100–1, 1206; and *Illinois Senate Journal, 67th Assembly*, p. 1065. Dorfman, "Report to ACLU." *Chicago Tribune*, 3 February 1951.

40. Dorfman, "Report to ACLU."

41. Ibid.

42. SAIC, *Report 1947–1948*, p. 138. *Chicago Tribune*, 26 October 1950. In 1947, an American Legion official accused the CHA of employing "definitely one or two communists" and having a secretary who was a "sympathizer." In 1950, a city alderman claimed that seventy percent of CHA employees belonged to the UPW, which he charged was subversive.

43. *Chicago Tribune*, 9, 23 December 1952. *Chicago Sun-Times*, 9, 27 December 1952. *Chicago Herald-American*, 26 December 1952.

44. *Chicago Tribune*, 27, 31 December 1952; 3, 13, 15, 22, 27 January; 5 February; 24 March 1953. *Chicago Sun-Times*, 13, 21 January 1953. Miscellaneous material is in Papers of the ACLU, Chicago chapter, box 8, University of Chicago.

45. The voters elected nine persons as council members. Citizens could vote for as many as nine candidates, and indicated their preference among the choices (first, second, third, etc.). All candidates exceeding the quota—for example, ten percent of the vote, plus one— were automatically elected. The other council members were elected by subtracting the quota from the leader's total. The remainder was then distributed to the other candidates, according to the voter's choice. In this way, nine persons ultimately met the quota.

    For example, if 10,000 people voted, then the quota would be 1001 (10% plus one). The leader might have amassed 1,500 votes, and he could be considered elected. The quota would be subtracted from his total (1,500 - 1,001 = 499), and then the 499 votes would be distributed to the other candidates. As each candidate went over the quota, the remainder of his votes would also be distributed to those under the mark until nine were elected. Ralph Straetz, *PR Politics in Cincinnati* (Washington Square: New York University Press, 1958), pp. 269–74.

46. *Cincinnati Enquirer*, 19, 20, 21, 22, 23 October 1947. Straetz, *PR Politics*, pp. 203–50.

47. *Cincinnati Enquirer*, 22 October; 1 November 1947.

48. *Cincinnati Enquirer*, 8, 27, 29 September 1949. *Cincinnati Post*, 26, 27, 28 September 1949.

49. *Cincinnati Enquirer*, 28 October; 3 November 1949. *Cincinnati Post*, 18, 25, 26, 29 October; 9 November 1949. *Cincinnati Times-Star*, 25, 31 October 1949. Straetz, *PR Politics*, pp. 205-7.

50. *Cincinnati Enquirer*, 12, 13, 14, 15, 16, 19, 22, 26 February; 5 March 1950. *Cincinnati Post*, 10 January; 14 February 1950.

51. *Cincinnati Enquirer*, 9, 12, 19, 23 March; 18 June; 13, 16, 24, 30 July; 14 September 1950. *Cincinnati Post*, 6, 9, 16, 23 March; 14 June; 14 September 1950.
    Robert Goldstein is wrong in citing this as an effect of increased tensions after the outbreak of the Korean War; *Political Repression* p. 359.

52. *Cincinnati Enquirer*, 29, 30 September 1953. *Cincinnati Times-Star*, 29, 30 September 1953. Straetz, *PR Politics*, p. 209. William H. Hessler, "It Didn't Work in Cincinnati," *The Reporter*, December 22, 1953, pp. 13-14.

53. *Cincinnati Enquirer*, 1, 2, 4, 6 October 1953. *Cincinnati Post*, 1, 2, October 1953. *Cincinnati Times-Star*, 1, 2 October 1953.

54. *Cincinnati Enquirer*, 6, 7, 8, 21 October 1953. *Cincinnati Post*, 8, 9 October 1953. Straetz, *PR Politics*, pp. 209-20. Hessler, "Cincinnati," pp. 15-17.

55. *Cincinnati Enquirer*, 4, 6, 9, 22, 29 October 1953. *Cincinnati Post*, 21, 30 October 1953. *Cincinnati Times-Star*, 24, 26, 27 October 1953.

56. *Cincinnati Enquirer*, 30 September; 7, 9, 11, 16, 19, 21, 22, 27, 28, 30 October; 1 November 1953. *Cincinnati Post*, 6, 21, 26, 28, 30 October 1953. *Cincinnati Times-Star*, 14 October 1953.

57. *Cincinnati Enquirer*, 3 November 1953. Wallace Collett to Jim Selcraig, n.d. (March 1980).

58. Robert Mowitz has argued that the scare arose particularly strong in Detroit because of its political structure—elections being held on a non-partisan basis. Supposedly, politicians did not have the backing of a party organization and needed any publicity they could get. Thus, they were willing to exploit the loyalty issue. Mowitz, "Michigan," p. 219. This argument has not been accepted in this chapter because Chicago and Cincinnati have shown that the scare also arose strongly where elections were held on a party basis. As a result, this chapter has emphasized the concept of a conservative movement (held together by ideology).

Chapter 4

1. SAIC, *Report 1947-1948*, pp. 127, 145.

2. Clarence Karier, *The Shaping of the American Educational State 1900 to the Present* (New York: Free Press, 1975), p. 82. Douglas T. Miller and Marion Nowak, *The Fifties: The Way We Really Were* (Garden City, N.Y.: Doubleday Co., 1977), pp. 253-54.

3. According to a 1950 poll, educational officials at both the state and local levels preferred to determine loyalty by maintaining "regular channels of contact," rather than creating any special procedures. E. Edmund Reutter, Jr., *The School Administrator and Subversive Activities* (New York: Bureau of Publications, Teachers College, Columbia University, 1951), pp. 83-88.

4. *Cleveland Plain Dealer*, 11, 24, 25, 26 May; 7 June 1949. *Cleveland News*, 24, 25 May 1949. Dworken v. Board of Education, Cleveland, 46 00 194, 62 OLA 10. *Canton Repository*, 7 June; 6 July 1950.

5. *Chicago Tribune*, 10 August; 12 October; 22 November 1950; 16 March; 12 April 1951. *Chicago Sun-Times*, 10 August 1950; 1, 16 March 1951. *Chicago Union Teacher*, April 1951, p. 5. Mary J. Herrick is wrong in asserting that the oath controversy was caused by Governor Stevenson's veto of a 1951 loyalty oath bill. Mary J. Herrick, *The Chicago Schools: A Social and Political History* (Beverly Hills: Sage Publishers, 1971), pp. 297–98.

6. *Chicago Tribune*, 27 June 1955. *Chicago Sun-Times*, 26 June; 2, 19, 20 July; 5 August 1955.

7. *Cleveland Plain Dealer*, 3, 8, 22, 23 December 1953. Edward Likover to Jim Selcraig, March 20, 1980.

8. U.S., Congress, House, Committee on Un-American Activities, *Communism in the Detroit Area*, 82nd Congress, 2nd session, pp. 2855–2860. *Detroit Free Press*, 26, 27, 28 February 1952. *Detroit News*, 26, 28 February 1952.

9. *Detroit Free Press*, 1, 11 March 1952. *Detroit News*, 4, 11 March 1952. Board of Education, Detroit, *Proceedings 1951–1952* (Detroit: n.p., 1952), pp. 364–69.

10. U.S., Congress, House, Committee on Un-American Activities, *Investigation of Communist Activities in the State of Michigan*, 83rd Congress, 2nd session, pp. 5049–83, 5286, 5295. Board of Education, Detroit, *Proceedings 1953–1954* (Detroit: n.p., 1954), pp. 305–10, 436. *Detroit News*, 4, 5, 6, 11 May; 2 July 1954. *Detroit Free Press*, 4, 11 May; 2 July 1954.

11. Committee on Un-American Activities, *Investigation in Michigan*, pp. 5063–69. *Garden City Review*, 6, 13, 20 May 1954. *Detroit News*, 7, 9 May 1954.

12. U.S., Congress, House, Committee on Un-American Activities, *Investigation of Communist Activities in the Dayton, Ohio Area*, 83rd Congress, 2nd session, pp. 7013–15. *Dayton Journal-Herald*, 16, 17, 23, 24 September 1954.

13. U.S., Congress, House, Committee on Un-American Activities, *Investigation of Communist Activities in the Ohio Area*, 84th Congress, 1st session, pp. 1419–35. *Canton Repository*, 9, 21 September 1954.

14. *Chicago Herald-American*, 24, 25, 26 May; 4, 7 June; 4, 9 October 1948. *Chicago Sun-Times*, 27, 28, 29 May; 5, 8 June 1948. Chicago, Board of Education, *Proceedings 1947–1948* (Chicago: n.p., 1948), pp. 1443–45. SAIC, *Report 1947–1948*, p. 187.

15. *Muskegon Chronicle*, 17, 20, 26 March; 9, 15, 16 April; 19 May 1948. Arthur Elder to Russel O. Parrington, 19 March 1948; Russel O. Parrington to Arthur Elder, 20 March 1948; Russel O. Parrington to Arthur Elder, 18 April 1948; all in Papers of the Michigan Federation of Teachers, box 10, Muskegon Federation of Teachers, Labor Affairs, Wayne. National Education Association, Committee on Tenure and Academic Freedom, *Report of 1948* (Washington, D.C.: National Education Association, 1948), pp. 16–17.

16. *Lansing State Journal*, 3, 4 December 1949. *Detroit Free Press*, 6 December 1949.

17. *Lansing State Journal*, 29 November; 4 December 1949. *Detroit Free Press*, 8 December 1949. American Legion, Department of Michigan, *Proceedings of the 32nd Annual Convention, August 22–27, 1950* (Detroit: n.p., 1950), pp. 92–98.

18. *Lansing State Journal*, 5, 7, 9, 10, 11, 16 December 1949. *Detroit Free Press*, 6, 8, 9, 11 December 1949.

19. *Chicago Tribune*, 7, 8, 9, 10, 11, 13, 26 October; 2, 3 November 1947.

20. *Chicago Tribune*, 16, 17 October 1947. Herrick, *Chicago Schools*, p. 295. The *Tribune's*

reports sparked a brief controversy in Delavan, Wisconsin, a small town near the Illinois border. A former resident and former Communist, Kenneth Goff, had been a major source for the *Tribune* series. He charged that the schools had Communist-slanted textbooks, and the school board held a mass meeting on the issue in late October. Goff claimed that nine students had become Communists because of such books, but he refused to disclose any names for fear of libel. He reiterated the charges against the textbooks, but his arguments were rejected by the president of the school board, the PTA president, a state education official, and various citizens. Eight months earlier, the school board had discontinued the use of one of the suspected books, *Land of the Soviets* published by the Institute of Pacific Relations. The board concluded that all the remaining books were objective. Indeed, the village newspaper declared that not only were the teachers "100% Americans," but that the textbooks were "conservative." No other school district had even this much controversy as a result of the *Tribune* series. *Delavan Enterprise,* 28 February; 17, 24, 31 October; 5 December 1947.

21. *Chicago Tribune,* 30 October; 1, 11 November 1949.

22. *Chicago Sun-Times,* 8 March 1953.

23. *Chicago Sun-Times,* 9 March 1953. For a more complete discussion of CASBO's educational philosophy, see Robert C. Morris, "Era of Anxiety: An Historical Account of the Effects and Reactions to Right-wing Forces Affecting Education during the Years 1949 to 1954" (Ph.D. dissertation, Indiana State University, 1976), pp. 253–56.

   In the fall of 1950, another brief controversy arose over a text. The *Tribune* charged that *I Want to Be Like Stalin* was a required book and was being used for indoctrination. Actually, the book was not required and was only being used for the study of propaganda. *Chicago Tribune,* 12, 13 October 1950.

24. *Chicago Sun-Times,* 23, 24, 25, 26 February; 8, 9, 10 March 1953. Kay Kamin, "A History of the Hunt Administration of the Chicago Public Schools, 1947–1953" (Ph.D. dissertation, University of Chicago, 1970), pp. 165–69.

25. *Lafayette Journal and Courier,* 14, 15 December 1951.

26. *Indianapolis Star,* 22, 23, 27, 30 December 1951; 1, 2, 3, 4, 6, 8, 9, 13 January 1952.

27. Frank Magruder, *American Government: A Consideration of the Problems of Democracy* (Boston: Allyn and Bacon, 1948), pp. 27, 45, 389, 482.

28. *Indianapolis Star,* 22, 25 December 1951; 8 January; 12 December 1952. *Indianapolis Times,* 11 December 1952. State of Indiana, Board of Education, Textbook Committee, "Minutes," 24 December 1951; 7 January; 7 August; 20 November; 5 December 1952.

29. Magruder, *American Government,* p. 719. William A. McClenaghan, rev., *Magruder's American Government* (Boston: Allyn and Bacon, 1953), pp. iii, 35–37, 720, 728, The Magruder text was banned in Georgia and in Houston, but was soon reinstated in both areas. Jackson, Michigan, and Trumbull County, Ohio, both defeated censorship attempts. Jack Nelson and Gene Roberts Jr., *The Censors and the Schools* (Boston: Little, Brown, 1963), pp. 41–49. Paul Blanshard, *The Right to Read: The Battle Against Censorship* (Boston: Beacon Press, 1955), p. 106.

30. *Indianapolis Star,* 29 November 1950; 18, 19 September 1952.

31. *Madison Capital-Times,* 31 March; 1, 2, 3, 4, April; 12 May 1953. *Wisconsin State Journal,* 1 April 1953.

32. *Peoria Journal,* 15, 18, 22 September 1950.

33. *Peoria Journal,* 17 November; 22 December 1950. *Peoria Star,* 17 November; 22 December 1950; 5, 11, 19 January 1951.

34. Maurice Boyd, "The Effect of Censorship Attempts by Private Pressure Groups on Public Libraries" (master's thesis, Kent State University, 1959), p. 59. Marjorie Fiske, *Book Selection and Censorship* (Berkeley: University of California Press, 1959), pp. 46, 62, 66, 123–25.

35. Ernest O. Melby and Morton Puner, eds., *Freedom and Public Education* (New York: Frederick A. Praeger, 1953), pp. 144–53, 160–82, 256–60.

36. Only censorship efforts that were successful are discussed in Caute, *Great Fear,* pp. 454–455; and Blanshard, *Right to Read,* pp. 63–69, 83. Miller and Nowak are wrong in declaring that the Robin Hood story was banned; *The Fifties,* p. 252.

37. Robert W. Iversen, *The Communists and the Schools* (New York: Harcourt, Brace, 1959), p. 344.

38. Frances FitzGerald makes this misinterpretation. She argues that history texts portrayed America as "perfect" and reflected "the National Association of Manufacturers' viewpoint." The texts bypassed vital events and issues, and, she strongly implies, brainwashed the students. She then finds it difficult to explain the texts' emphasis on responsibility, and she completely misses how such exhortations could be channeled into reform activities. Her book tells us nothing new, and is merely a polemic from the Left. Frances FitzGerald, *America Revised: History Schoolbooks in the Twentieth Century* (Boston: Little, Brown, 1979), pp. 10, 37, 57, 67, 114, 120.

Chapter 5

1. One conservative organization tried to combine a loose structure and a national organization. The Minute Women did not act as a pressure group, but rather informed its members of leftist activities and urged them as individuals to write letters, picket meetings, and lobby. The organization only established chapters in a few larger cities. Carleton, "Houston," p. 106.

2. *Yellow Springs News,* 15 January; 18 March; 29 April 1948; 16 June 1949; 24 July; 25 September 1952; 15 January; 9 April; 17 September 1953. *Yellow Springs American,* 11 June 1953 to 15 April 1954. Nancy Bishop, "The Yellow Springs American" (seminar paper, Antioch College, 1956), pp. 2–12, Antiochiana, Antioch College, Yellow Springs, Ohio (hereafter referred to as Antiochiana).

3. *Barron County News-Shield,* 17 March; 14 April; 5, 19 May 1949. *Rice Lake Chronotype,* 23, 30 March; 20 April 1949. William S. Fairfield, "How the Reds Came to Haugen, Wisconsin," *The Reporter,* 5 January 1954, pp. 24–26.

4. *Milwaukee Sentinel,* 23, 24, 25, 26, 27, 29, 30, 31 July 1950.

5. *Chicago Sun-Times,* 13, 14 April 1953. Other cases of violence include the stoning of a Progressive party candidate in West Frankfurt, Illinois, and the beating and forceable ejection of several workers who had invoked the Fifth Amendment before HUAC in Detroit. *Chicago Tribune,* 3 September 1948. *Detroit News,* 1, 2, 3, 4, 5, 6, 7 March 1952.

6. *Peoria Star,* 15, 18, 20, 21 October 1950. *Peoria Journal,* 15, 25, 26, 28 October 1950. David Caute wrongly declares that the boycott closed the play; *Great Fear,* p. 536.

7. The four musicans were Lee Hays, Pete Seeger, Fred Hellerman, and Ronnie Gilbert.

Columbus Citizen, 17, 19, 25, 26, 27 August 1951. *Counterattack*, 1 June; 14 September 1951. David King Dunaway, *How Can I Keep From Singing: Pete Seeger* (New York: McGraw-Hill, 1981), pp. 150–56.

8. *Cleveland Plain Dealer*, 2 February 1952.

9. *Legion News*, 6, 13, 20, 27 March; 3 April 1953. Milwaukee County American Legion to Harry MacDonald, 26 February 1953; and Robert G. Wilke to Milwaukee County American Legion, 27 April 1953; Papers of the American Legion, Department of Wisconsin, box 50, the Wisconsin State Historical Society, Madison. *Columbus Citizen*, 7 February 1953.

10. Herbert Biberman, *Salt of the Earth: The Story of a Film* (Boston: Beacon Press, 1965), pp. 178–83.

11. Biberman, *Salt of the Earth*, pp. 185–212. Edward Clamage to Cinema Annex, 12 May 1954; Herbert Biberman to ACLU, n.d.; June Sak to ACLU, 18 September 1954; "On the Live Wire;" and Independent Productions Corporation v. CMPOU; Papers of the ACLU, Chicago chapter, box 36, University of Chicago. *New York Times*, 1 November 1965.

12. American Legion, Department of Illinois, *Report of the 33rd Annual Convention* (Chicago: n.p., 1951), p. 39. American Legion, Department of Illinois, *Report of the 34th Annual Convention* (Chicago: n.p., 1952), p. 57. *Chicago Tribune*, 20 June; 26 August; 2, 5, 6, 7, 10 September; 1 October 1951. Sorenson, "Anti-Communist Impulse," chap. 6, pp. 17–25.

13. Ralph S. Brown, Jr., *Loyalty and Security: Employment Tests in the United States* (New Haven: Yale University Press, 1958), p. 118. *Indianapolis Star*, 17, 19, 21 November 1953. *Indianapolis Times*, 18, 19 21 November 1953; 25, 26 March; 13, 15, 16, 26 May 1955. Robert Goldstein is wrong in stating that the city of Indianapolis barred the ACLU; *Political Repression*, p. 359.

14. *Lansing State Journal*, 14, 15, 16 April 1950. *Madison Capital-Times*, 1 March 1948. Clutter, "Indiana Legion," pp. 267–268. Many other examples of seminars could also be cited.

15. *Mosinee Times*, 12, 19, 26 April 1950.

16. *Red Star*, 1 May 1950.

17. *Indianapolis Star*, 2 December 1951. The Veterans of Foreign Wars helped to plan this event.

18. Ben H. Bagdikian, "What Happened to the Girl Scouts?" *Atlantic*, May 1950, pp. 63–64. Blanshard, *Right to Read*, pp. 127–29. American Legion, Department of Illinois, *Report of the 36th Annual Convention* (Chicago: n.p., 1954), p. 98. The national Legion rejected the boycott proposal, but it did criticize the handbook.

19. Thomas C. Reeves, *Freedom and the Foundation: The Fund for the Republic in the Era of McCarthyism* (New York: A. A. Knopf, 1969), p. 107. Charles Komaiko and Jean Komaiko, "The Illinois Legion and 'Positive Americanism,'" *The Reporter*, 7 April 1955, pp. 34–36.

20. Reeves, *Fund for the Republic*, pp. 124–27. "The Reporter's Notes," *The Reporter*, 6 October 1955, p. 4. *Illinois State Journal*, 3 September 1955. *Illinois State Register*, 3 September 1955. *Chicago Sun-Times*, 3 September 1955.

21. Clutter, "Indiana Legion," pp. 268–69, 305. Sorenson, "Anti-Communist Impulse in Indiana," chap. 7, pp. 25–26.

22. August Meier and Elliott Redwick, *CORE* (New York: Oxford University Press, 1973), pp. 31–32, 62–65, 71.

23. MacDougall, *Gideon's Army*, pp. 125–26. State Central Committee (IVI) "Minutes, 20 January 1947 and 28 February 1947;" and Board of Directors, "Minutes, 6 February 1947;" Papers of the Independent Voters of Illinois, box 1, Chicago Historical Society, Chicago. Frank W. McCulloch to James Loeb, 19 April 1947; and Richard A. Meyer to James Loeb, 23 April 1947; Papers of the Americans for Democratic Action, box 13, Wisconsin State Historical Society, Madison.

24. *Civil Liberties News*, 7, 28 June; 5 July; 25 October 1946. Ruth Ziegler, "The Chicago Civil Liberties Committee, 1929–1938" (master's thesis, University of Chicago, 1938) gives the early history of the organization.

25. *Civil Liberties News*, 15, 22 October; 31 December 1946; 22 April 1947; 9 January; 1 August; 1 October 1948. (CCLC) Weekly Board Minutes, 1 March; 1 November 1948; Papers of Ira Latimer, Chicago Historical Society, Chicago. *Chicago Tribune*, 7 August 1948.

26. *Wisconsin Farmer Union News*, 10, 24 December 1945; 14 April; 27 October 1947; 26 April; 10 May 1948; 28 February 1949. State Board (WFU), "Minutes, 12 December 1946" and "Minutes, 30 March 1948;" miscellaneous letters and resolutions; Papers of Kenneth W. Hones, box 1, folders 3 and 5, Wisconsin State Historical Society, Madison. Alonzo L. Hamby, *Beyond the New Deal: Harry S. Truman and American Liberalism* (New York: Columbia University Press, 1973), pp. 33–34, 149–50, 165, 223, 257. *Milwaukee Sentinel*, 3 October 1946.

27. Executive Board, National Lawyers Guild, Detroit, "Minutes, 1950;" Harold Cranefield to Guild Members, 5, 11, October 1950; Robert J. Silberstein to Harold Norris, 2 October 1950; Harold Norris to Robert Silberstein, 14 October 1950; Papers of Harold Norris, box 1, September 1950 and October–December 1950, Bentley, UM.

28. Liberal defenders include Eric Goldman, *Rendezvous with Destiny: A History of Modern American Reform* (New York: Vintage Books, 1955), pp. 324–325; and Hamby, *Beyond the New Deal*, pp. 383, 386, 401, 470, 505–507. A recent critic of the liberal response is Mary McAuliffe, *Crisis on the Left: Cold War Politics and American Liberals* (Amherst: University of Massachusetts Press, 1978), pp. 81–82, 86, 147.

29. The quotation comes from Richard Hofstadter, *The Progressive Historians*, p. 454.

30. Griffith, "American Politics," p. 14.

Chapter 6

1. Joseph McCarthy, *McCarthyism: The Fight for America* (New York: Devin-Adair, 1952), p. 101.

2. Philip Altbach, *Student Politics in America: A Historical Analysis* (New York: McGraw-Hill Co., 1974), p. 118.

3. Slavery was a much more repressive environment than a midwestern university, but even there, Eugene Genovese has pointed out how paternalism softened the effects of that system. Eugene Genovese, *Roll, Jordan, Roll, The World the Slaves Made* (New York: Vintage Books, 1972), p. 4–7.

4. *Ohio State Lantern*, 5, 10, 12, 16, 17, 22, 23 April 1946. James E. Pollard, *The History of The Ohio State University, The Bevis Administration, 1940–1956: The Postwar Years and*

the Emergence of the Greater University, vol. 8, part 2 (Columbus: Ohio State University Press, 1970), pp. 127–28. Miscellaneous materials are in the Papers of Howard Bevis, Ohio State Youth for Democracy, 3/h/39, University Archives, Ohio State University, Columbus (hereafter referred to as OSU Archives).

5. *Michigan State News*, 7, 12, 13, 14 November 1946.

6. *Michigan State News*, 31 January; 1, 4, 5, 7 February 1947. *Lansing State Journal*, 31 January; 1, 2, 3, 4, 5, 6 February 1947.

7. *Detroit Free Press*, 11, 21 December 1948; 14 January 1949.

8. *Detroit Collegian*, 29, 31 October 1946. Student Activities Committee to Victor Spathelf, 7 February 1947, Papers of Clarence Hilberry, box 4, AYD, University Archives, Wayne State University, Detroit (hereafter referred to as Wayne Archives). David D. Henry to Eugene C. Keyes, 12 February 1947, Papers of Arthur A. Neef, Wayne Archives. Victor Spathelf, "AYD Boesky Restaurant Incident," Papers of the Division of Student Personnel, box 28, general AYD, Wayne Archives.

9. Recognitions Subcommittee, Student Activities Committee, "Report 28 February 1947;" and Victor Spathelf to George Shenkar, 3 March 1947; Papers of Clarence Hilberry, box 4, AYD, Wayne Archives. Harold E. Stewart, "Report;" Victor Spathelf, "Report;" Victor Spathelf, "Report;" Papers of the Division of Student Personnel, box 28, general, Marxian Study Society, Wayne Archives.
   Detroit Collegian, 2, 3, 14, 17 March 1947. George Shenkar to Jim Selcraig, February 9, 1980.

10. Colin L. Smith, "Press Statement;" David D. Henry, "Notes for Members of the Board of Education, 25 March 1947;" and Theron L. Caudle to David D. Henry, 24 March 1947; Papers of Arthur A. Neef, box 40, Callahan Commission, Wayne Archives. David D. Henry, "Testimony Before the Callahan Commission," n.d.; Papers of Clarence Hilberry, box 4, AYD, Wayne Archives. David D. Henry to the Board of Education, Detroit, 19 March 1947, Vertical file, Communism, Wayne Archives.

11. George Schermer to David D. Henry, 17 March 1947; Douglas W. McGregor to David D. Henry, 3 April 1947; Clarence Hilberry to A. J. Brumbaugh, 20 October 1949; Papers of Clarence Hilberry, box 4, AYD, Wayne Archives. David D. Henry to University Council, 9 April 1947, Papers of Arthur A. Neef, box 40, Callahan Commission, Wayne Archives. A. H. Kelly to David D. Henry, 14 April 1947, Papers of the Division of Student Personnel, box 28, general AYD, Wayne Archives. Detroit, Board of Education, *Proceedings 1946–1947* (Detroit: n.p., 1947), p. 425–525. Leslie Hanawalt, *A Place of Light: The History of Wayne State University* (Detroit: Wayne State University Press, 1968), p. 485 n. 4.

12. Committee on Student Affairs, "The Student in the University," 24 October 1949, Papers of Division of Student Personnel, box 28, general, political and social action groups, Wayne Archives. Victor Spathelf to John Cherveny, 14 January 1948 (handwritten notation by David D. Henry?), Papers of Division of Student Personnel, box 20, general, Collegian Club, Wayne Archives. *Detroit Collegian*, 15 April; 16, 17 December 1947. George Shenkar to Jim Selcraig.

13. *Ann Arbor News*, 4, 5, 6 February; 22, 30 April 1947. For miscellaneous material on the AYD, see the Papers of Alexander G. Ruthven, box 58, folder 6, AYD, Bentley, UM.

14. *Michigan Daily*, 13, 16 December 1947.

15. *Michigan Daily*, 20, 25 February; 6, 18, 22 March 1948. For miscellaneous material, see

the Papers of Alexander G. Ruthven, box 58, folder 6; and the Papers of John L. Brumm, box 1, academic freedom; Bentley, UM.

16. Fred Turner to George Stoddard, 5 February 1947, Papers of George Stoddard, general correspondence, 1946–1947, Dean of Students, the Archives, University of Illinois, Urbana (hereafter referred to as Illinois Archives).

17. *Daily Illini*, 13, 15, 23, 26 February; 15, 19, 20, 21, 22, 23, 26, 27, 29, 30 March; 3, 9, 16, 17, 19, 24 April 1947.

18. *Daily Illini*, 14, 15, 16, 23, 28 May; 9, 15 August 1947. George Stoddard to Dwight Green, 7 August 1947, Papers of Fred Turner, general correspondence, box 9, Illinois Archives. House Bill 711 in *Illinois House Journal, 65th Assembly*, pp. 166, 879; and *Illinois Senate Journal, 65th Assembly*, p. 1588.

19. *Daily Cardinal*, 3, 4, 5, 10 December 1947. *Madison Capital-Times*, 3, 4, 10 December 1947. *Milwaukee Journal*, 15 May 1947.

20. William V. Morgenstern to E. C. Colwell, 5 February 1947; William Morgenstern to Howard H. Moore, 21 February 1947; Howard Moore to William Morgenstern, 27 February 1947; E. C. Colwell to William Morgenstern, 8 April 1947; Presidential Papers 1950–1955, Communism 1947–1954, University of Chicago. Robert M. Strozier to A. W. Sherer, 22 December 1947, Presidential Papers 1945–1950, Student Government, Organizations, and Activities, 1946–1949, University of Chicago. *Chicago Maroon*, 14 November; 9 December 1947.

21. *Daily Illini*, 5, 6, 18 November; 3, 4, 9, 15, 18 December 1948; 7, 11, 14, 18 January 1949. George Stoddard to Fred Turner, n.d., Papers of George Stoddard, general correspondence, 1947–1948, Dean of Students, Illinois Archives. Joseph Ewers to R. H. Linkins, 25 March 1949, Papers of Fred Turner, general correspondence, box 9, Illinois Archives.

22. *Daily Illini*, 3 August; 13 December 1949; 19 August; 14, 30 September; 4 October; 7 December 1950. Joseph Ewers to Fred Turner, 6 October 1950, Papers of Fred Turner, general correspondence, box 13, Illinois Archives. Fred Turner to Ivan Elliott, 18 October 1950, Papers of George Stoddard, general correspondence, 1950–1951, Dean of Students, Illinois Archives.

23. *Ohio State Journal*, 25, 29, 30, 31 March 1948. *Columbus Dispatch*, 19, 24, 29, 30, 31 March; 1 April 1948.

24. *Ohio State Lantern*, 30, 31 March; 1, 2, 5, 8 April 1948. *Columbus Dispatch*, 24, 31 March 1948.

25. *Ohio State Lantern*, 12, 14, 16 April 1948. Pollard, *Bevis Years*, pp. 130–132.

26. *Ohio State Lantern*, 16, 19, 20, 22 April; 11 May; 4 June 1948. The *Columbus Dispatch* accused the campus YMCA of "Communist party activity," but an official university investigation cleared the group. Admissions Commission, "Report on the Ohio State University YMCA," Papers of Howard Bevis, YMCA 1948–1954, OSU Archives.

27. *Columbus Dispatch*, 12 August; 7 October 1951. Steven P. Gietschier, "Limited War and the Home Front: Ohio during the Korean War" (Ph.D. dissertation, Ohio State University, 1977), pp. 163–76. Ohio State University also had two smaller incidents concerning speakers and group recognition. In February 1948, Students for Wallace were denied hearing Lewis Hahn because of a trustees' rule barring "candidates for public office." Hahn was not a candidate but the state campaign director for Henry Wallace. Two

years later, Students for Wallace was banned after some of its members heard Herbert Phillips speak on campus. The students claimed that Phillips spoke only informally, but to no avail. *Ohio State Lantern*, 9, 25 February 1948; 2 March; 7, 13, April; 11, 20, 23, 26 May 1949.

28. Gietschier, "Limited War," pp. 176–80. Pollard, *Bevis Years*, pp. 142–51. Harry G. Good, *The Rise of the College of Education of The Ohio State University* (Columbus: Ohio State University Press, 1960), pp. 225–26. Newspapers critical of the "gag rule" included the *Columbus Citizen*, *Cleveland Press*, *Akron Beacon-Journal*, and *Toledo Blade*.

29. Gietschier, "Limited War," pp. 183–87. Good, *College of Education*, p. 227.

30. Gietschier ("Limited War," p. 188) and Good (*College of Education*, p. 226) both claim that no other speakers were banned after Cecil Hinshaw. See, however, the testimony given by Sidney Isaacs, n.d., Papers of the Ohio Un-American Activities Committee, Ohio Historical Society.

31. *Detroit Collegian*, 20, 24, 29 March; 6, 26 April; 1, 3 May 1950. *Detroit Free Press*, 29 March; 29 April 1950. *Detroit Times*, 26 April 1950. Wayne University also had a smaller "speaker incident" in late 1948. The Special Programs Committee rejected an attempt by an ad hoc group to bring the Very Rev. Hewlett Johnson, Dean of Christ Church, Canterbury, as a speaker. Johnson was a leftist, but the official reason was that the group had no official status at the university. *Detroit Collegian*, 23, 24, 30 November; 1, 6 December 1948.

32. *Detroit Collegian*, 5, 8, 9 May 1950.

33. *Michigan Daily*, 30, 31 March; 6, 18, 20, 26, 28 April 1950. Two smaller "speaker" controversies also occurred on campus, affecting Carl Marzani in the spring of 1948 and James Zarichny in the spring of 1949. Both spoke off campus. *Michigan Daily*, 22, 26 May 1948; 1, 9, 10 March 1949.

34. *Michigan Daily*, 2, 4, 7 March 1952.

35. Faculty-Student Committee, "Report," 18 March 1952, Papers of Alexander Ruthven, box 58, folder 4—McPhaul, Bentley, UM. *Michigan Daily*, 8, 20 March; 18, 22 April 1952.

36. Joint Judiciary Council, "Findings and Recommendations," 28 April 1952, Papers of Alexander Ruthven, box 58, folder 4, Bentley, UM. *Michigan Daily*, 22, 26 April; 4 May 1952.

37. Deborah Bacon to Alexander Ruthven, Papers of Alexander Ruthven, box 58, folder 4, Bentley, UM. *Michigan Daily*, 7 March; 11, 15, 25 November; 6 December 1952; 7 January; 16 April 1953; 20 November 1954; 21 April 1955; 13 November 1956.

38. Malcolm Sharp to Robert Strozier, 11 September 1950, Presidential Papers 1950–1955, Student Government, Organizations, and Activities, 1950–1954, University of Chicago. Malcolm Sharp to Robert Strozier, 18 June 1951, in Presidential Papers 1950–1955, Labor Youth League, University of Chicago.

39. The court case that Sharp was concerned about was Garner v. Board of Public Works, 341 US 716 (1951), in which the court read scienter, knowledge and intent, into a loyalty oath. Malcolm Sharp to Robert Strozier, 18 June 1951; Laird Bell to Lawrence Kimpton, 13 July 1951; Robert Strozier to Lawrence Kimpton, 23 July 1951; Labor Youth League, "Statement, 8 October 1951;" Harry Kalven Jr. to William Josephson, 5 December 1951; Edward Levi to Lawrence Kimpton, 4 January 1952; Presidential Papers 1950–1955, Labor Youth League, University of Chicago.

40. Laird Bell to Lawrence Kimpton, 4 January 1952; Donald Meikeljohn to Lawrence Kimpton, 4 January 1952; Robert Strozier to Student Government, 4 February 1952; Presidential Papers 1950–1955, Labor Youth League, University of Chicago. *Chicago Maroon*, 9 February; 11 May; 16, 23 November; 7 December 1951; 18, 25 January; 8 February 1952; 13 February 1953.

41. *Daily Cardinal*, 8 March 1950; 15 January 1953. *Madison Capital-Times*, 14, 15 January 1953.

42. *Madison Capital-Times*, 13 March 1953. *Wisconsin State Journal*, 1 April 1953. *Daily Cardinal*, 2 October 1956. Subcommittee on General Student Organization and Politics, "Report, 13 February 1953," Papers of the Divisions of Student Affairs, Student Life and Interest Commission, University Archives, University of Wisconsin, Madison. Student Life and Interest Commission, "Annual Report, 1953," Papers of the American Legion, Department of Wisconsin, box 40, folder 4, Wisconsin State Historical Society, Madison.

43. *Michigan State News*, 22 June 1950. *Lansing State Journal*, 16, 20 June 1950.

44. *Lansing State Journal*, 26, 27 June 1950. Administrative Group, "Minutes of Special Meeting, 27 June 1950," Papers of John A. Hannah, University Archives, Michigan State University, East Lansing.

45. *Chicago Maroon*, 9 October 1951, *Chicago Sun-Times*, 5 October 1951. *Chicago Tribune*, 5, 6 October 1951. *Chicago Herald-American*, 9 October 1951.

46. *Chicago Maroon*, 19 October 1951. *Chicago Sun-Times*, 11, 12 October 1951. *Chicago Tribune*, 11 October 1951. Fourteen Faculty Members to the President of Student Government, 9 October 1951; Special Executive Committee on the University of Chicago *Maroon*, "Minutes, 23 October 1951;" "Report to the Executive Committee of the ACLU on the *Maroon*," n.d.; Papers of the American Civil Liberties Union, Chicago Chapter, box 29, folder 7, University of Chicago.

47. Ibid. *Chicago Maroon*, 11 January 1952.

48. *Michigan State News*, 12, 14, 15, 16, 17, 21 April 1948.

49. *Michigan State News*, 20, 21 May 1948. *Muskegon Chronicle*, 28, 29 April 1948. *Michigan Senate Journal*, 1948, pp. 208–11, 302–16, 332–66.

50. SAIC, *Investigation of University of Chicago*, pp. 55–61, 119–28. The SAIC also subpoenaed another student, Paul Lerman, but he did not testify.

51. U.S., Congress, Senate, Committee on the Judiciary, Subcommittee to Investigate the Administration of the Internal Security Act, *Subversive Influence in the Educational Process*, 83rd Congress, 1st session, pp. 1086–91.

52. Committee on Un-American Activities, Investigation in Michigan, pp. 5388–413. *Michigan Alumnus*, June 5, 1954, pp. 349–51.

53. The testimony is found in the Papers of the Ohio Un-American Activities Committee, 20 May 1952, Ohio Historical Society, Columbus. Norval H. Luxon to John H. Slocum, 14 August 1953, Papers of Howard Bevis, subversive activities 1953–1954, University Archives, Ohio State University, Columbus.

54. Committee on Un-American Activities, *Investigation in Detroit*, pp. 2910–14. *Detroit Free Press*, 29 February; 8, 14 March 1952. *Detroit Collegian*, 29 February; 5, 7, 10, 14 March 1952. David D. Henry to Seymour Goldman, 20 March 1952; Arthur Neef to Victor Rapport, 12 March 1952; Papers of Arthur Neff, box 30, communism 1952, Wayne

Archives. Seymour Goldman to Committee on Non-Academic Discipline; Student Government, "Resolution," n.d.; C. E. Page to Board of Education; Papers of Arthur Neef, p. 16, loose material, Wayne Archives. Committee on Non-Academic Discipline, "Report," in vertical file, communism—Lorraine Meisner, Wayne Archives.

55. David D. Henry to Antonia Kolar, 25 April 1952, Papers of Arthur Neef, box 30, communism 1952, Wayne Archives. *Detroit Collegian*, 7 March 1952.

56. Altbach, *Student Politics*, p. 112, 118. Seymour M. Lipset, *Passion and Politics: Student Activism in America* (Boston: Little, Brown, 1971), p. 185.

57. Irwin Unger does not even mention these three groups in discussing the origins of the 1960s Movement; *The Movement: A History of the American New Left, 1959–1972* (New York: Dodd, Mead, and Co., 1974), pp. 13–17. Philip Altbach points to religious groups, like the YMCA, as the most effective forum on and force for social change during these years. Philip Altbach, "Before Berkeley," *The New Pilgrims: Youth Protest in Transition*, ed. Philip Altbach and Robert Laufer (New York: McKay Co., 1972), p. 27.

58. "Athenean," quoted in the *Milwaukee Journal*, 10 April 1951. William H. Whyte, "The Class of '49," *Fortune*, June 1949, p. 85. "U.S. Campus Kids of 1953," *Newsweek*, 2 November 1953, p. 52. Altbach, *Student Politics*, p. 116.

59. Charles Lerner, "Students for America: McCarthy's Class of '54," *New Foundations* 7 (Spring 1954):13–18.

60. David Riesman, "The Found Generation," *American Scholar* 25 (Autumn 1956):433–34. "Campus Kids," p. 54. Altbach, *Student Politics*, pp. 126, 164. Lipset, *Passion and Politics*, p. 188.

Chapter 7

1. Caute, *Great Fear*, pp. 405–6. Robert MacIver, *Academic Freedom in Our Time* (New York: Columbia University Press, 1955), pp. 34, 120. William Preston, "Shadows of War and Fear," *The Pulse of Freedom: American Liberties, 1920–1970s*, ed. Alan Reitman (New York: W. W. Norton, 1975), p. 131. *New York Times*, 11 May 1951.

2. In one case, the professor resigned after being named as a Communist before HUAC. In July 1950, two witnesses identified Dr. Samuel Rappaport and his wife, both of whom were doctors at the Children's Hospital in Cincinnati. He was also a professor of pediatrics at the Medical School at the University of Cincinnati. Shortly thereafter, he resigned the position that he had held since 1937. Reginald McGrane, *The University of Cincinnati: A Success Story in Higher Education* (New York: Harper and Row, 1963), pp. 312–13.

3. Testimony of 20 May 1952 in the Papers of the Ohio Un-American Activities Committee, Ohio Historical Society, Columbus. *Ohio State Lantern*, 30 January 1953.

4. U.S., Congress, House, Committee on Un-American Activities, *Communist Methods of Infiltration (Education)*, 83rd Congress, 1st session, pp. 129–153.

5. Gietschier, "Limited War," pp. 192–97. *Columbus Citizen*, 18 March; 1, 2 April 1953.

6. Gietschier, "Limited War," pp. 199–204. *Columbus Citizen*, 4 April 1953.

7. *Columbus Citizen*, 8, 18, 20 April 1953. Ohio State University, Board of Trustees, *Proceedings*, 20 April 1953 (Columbus: Ohio State University Press, 1953). American Association of University Professors (AAUP), Special Committee, "Academic Freedom

and Tenure in the Quest for National Security: Ohio State University," *AAUP Bulletin* 42 (Spring 1956):81–83. Pollard, *Bevis Years*, pp. 167–70.

8. Gietschier, "Limited War," pp. 207–208. *Columbus Citizen*, 16 May 1953. U.S., Congress, House, Committee on Un-American Activities, *Investigation of Communist Activities in the Columbus, Ohio Area*, 83rd Congress, 1st session, pp. 1783–838.

9. Committee on Un-American Activities, *Investigation in Michigan*, pp. 5012–47. "University Procedure Under the Trucks Act," *Faculty Bulletin*, April 21, 1954, p. 1. Detroit, Board of Education, *Proceedings 1953–1954* (Detroit: n.p., 1954), pp. 305–10.

10. President's Advisory Committee on Loyalty, "Report with Reference to Dr. Gerald Harrison," Papers of Arthur A. Neef, box 45, Dr. Gerald Harrison, Wayne Archives. Emilie A. Newcomb to Committee on Rights and Responsibilities, 9 June 1954, Papers of Arthur A. Neef, p. 16, loose material, Wayne Archives.

11. Committee of Rights and Responsibilities, "Report with Reference to Gerald Harrison, 9 November 1954," Papers of Arthur A. Neef, p. 16, untitled folder, Wayne Archives. Committee of Rights and Responsibilities to Clarence Hilberry, 14 December 1954, Papers of Arthur A. Neef, p. 16, loose materials, Wayne Archives. Committee of Rights and Responsibilities, "Report," n.d. (May 1955?), Papers of Clarence Hilberry, box 47, Committee of Rights and Responsibilities, Wayne Archives.

12. President's Advisory Committee on Loyalty, "Report, 6 July 1954," Papers of Clarence Hilberry, box 31, Report with Reference to Irving Stein, Wayne Archives. Vaden Miles, et al., to President Hilberry, Papers of Arthur A. Neef, p. 16, Exhibits in Irving Stein Hearings, Wayne Archives.

13. Committee on Un-American Activities, *Investigation in Michigan*, pp. 5331–87.

14. Special Advisory Commission to the President, "Report," Papers of Marvin Niehuss, topical file, box 6, The Three, Bentley, UM. AAUP, Committee A, "University of Michigan," *AAUP Bulletin* 44 (March 1958):57–66.

15. Special Advisory Commission, "Report," Committee A, "University of Michigan," pp. 79–94. Horace Davis, "To the Special Advisory Commission of the President, 14 June 1954," and Horace Davis, "Letter to the Faculty, 31 July 1954," Papers of the American Association of University Professors, University of Michigan chapter, box 2, Nickerson and Davis cases, folder one, Bentley, UM.

16. Ibid.

17. Ibid.

18. Ibid. Chandler Davis spent six months in jail for contempt of Congress. He could not find any other permanent teaching position, although he did obtain a few temporary jobs as an instructor and a position as an editor. In 1962, he was hired by Toronto University in Canada. Mark Nickerson immediately found employment at the University of Manitoba. Caute, *Great Fear*, pp. 552–53, 572 n. 23. Chandler Davis to Jim Selcraig, 30 December 1980.

19. Subcommittee to Investigate the Internal Security Act, *Subversive Influences in Educational Process*, pp. 1080–113.

20. Sidney J. Socolar to Jim Selcraig, 2 March 1980. *Chicago Maroon*, 3, 31 July 1953.

21. Committee on Un-American Activities, *Investigation in Dayton*, pp. 6978–83. *Dayton Journal Herald*, 17 September 1954. Frank J. Donner, *The Un-Americans* (New York: Ballantine Books, 1961), pp. 173–174. *Yellow Springs News*, 7 July 1954. For many papers

on the Robert Metcalf case, see Antiochiana. Metcalf went through some legal difficulties after the hearing. He was indicted for contempt, saw the case dismissed, was reindicted, and again saw the case dismissed. Some faculty members helped to pay for his attorneys' fees.

22. Clark, *Indiana University*, pp. 294–302. Clutter, "Indiana Legion," pp. 253–56.

23. SAIC, *Investigation of the University of Chicago.* Harsha, "Broyles Commission," pp. 88–139. In Michigan, the state legislative committee, known as the Callahan Commission, questioned only one professor, Leroy Waterman of the University of Michigan. Waterman answered all questions, denied that he was a Communist, supported his political activities, but apologized if his title of professor had been used in his political activities. *Michigan Senate Journal of 1948*, p. 26.

24. MacDougall, *Gideon's Army*, pp. 369–370. Karl Schmidt, *Henry Wallace: Quixotic Crusade* (Syracuse: Syracuse University Press, 1960), p. 87.

25. MacDougall, *Gideon's Army*, p. 728.

26. AAUP, Committee A on Academic Freedom and Tenure, "Academic Freedom and Tenure: Evansville College," *AAUP Bulletin* 35 (Spring 1949):81–83.

27. Committee A, "Evansville College," p. 84. *Evansville Courier*, 4, 5, 6, 7, 23 April 1948.

28. Committee A, "Evansville College," pp. 88–96, 102–104. *Evansville Courier*, 9, 10, 11, 12, 13 April 1948.

29. *Evansville Courier*, 13, 15 April 1948.

30. Harold F. Williamson and Payson S. Wild, *Northwestern University, A History, 1850–1975* (Evanston: Northwestern University Press, 1976), pp. 216–217. *Chicago Tribune*, 28 April 1948.

31. MacDougall, *Gideon's Army*, pp. 400, 438. *Cleveland Plain Dealer*, 12 June 1948.

32. *Daily Illini*, 7 May 1949. *Champaign-Urbana News-Gazette*, 18 May 1949.

33. *Champaign-Urbana News-Gazette*, 8, 9, 12 June 1949. Phillips Bradley to George Stoddard, 9 June 1949, Papers of George Stoddard, general correspondence, box 28, Illinois Archives.

34. *Champaign-Urbana News-Gazette*, 14 June 1949. Phillips Bradley, "Report on the Meeting with Legislators, 14 June 1949," Papers of George Stoddard, general correspondence, box 28, Illinois Archives.

35. Phillips Bradley, "Report of the Meeting in Rockford, 22 June 1949;" R. G. Soderstrom to George Stoddard, 28 June 1949; Frank M. White to George Stoddard, 11 August 1949; Papers of George Stoddard, general correspondence, box 28, Illinois Archives. University of Illinois, Board of Trustees, *45th Report 1948–1950* (Urbana: University of Illinois Press, 1950), pp. 492, 816.

36. U.S., Congress, House, Committee on Labor and Education, *Extension Service*, 80th Congress, 2nd session, pp. 307–56. Commission of Inquiry on the Worker Education Service, "Report," Papers of Alexander G. Ruthven, box 59, Worker Education Service, Bentley, UM. *Michigan Daily*, 20 May 1948.

37. Commission of Inquiry, "Report," *Michigan Daily*, 20, 21 May 1948. For various papers on the case, see the Papers of Arthur Elder, box 20, Labor Affairs, Wayne.

38. Alexander Ruthven to the Board of Trustees, 21 September 1948, Papers of Alexander Ruthven, box 59, WES, Bentley, UM.

39. "History of the WES Controversy," Papers of Alexander Ruthven, box 59, WES, Bentley, UM. University of Michigan, Board of Regents, *Proceedings 1948–1949* (Ann Arbor: University of Michigan Press, 1949), p. 113. *Detroit Free Press*, 17, 21 October 1948; 10 January; 8 February 1949.

40. *Champaign-Urbana News-Gazette*, 8, 9, 11, 13, 14, 17, 21 May 1950.

41. *Champaign-Urbana News-Gazette*, 18 May 1950. Harno Committee, "Report," Papers of George Stoddard, general correspondence, box 46, Illinois Archives.

42. *Champaign-Urbana News-Gazette*, 18, 23, 25, 28 May; 2, 4, 11 June 1950.

43. *Illinois State Journal*, 28 May 1950. *Daily Illini*, 30 May 1950. *Chicago Tribune*, 28, 30 May; 6, 15, 21 June 1950.

44. *Daily Illini*, 26 June 1950. *Champaign-Urbana Courier*, 5, 23 July 1950. Howard Bowen, "Statement to the Press, 22 June 1950;" and George Stoddard, "Report to the Board of Trustees on Conditions in the Department of Economics and the College of Commerce and Business Administration, 22 June 1950;" Papers of George Stoddard, general correspondence, box 47, Illinois Archives.

45. *Illinois State Journal*, 25 June 1950. *Chicago Tribune*, 23, 28 June 1950. *Peoria Star*, 27 June 1950. *Champaign-Urbana News-Gazette*, 23 June 1950.

46. *Champaign-Urbana News-Gazette*, 10 August 1950.

47. *Champaign-Urbana News-Gazette*, 11, 12, 13, 20 August 1950. *Chicago Tribune*, 12 August 1950. *Alton Telegraph*, 12, 18 August 1950.

48. George Stoddard to Ora Dillavou, 14 August 1950; Ora Dillavou to George Stoddard, 15 August 1950; and George Stoddard to Ora Dillavou, 17 August 1950; Papers of George Stoddard, general correspondence, 1949–1950, Con-Fi, Illinois Archives.

49. *Daily Illini*, 30 September 1950. *Champaign-Urbana Courier*, 14, 20 August; 5 November 1950. *Peoria Star*, 14 October 1950. *Chicago Tribune*, 4 November 1950. *Champaign-Urbana News-Gazette*, 5, 6 November 1950. George Stoddard, "The State of the University," Papers of George Stoddard, general correspondence, box 47, Illinois Archives.

50. *Champaign-Urbana News-Gazette*, 8 November 1950.

51. *Champaign-Urbana News-Gazette*, 19, 24, 25, 26 November; 29 December 1950. *Daily Illini*, 4 January 1951. Executive Committee of the College of Commerce and Business Administration, "Press Release, 10 October 1950;" Howard Bowen, "Statement to the Trustees, 24 November 1950;" University Council, Executive Committee, "Report, 11 December 1950;" Papers of George Stoddard, general correspondence, box 47, Illinois Archives. University of Illinois, Board of Trustees, *46th Report 1950–1952* (Urbana: University of Illinois Press, 1952), pp. 460–61, 484–87.

52. *Daily Illini*, 25, 28 July; 2 August 1951; 10 May 1952. *Champaign-Urbana Courier*, 24 July 1951; 13 April 1953. *Champaign-Urbana News-Gazette*, 31 December 1950. *Chicago Tribune*, 31 December 1950; 29, 30 July 1951.

53. D. Chris Goettelmann, "The History of the Rempfer Case," (History of Western Civilization Paper, Antioch College, 21 May 1955), pp. 3–7. Robert Rempfer, "To Have and to Hold;" "On Democratic Living;" and "Criticisms of my Political Action of the Past 2½ Years," Papers on the Robert Rempfer case, Antiochiana.

54. Douglas McGregor, Confidential, 9 April 1953; W. Boyd Alexander to the Board of Review, 2 June 1953; Douglas McGregor to Robert Rempfer, 9 February 1953; and

Douglas McGregor to G. P. Shannon, n.d. (late April 1953?), Papers on the Robert Rempfer case, Antiochiana.

55. Goettelmann, "Rempfer Case," pp. 14–22; Robert Rempfer, "Dear Friends, 11 April 1953," both in Papers on the Robert Rempfer case, Antiochiana. Testimony by Sidney Isaacs, n.d., Papers of the Ohio Un-American Activities Committee, Ohio Historical Society. Rempfer found another position at Fisk University.

56. Parker Hamilton to Adcil, 14 April 1953, Papers on the Robert Rempfer case, Antiochiana. U.S., Congress, Senate, Committee on the Judiciary, Subcommittee to Investigate the Administration of the Internal Security Act, *Communist Tactics in Controlling Youth Organizations*, 83rd Congress, 2nd session, p. 226. Testimony by Douglas McGregor, 19 May 1952, Papers of the Ohio Un-American Activities Committee, Ohio Historical Society.

There is a question whether this incident should be classified as a Red Scare controversy. An Antioch faculty member denied that it constituted a "McCarthy-like incident." This is in part a question of semantics. Rempfer obviously had the right to appeal his case and present his evidence in a manner that many of McCarthy's victims did not. Yet some of the charges raised against Rempfer carried political overtones. Moreover, the issues were raised in a climate of McCarthyism so that those overtones became more pronounced. I believe that this case contrasts well with those at the University of Illinois and Olivet College. All the cases were not pure academic freedom cases, but all had similar aspects that became accentuated perhaps because of the time in which they occurred. Valdemar Carlson to Jim Selcraig, 20 May 1980.

57. Olivet College Faculty Meeting "Minutes, 18 February 1947"; and Roy Thomas to Frank W. Blair, n.d. (October 1948?); Olivet College Archives, Olivet College Library, Olivet, Michigan (hereafter referred to as Olivet Archives). Ethelyn Sexton to Governor Kim Sigler, 24 April 1947; Harry Kellogg to Governor Kim Sigler, 15 May 1947; and Victor Anderson to Harry Kellogg, 15 May 1947; Papers of Governor Kim Sigler, Correspondence of the Legal Advisor Relating to Communism, Michigan Historical Division. *Olivet Optic*, 27 February 1947. *Detroit Free Press*, 21 February 1947.

58. Roy Thomas to Frank Blair, n.d.; Frank Blair to R. Norris Wilson, 7 September 1948; Olivet College Faculty List, 29 March 1949; Olivet Archives. *Olivet Echo*, 20 February; 24 March 1948. James A. Richards Jr., "The Distintegration of a Christian College," *The Progressive*, March 1949, pp. 19–21.

59. Roy Thomas to Frank Blair, n.d., Olivet Archives. *Detroit Free Press*, 18 September 1948. The non-conformity aspect is emphasized in Milton Mayer, "The Professor's Beret," *Nation*, November 27, 1948, p. 605; "The Bung and the Trough," *Time*, October 18, 1948, p. 63; and MacIver, *Academic Freedom in Our Time*, pp. 148–49. One problem in emphasizing the nonconformity aspect is that it ignores that much of the support for the purge came from outside of the village and even from large metropolitan areas, such as Detroit.

60. Student Action Committee, "Dear Friends, 24 September 1948;" Student Action Committee to President Ashby, 24 September 1948; President Ashby to Robert DeYoung, et al., 17 September 1948; President Ashby to Glen H. Allison, et al., 27 September 1948; "Procedure," 30 September 1948; President Ashby to Ray Ayer, et al., n.d.; Olivet Archives. "Bung and Trough," p. 63. *Olivet Optic*, 23, 30 September 1948. *Detroit Free Press*, 18, 20, 21, 22, 23, 24 September; 4 October 1948. Tucker P. Smith to Irvin Kuenzli, 27 September 1948; Papers of the Michigan Federation of Teachers, box 10, Olivet College Teachers Union, Labor Affairs, Wayne.

61. Student Petition, 18 October 1948; and Roy Thomas to Frank Blair, n.d.; Olivet Archives.

Olivet Echo, 17 November 1948. *Olivet Optic*, 7 October 1948. *Detroit Free Press*, 6 November 1948.

62. Olivet College Teachers Union to President Ashby, 6 December 1948; and Tucker Smith to Arthur Elder, 8 December 1948; Labor Affairs, Wayne. *Olivet Echo*, 19 January 1949. *Battle Creek Enquirer*, 12 February 1949. *Detroit Free Press*, 9, 10, 29 January 1949. *Olivet Optic*, 13, 27 January; 3 February 1949.

63. *Battle Creek Enquirer*, 14 March 1949. *Olivet Echo*, 29 April 1949. *Detroit Free Press*, 4 March; 6, 23 April; 8 May; 19 June 1949. President's Report, 28 January 1952, Olivet Archives.

64. *Cleveland Plain Dealer* 17 April 1947. *Cincinnati Enquirer*, 5 August 1951. SAIC, *Report 1947–1948*, p. 173. Joseph Ewers to George Stoddard, 19 January 1953; and George Stoddard to Joseph Ewers, 20 January 1953; Papers of George Stoddard, general correspondence, box 71, Dean of Students, Illinois Archives. I was unable to find if Frank Kornacker became involved in any other incidents, but Norman Cazden was questioned by HUAC in the spring of 1954.

65. J. B. Matthews, "Communism and the Colleges," *American Mercury*, May 1953, pp. 111–44. For the DeBoer charges, see the *Champaign-Urbana News-Gazette*, 10 June 1949; *Illinois State Journal*, 10 June 1949; *Daily Illini*, 2 May 1951; and Joseph Ewers to George Stoddard, 19 January 1953, Papers of George Stoddard, general correspondence, box 71, Dean of Students, Illinois Archives.

66. Preston, "War and Fear," p. 131. Chap. 6, n. 3 suggests others who would accept Preston's arguments.

67. In a slightly different context, William Spinrad points to decisionmaking resulting from four interrelated variables: "a set of values, specially involved roles, kinds of institutional structures and processes, and concrete situational factors;" *Civil Liberties*, p. 85.

68. Paul Lazarsfeld and Walter Thielens Jr., *The Academic Mind: Social Scientists in a Time of Crisis* (Glencoe, Il: Free Press, 1958), pp. 35, 85, 378.

Chapter 8

1. Two historians define "movement" narrowly, that is, requiring a formal organization. They thus deny that the scare was characterized by a movement. My quarrel with them is partially semantic. Seymour M. Lipset and Earl Raab, *The Politics of Unreason: Right-wing Extremism in America, 1790–1970* (New York: Harper and Row, 1970), pp. 209, 220. Sprinrad, *Civil Liberties*, p. 101.

2. Rogin, *Intellectuals and McCarthy*.

3. This is the only way that the concept of "relative deprivation" can be used in interpreting this period—in a political sense, not an economic one.

4. In the fall of 1945, a Unitarian minister in Dayton, Ohio, ran for the school board. Rumors linked Rev. Harold Marley to leftist causes, and he finished fifth in the election. A few weeks later, Marley's chances were revived when one of those who had been elected moved out of the city and resigned his position on the board. The decision on the vacancy was to be made by the school board. Rumors about Marley's leftist activities continued to circulate, and the school board president wrote to HUAC for information on the minister. The HUAC report, which was released to the press on January 11, 1946, listed six alleged Communist front affiliations. Marley admitted them, but interpreted them as legitimate

political expression of a liberal tendency. The *Dayton Journal* agreed with Marley's position, but the school board did not. By a five-to-one vote, it picked the PTA president, who had not run in the fall campaign. *Dayton Journal*, 3, 7, 8, 11, 12, 16, 24, 25 January 1946.

5. *Ann Arbor News*, 14 May to 4 June 1946. This paper was part of the Booth Publication Company, which owned several newspapers in Michigan. The series was designed to raise an alarm about Communist activities, but it was not sensational. It tried to be specific and to differentiate between leftists and Communists.

6. Griffith, "American Politics," pp. 14–16. Goldstein, *Political Repression*, pp. 348–49. Theoharis, "Rhetoric of Politics." Goldstein, *Political Repression*, p. 306. Freeland, *Truman Doctrine and McCarthyism*, p. 359. McAuliffe, *Crisis on the Left*, p. 2. Alan Yarnell, *Democrats and Progressives: The 1948 Presidential Election as a Test of Postwar Liberalism* (Berkeley: University of California Press, 1974), p. 107.

7. See V. O. Key's comment in footnote 60 of chapter 2.

8. George Gallup, *The Gallup Poll: Public Opinion, 1935-1971* (New York: Random House, 1972), pp. 587, 593, 639, 690, 736. Samual Stouffer, *Communism, Conformity, and Civil Liberties* (Garden City, New York: Doubleday and Co., 1954), pp. 75, 83, 86–87.

9. Theoharis cites a poll from February 1948 which supposedly reveals that 40% felt that the CP "posed *no* threat to the U.S." (his emphasis). The poll, which gave four choices, can be interpreted quite differently however:

   1. The CP is far too weak to have any power in the U.S.   —12%
   2. The CP in the U.S. is still comparatively weak, but it does have some power in a few industries and unions   —28%
   3. The CP in the U.S. is getting stronger, and it already controls a good many industries and unions.   —35%
   4. The CP in the U.S. is rapidly getting to the point where it can dominate the whole country.   —10%

   Theoharis combines #1 and #2 to get his 40% who totally deny that the CP is a threat, but it is just as valid to combine #2, 3, and 4 to find that 73% perceived the CP as some kind of threat. Theoharis, "Rhetoric of Politics," p. 233f.

10. Rogin, *Intellectuals and McCarthy*, p. 31.

11. Donald F. Crosby, *God, Church, and Flag: Senator Joseph R. McCarthy and the Catholic Church, 1950-1957* (Chapel Hill: University of North Carolina), p. 25.

12. Rogin, *Intellectuals and McCarthy*, p. 225.

13. Holmes, "Communism in Hawaii," p. xiii. Carleton, "Crisis of Rapid Change," pp. 66–68.

14. *International Encyclopedia of the Social Sciences*, s.v. "Elites," by Suzanne Keller. Suzanne Keller, *Beyond the Ruling Class: Strategic Elites in Modern Society* (New York: Random House, 1963), pp. 5, 20, 58. The theory that a single elite holds controlling power in the country has recently been convincingly critiqued in Nelson Polsby, *Community Power and Political Theory: A Further Look at Problems of Evidence and Inference*, 2d enlarged edition, (New Haven: Yale University Press, 1980).

15. V. O. Key, Jr., *Politics, Parties, and Pressure Groups*, (New York: Thomas Y. Crowell, 1958), p. 158.

16. Frank J. Donner, who is a severe critic of all Red Scare activities, admits that limitations occurred on the national level as well. Only 145 Communists were indicted for violating

the Smith Act, and only 29 were jailed. Frank J. Donner, *The Age of Surveillance: The Aims and Methods of America's Political Intelligence System* (New York: A. A. Knopf, 1980), p. 21.

Carey McWilliams, another leftist, also notes the mixed nature of the Scare. "Dissent was never wholly suppressed. . . . Most of the victims survived; not too many went to jail; not all those 'fingered' lost their jobs. . . . But it was a brutal business just the same." Carey McWilliams, *The Education of Carey McWilliams* (New York: Simon and Schuster, 1978), pp. 169, 185.

17. Spinrad, *Civil Liberties*, p. 310 n.9.

18. William A. Williams quoted in Christopher Lasch, *The Agony of the American Left* (New York: Vintage Books, 1969), p. 41f. Robert Goldstein also believes that the U.S. is heading toward a "totalitarian abyss:" *Political Repression*, p. 574.

Beneath this leftist rhetoric lies a difficult question: was the Second Red Scare more repressive than the first, which occurred after the First World War? Scholars need to begin comparative work on these two cases, and suggest some answers.

19. James T. Patterson, *The New Deal and the States: Federalism in Transition* (Princeton: Princeton University Press, 1969), p. 202.

20. This conclusion points to mood, or more precisely, political culture, as the central scholarly question. It is legitimate to analyze the rise of the scare: socio-economic changes (status anxiety), the activity of elites, the impact of the Cold War, the effect of rhetoric by national political leaders, etc. Most of the historical work has focused on this issue. Less has been done on the decline of the scare (the limitations of the conservative movement). Ultimately, the study of the scare must point to its relationship to the postwar era as a whole. This is the crux of the issue. From the rhetoric of conservatives at this time, they see themselves as outsiders. Yet liberals see themselves in the same way. So, who is in charge? Can historians give a noncontradictory answer to what constituted the political culture? The scare's depth, duration, and significance are not closed questions but matters of necessary debate.

Bibliography

Primary Sources

A. Manuscripts

Antiochiana, Antioch College, Yellow Springs, Ohio.
    Papers on the Robert Metcalf case
    Papers on the Robert Rempfer case
Archives of Labor and Urban Affairs, Wayne State University, Detroit.
    Civil Rights Congress
    Arthur Elder
    Richard Frankensteen
    Stanley Nowak
    Michigan Federation of Teachers
    Yale Stuart
Burton Historical Collection, Detroit Public Library, Detroit.
    Mayor's Papers (includes Edward Jeffries, Jr., Eugene Van Antwerp, and Albert Cobo)
    1945–1957
Chicago Historical Society, Chicago.
    Chicago Teachers Union
    Independent Voters of Illinois
    Ira H. Latimer
Department of Special Collections, University of Chicago, Chicago.
    American Civil Liberties Union, Chicago
    Office of Student Activities
    Presidential Papers, 1944–1962
    Presidential Papers, 1950–1955
Michigan Historical Collections, Bentley Historical Library, University of Michigan, Ann
    Arbor
    American Legion, Department of Michigan
    American Association of University Professors, UM
    John L. Brumm
    Henry H. Crane
    Donald Leonard
    Ralph Muncy
    Marvin L. Niehuss
    Harold Norris
    Alexander G. Ruthven

Special Advisory Committee on the Suspension of Drs. H. Chandler Davis, Mark
    Nickerson, and Clement I. Markert
G. Mennen Williams
Ohio Historical Society, Columbus.
    American Civil Liberties Union, Cleveland
    State of Ohio, Department of Education, Department of Film Censorship
    Ohio Socialist Labor Party
    Ohio Un-American Activities Committee
Olivet College Archives, Olivet, Michigan
    Administrative Papers 1946–1951
State Archives, Michigan Historical Division, Department of State, State of Michigan,
    Lansing.
    Kim Sigler
    Attorney General Records
State Archives, State of Illinois, Springfield.
    William Stratton
State Archives, State of Indiana, Indianapolis.
    Henry F. Schricker
University Archives, Ohio State University, Columbus.
    Howard Bevis
University Archives, University of Illinois, Urbana.
    American Association of University Professors, UI
    John J. DeBoer
    Coleman R. Griffith
    David D. Henry
    Wayne Johnston
    Lloyd Morey
    George Stoddard
    Harry Tiebout
University Archives, University of Wisconsin, Madison.
    American Association of University Professors
    Division of Student Affairs
    President E. B. Fred
University Archives, Wayne State University, Detroit.
    Division of Student Personnel
    Clarence Hilberry
    Arthur A. Neef
    Vertical File
Wisconsin State Historical Society, Madison.
    Americans for Democratic Action
    American Legion, Department of Wisconsin
    Fred B. Blair
    William Evjue
    Kenneth W. Hones

B. Newspapers

Ohio
    Akron Beacon Journal
    Canton Repository
    Cincinnati Enquirer

Cincinnati Post
Cincinnati Times Star
Cleveland News
Cleveland Plain Dealer
Columbus Citizen
Columbus Dispatch
Dayton Journal
Galion Inquirer
Ohio State Journal
Ohio State University Lantern
Yellow Springs American
Yellow Springs News
Illinois
    Champaign-Urbana Courier
    Champaign-Urbana News-Gazette
    Chicago Daily News
    Chicago Maroon (University of Chicago)
    Chicago Sun-Times
    Chicago Tribune
    Daily Illini (University of Illinois)
    Illinois State Journal
    Illinois State Register
    Peoria Journal (and Transcript)
    Peoria Star
Indiana
    Bloomington World
    Evansville Courier
    Gary Post-Tribune
    Indianapolis News
    Indianapolis Star
    Indianapolis Times
    Lafayette Journal
    Terre Haute Star
    Terre Haute Tribune
Michigan
    Ann Arbor News
    Battle Creek Enquirer
    Detroit Free Press
    Detroit News
    Detroit Times
    Ferndale Gazette
    Flint Journal
    Garden City Review
    Jackson Citizen Patriot
    Lansing State Journal
    Michigan Chronicle
    Michigan Daily (University of Michigan)
    Michigan State News
    Muskegon Chronicle
    Olivet Optic
    Wayne Collegian

Wisconsin
>   *Barron County Shield*
>   *Daily Cardinal* (University of Wisconsin)
>   *Delavan Enterprise*
>   *Madison Capital Times*
>   *Milwaukee Journal*
>   *Milwaukee Sentinel*
>   *Rice Lake Chronotype*
>   *Wisconsin State Journal*

C. Correspondence

Irwin Abrams
Howard Bowen
David Broder
Edward C. Budd
Wallace Collett
John V. Corrigan
H. Chandler Davis
Samuel Devine
Ann F. Ginger
Richard Guttman
Morse Johnson
Edward Likover
Carleton Mabee
George D. Pappas
George F. Parker
William Proxmire
James A. Richards, Jr.
George Shenkar
Sidney J. Socolar
La Rue Spiker
Edwin K. Steers

D. Interviews

Henrietta DeBoer
Harry Hilton
Harry Tiebout
George Stoddard (by Blair Kling)
Charles Shattuck (by Cathryn Corcoran)
John Due (by Renea Jones)

E. Governmental Hearings

U.S. Congress. House. Committee on Un-American Activities.
>   *Investigation of Un-American Propaganda Activities in the United States*, 80th Congress,
>   1st session, 1947.
>   *Hearings Regarding Communist Activities in the Cincinnati, Ohio Area*, 81st Congress,
>   2nd session, 1950.
>   *Communism in the Detroit Area*, 82nd Congress, 2nd session, 1952.

Investigation of Communist Activities in the Columbus, Ohio Area, 83rd Congress, 1st session, 1953.
Communist Methods of Infiltration (Education), 83rd Congress, 1st session, 1953.
Investigation of Communist Activities in the Dayton, Ohio Area, 83rd Congress, 2nd session, 1954.
Investigation of Communist Activities in the Chicago Area, 83rd Congress, 2nd session, 1954.
Investigation of Communist Activities in the State of Michigan, 83rd Congress, 2nd session, 1954.
Investigation of Communist Activities in the Ohio Area, 84th Congress, 1st session, 1955.
U.S. Congress. House. Committee on Education and Labor.
Labor Education Extension Service. 80th Congress, 2nd session, 1948.
U.S. Congress. Senate. Committee on the Judiciary. Subcommittee to Investigate the Administration of the Internal Security Act.
Communist Tactics in Controlling Youth Organizations. 82nd Congress, 1st session, 1951.
Subversive Influences in the Educational Process. 83rd Congress, 1st session, 1953.

F. Other Governmental Documents

The Book of the States. Chicago: Council of State Governments, 1948-49, 1950-51, 1952-53, 1954-55, 1956-57.
Illinois, Seditious Activities Investigating Commission. *Report, 1947-1948*. Springfield: State of Illinois, 1949.
Illinois, Seditious Activities Investigating Commission. *Report of the Investigation of the University of Chicago and Roosevelt College*. Springfield: State of Illinois, 1949.
Journal of the House of Representatives of the 65th General Assembly of the State of Illinois. Springfield: State of Illinois, 1947. 66th session, 1949; 67th session, 1951; 68th session, 1953; and 69th session, 1955.
Journal of the House of Representatives of the 97th General Assembly of the State of Ohio. Columbus: F. J. Heer Printing Co., 1947. 98th session, 1949; 99th session, 1951; 100th session, 1953; 101st session, 1955.
Journal of the House of Representatives of the State of Michigan, 1947 Regular session. Lansing: Franklin de Kleine Co., 1947. 1948 extra session, 1949 regular session, 1950 extra session, 1951 regular session, 1952 extra session, 1953 regular session, 1954 regular session, 1955 regular session.
Journal of the Indiana House of Representatives of the State of Indiana, 85th session of the General Assembly. Indianapolis: Bookwalter Co., 1947. 86th session, 1949; 87th session, 1951; 88th session, 1953; 89th session, 1955; 90th session, 1957.
Journal of the Indiana Senate of the State of Indiana, 85th session of the General Assembly. Indianapolis: Bookwalter Co., 1947. 86th session, 1949; 87th session, 1951; 88th session, 1953; 89th session, 1955; 90th session, 1957.
Journal of the Proceedings of the 68th session of the Wisconsin Legislature: Assembly. Madison: Democratic Printing Co., 1947. 69th session, 1949; 70th session 1951; 71st session, 1953; 72nd session, 1955.
Journal of the Proceedings of the 68th session of the Wisconsin Legislature: Senate. Madison: Democratic Printing Co., 1947. 69th session, 1949; 70th session 1951; 71st session, 1953; 72nd session, 1955.
Journal of the Senate of the 65th General Assembly of the State of Illinois. Springfield: State of Illinois, 1947. 66th session, 1949; 67th session, 1951; 68th session, 1953; 69th session, 1955.
Journal of the Senate of the 97th General Assembly of the State of Ohio. Columbus: F. J. Heer

Printing Co., 1947. 98th session, 1949; 99th session, 1951; 100th session, 1953; 101st session, 1955.

Journal of the Senate of the State of Michigan, 1947 Regular session. Lansing: Franklin de Kleine Co., 1947. 1948 extra session; 1949 regular session; 1950 extra session; 1951 extra session; 1952 extra session; 1953 regular session; 1954 extra session; 1955 regular session.

G. Court Cases

Albertson v. Attorney General, State of Michigan, 345 Mich 519, 77 NW 2d 104 (1956).
Albertson v. Millard, 106 F.Supp 635, 345 US 242, 73 SCt 600.
Chicago Housing Authority v. Blackman, 4 Ill 2d 319, 122 NE 2d 522 (1954).
Dworken v. Board of Education, Cleveland, 42 Ohio Opinions 240, 46 00 194, 57 OLA 449, 63 OLA 10.
Dworken v. Collopy, 56 OLA 513, 91 NE 2d 564 (1950).
In re Anastaplo, 3 Ill 2d 471, 121 NE 2d 826 (1954), 18 Ill 2d 182, 348 US 946, 366 US 82 (1961).
MacDougall v. Green 335 US 281 (1948).
Pickus v. Board of Education, City of Chicago, 9 Ill 2d 599, 138 NE 2d 532 (1956).
Slagle v. State of Ohio, 170 Ohio St 216, 163 NE 2d 177, 366 US 259, 81 SCt 1076.
State of Ohio v. Arnold, 69 OLA 148, 124 NE 2d 473 (1954).
State of Ohio v. Morgan, 164 OS 529, 133 NE 2d 104, 354 US 929, 147 NE 2d 847, 360 US 423.
State of Ohio v. Raley, 100 OA 75, 136 NE 2d 295, 164 OS 529, 360 US 423, 79 SCt 1257.
State, ex. rel. Beck v. Hummel, 150 OS 127, 80 NE 2d 899 (1948).
State, ex. rel. Smilack v. Bushong 159 OS 259, 111 NE 2d 918 (1953).

H. Reports, Proceedings, and Other Miscellaneous Material

American Civil Liberties Union. *Annual Report 1951–1953.* New York: n.p., 1953.
American Civil Liberties Union. *Annual Report 1954–1955.* New York: n.p., 1955.
American Legion, Department of Illinois. *Report of the 29th Annual Convention.* Chicago: n.p., 1947.
American Legion, Department of Illinois. *Report of the 30th Annual Convention.* Chicago: n.p., 1948.
American Legion, Department of Illinois. *Report of the 31st Annual Convention.* Chicago: n.p., 1949.
American Legion, Department of Illinois. *Report of the 32nd Annual Convention.* Chicago: n.p., 1950.
American Legion, Department of Illinois. *Report of the 33rd Annual Convention.* Chicago: n.p., 1951.
American Legion, Department of Illinois. *Report of the 34th Annual Convention.* Chicago: n.p., 1952.
American Legion, Department of Illinois. *Report of the 35th Annual Convention.* Chicago: n.p., 1953.
American Legion, Department of Illinois. *Report of the 36th Annual Convention.* Chicago: n.p., 1954.
American Legion, Department of Illinois. *Report of the 37th Annual Convention.* Chicago: n.p., 1955.
American Legion, Department of Michigan. *Proceedings of the 29th Annual Convention.* Detroit: n.p., 1947.
American Legion, Department of Michigan. *Proceedings of the 30th Annual Convention.* Detroit: n.p., 1948.
American Legion, Department of Michigan. *Proceedings of the 31st Annual Convention.* Detroit: n.p., 1949.

American Legion, Department of Michigan. *Proceedings of the 32nd Annual Convention.* Detroit: n.p., 1950.

American Legion, Department of Michigan. *Proceedings of the 33rd Annual Convention.* Detroit: n.p., 1951.

American Legion, Department of Michigan. *Proceedings of the 34th Annual Convention.* Detroit: n.p., 1952.

American Legion, Department of Michigan. *Proceedings of the 35th Annual Convention.* Detroit: n.p., 1953.

American Legion, Department of Michigan. *Proceedings of the 36th Annual Convention.* Detroit: n.p., 1954.

American Legion, Department of Michigan. *Proceedings of the 37th Annual Convention.* Detroit: n.p., 1955.

The Brief.

Chicago, Board of Education. *Proceedings 1947-1948.* Chicago: n.p., 1948.

Chicago Union Teacher.

Civil Liberties Docket.

Civil Liberties News.

Counterattack

Detroit, Board of Education. *Proceedings 1945-1946.* Detroit: n.p., 1946.

Detroit, Board of Education. *Proceedings 1951-1952.* Detroit: n.p., 1952.

Detroit, Board of Education. *Proceedings 1953-1954.* Detroit: n.p., 1954.

McCarthy, Joseph R. *McCarthyism: The Fight for America.* New York: Devin-Adair, 1952.

McClenaghan, William A., rev. *Magruder's American Government.* Boston: Allyn and Bacon, 1953.

Magruder, Frank A. *American Government: A Consideration of the Problems of Democracy.* Boston: Allyn and Bacon, 1948.

National Education Association, Committee on Academic Freedom and Tenure. *Report of 1948.* Washington, D.C.: n.p., 1948.

Ohio State University, Board of Trustees. *Proceedings, 1952-1953.* Columbus: Ohio State University Press, 1953.

United States, Library of Congress, Legislative Reference Service, American Law Division. *Internal Security and Subversion: Principal State Laws and Cases.* Washington, D.C.: U.S. Government Printing Office, 1965.

University of Illinois, Board of Trustees. *45th Annual Report, 1948-1950.* Urbana: University of Illinois Press.

University of Illinois, Board of Trustees. *46th Annual Report, 1950-1952.* Urbana: University of Illinois Press.

University of Illinois, Board of Trustees. *47th Annual Report, 1952-1954.* Urbana: University of Illinois Press.

University of Illinois, Board of Trustees. *48th Annual Report, 1954-1956.* Urbana: University of Illinois Press.

University of Michigan, Board of Regents. *Proceedings, 1948-1949.* Ann Arbor: University of Michigan Press, 1949.

Secondary Works

A. The Midwest

American Association of University Professors, Committee A on Academic Freedom and Tenure. "Academic Freedom And Tenure, Evansville College." *AAUP Bulletin* 35 (Spring 1949):74-111.

———. "University of Michigan." *AAUP Bulletin* 44 (March 1958):53-101.

————, Special Committee, "Academic Freedom and Tenure in the Quest for National Security—Ohio State University." *AAUP Bulletin* 42 (Spring 1956):81–83.

————. "Academic Freedom and Tenure in the Quest for National Security—University of Michigan." *AAUP Bulletin* 42 (Spring 1956):89–92.

————, "Academic Freedom and Tenure in the Quest for National Security—Wayne University." *AAUP Bulletin* 42 (Spring 1956):87–89.

Andrew, William D. "Factionalism and Anti-Communism: Ford Local 600." *Labor History* 20 (Spring 1979):227–55.

Bagdikian, Ben H. "What Happened to the Girl Scouts?" *Atlantic*, May 1955. pp. 63–64.

Bartholomew, Paul C. *The Indiana Third Congressional District*. South Bend: University of Notre Dame Press, 1970.

Boyd, Maurice R. "The Effect of Censorship Attempts by Private Pressure Groups on Public Libraries." Master's thesis, Kent State University, 1959.

"The Bung and the Trough." *Time*, October 18, 1948, p. 63.

Christenson, Leo M. "The Power of the Press: The Case of the *Toledo Blade*." *Midwest Journal of Political Science* 3 (August 1959):227–40.

Clutter, Richard M. "The Indiana American Legion, 1919–1960." Ph.D. dissertation, Indiana University, 1974.

Clark, Thomas D. *Indiana University, Midwestern Pioneer: Years of Fulfillment*. Bloomington: Indiana University Press, 1977.

Clive, Alan G. "The Society and Economy of Wartime Michigan, 1939–1945." Ph.D. dissertation, University of Michigan, 1976.

Conot, Robert. *American Odyssey*. New York: Morrow and Co., 1974.

Current, Richard N. *Wisconsin*. New York: Norton, 1977.

Davis, Kenneth. "East is East and Midwest is Midwest." *New York Times Magazine*, November 20, 1949, p. 17.

Demartini, Joseph R. "Student Protest during Two Periods in the History of the University of Illinois, 1867–1894 and 1929–1942." Ph.D. dissertation, University of Illinois, 1974.

Derge, David R. "Metropolitan and Outstate Alignments in the Illinois and Missouri Legislative Delegations." *American Political Science Review* 52 (December 1958):1051–1065.

Donovan, Leo. "Detroit: City of Conflict." In *Our Fair City*, pp. 148–67. Edited by Robert Allen. New York: Vanguard Press, 1947.

Douglas, Paul H. *In The Fullness of Time: Memoirs*. New York: Harcourt, Brace, Jovanovich, 1971.

Downing, Francis. "Stockholm and Detroit." *Commonweal*, August 18, 1950, pp. 458–60.

Dunbar, Willis F. *Michigan: A History of the Wolverine State*. Grand Rapids: William B. Eerdmans Publ. Co., 1965.

Ebert, Roger, ed. *An Illini Century: 100 Years of Campus Life*. Urbana: University of Illinois Press, 1967.

Epstein, Leon. *Politics in Wisconsin*. Madison: University of Wisconsin Press, 1958.

Fairfield, William S. "How the Reds Came to Haugen, Wisconsin." *The Reporter*, January 5, 1954, pp. 24–26.

Feer, Robert. "Academic Freedom at State Universities: The University of Illinois, 1867–1950, as a Case Study." Master's thesis, Harvard University, 1950.

Fenton, John H. *Midwest Politics*. New York: Holt, Rinehart and Winston, 1960.

Ferguson, LeRoy C., and Smuckler, Ralph M. *Politics in the Press: An Anlysis of Press Content in the 1952 Senatorial Campaigns*. East Lansing: Michigan State College Press, 1954.

Fetter, Frank W. "Witch Hunt in the Lincoln Country." *AAUP Bulletin* 41 (Summer 1955):231–40.

Flinn, Thomas A. "Continuity and Change in Ohio Politics." *Journal of Politics* 24 (August 1962):521–44.

_____. "The Outline of Ohio Politics." *Western Political Quarterly* 13 (September 1960): 702–21.

Gatherum, Patricia N. "Film Censorship in Ohio: A Study in Symbolism." Seminar Paper, Ohio State University, 1974.

Gietschier, Steven P. "Limited War and the Home Front: Ohio during the Korean War." Ph.D. dissertation, Ohio State University, 1977.

Good, Harry G. *The Rise of the College of Education of The Ohio State University.* Columbus: Ohio State University Press, 1960.

Griffith, Robert. "The General and the Senator: Republican Politics and the 1952 Campaign in Wisconsin." *Wisconsin Magazine of History* 54 (Autumn 1970):23–29.

Hanawalt, Leslie L. *A Place of Light: The History of Wayne State University.* Detroit: Wayne State University Press, 1968.

Haney, Richard C. "A History of the Democratic Party of Wisconsin since World War Two." Ph.D. dissertation, University of Wisconsin, 1970.

Harsha, E. Houston. "Illinois: The Broyles Commission." In *The States and Subversion,* pp. 54–139. Edited by Walter Gellhorn. Ithaca: Cornell University Press, 1952.

Herrick, Mary J. *The Chicago Schools: A Social and Political History.* Beverly Hills: Sage Publications, 1971.

Hessler, William H. "It Didn't Work in Cincinnati." *The Reporter* 9 (December 22, 1953): 131–70.

Hill, Dietrich, A. "Meeting the Charge of Communism: A Study of the Speech Given by Paul H. Douglas September 22, 1948 at Urbana, Illinois." Master's thesis, University of Illinois, 1949.

Hill, Warren P. "A Critique of Recent Ohio Anti-Subversive Legislation." *Ohio State Law Journal* 14 (Autumn 1953):439–93.

Howard, Robert P. *Illinois: A History of the Prairie State.* Grand Rapids: William B. Eerdmans Publishing Company, 1972.

Jensen, Richard H. *Illinois.* New York: Norton, 1978.

Johnson, Walter, ed. *The Papers of Adlai Stevenson: Governor of Illinois, 1949–1953.* Boston: Little, Brown, 1973.

Jones, James T. "The Progressive Party in Illinois, 1947–1948." Master's thesis, University of Illinois, 1953.

Kamin, Kay H. "A History of the Hunt Administration of the Chicago Public Schools, 1947–1953." Ph.D. dissertation, University of Chicago, 1970.

Keefe, William J. "Party Government and Lawmaking in the Illinois General Assembly." *Northwestern University Law Review* 47 (March-April 1952):55–71.

Knepper, George. *New Lamps for Old: 100 Years of Urban Higher Education at the University of Akron.* Akron: University of Akron Press, 1970.

Komaiko, Charles, and Komaiko, Jean. "The Illinois Legion and 'Positive Americanism.'" *The Reporter,* April 7, 1955, pp. 34–36.

LaPalombara, Joseph. *Guide to Michigan Politics.* East Lansing: Michigan State University Press, 1960.

London, Ephraim S. "Heresy and the Illinois Bar: The Application of George Anastaplo for Admission." *Lawyers Guild Review* 12 (Fall 1952):163–76.

McGrane, Reginald C. *The University of Cincinnati: A Success Story in Urban Higher Education.* New York: Harper and Row, 1963.

Maher, Richard L. "Ohio: Oxcart Government." In *Our Sovereign State,* pp. 166–88. Edited by Robert S. Allen. New York: Vanguard Press, 1949.

Martin, John Bartlow. *Adlai Stevenson of Illinois.* Garden City, N.Y.: Doubleday, 1976.

Mayer, Martin. "The Professor's Beret." *Nation,* November 27, 1948, pp. 605–6.

Mowitz, Robert J. "Michigan: State and Local Attacks on Subversion." In *The States and Subversion,* pp. 184–230. Edited by Walter Gellhorn. Ithaca: Cornell University Press, 1952.

Munger, Frank. *The Struggle for Republican Leadership in Indiana, 1954*. New York: McGraw-Hill, 1960.

Neikind, Clair. "U.S. Communists—1950." *The Reporter*, June 6, 1950, pp. 7–10.

Nesbit, Robert C. *Wisconsin: A History*. Madison: University of Wisconsin Press, 1973.

Nikoloric, L.A. "AVC—Innocent No More." *Progressive*, May 1949, pp. 11–13.

O'Brien, Michael J. "The Anti-McCarthy Campaign in Wisconsin, 1951–1952." *Wisconsin Magazine of History* 56 (Winter 1972–73):91–108.

―――. "McCarthy and McCarthyism: The Cedric Parker Case, November 1949." In *The Specter: Original Essays on the Cold War and the Origins of 'McCarthyism,'* pp. 224–39. Edited by Athan Theoharis and Robert Griffith. New York: Franklin Watts, 1974.

―――. *McCarthy and McCarthyism in Wisconsin*. Columbia: University of Missouri Press, 1980.

―――. "Senator Joseph McCarthy and Wisconsin, 1947–1957." Ph.D. dissertation, University of Wisconsin, 1971.

Oshinsky, David M. *Senator Joseph McCarthy and the American Labor Movement*. Columbia: University of Missouri Press, 1976.

Patterson, James T. *Mr. Republican: A Biography of Robert A. Taft*. Boston: Houghton Mifflin Co., 1972.

Peckham, Howard H. *Indiana*. New York: Norton, 1978.

―――. *The Making of the University of Michigan, 1817–1967*. Ann Arbor: University of Michigan Press, 1967.

Petrovich, Peter B. "Taft and the Ohio Press," *The Reporter*, December 12, 1950, pp. 36–37.

Pevos, Daniel N. "The Present Status of Michigan Anti-Subversive Legislation." *Wayne Law Review* 2 (Summer 1956):221–28.

Pierce, Martin G. "Red-Hunting in Illinois, 1947–1949: The Broyles Commission." Master's thesis, University of Wisconsin, 1959.

Plochman, George K. *The Ordeal of Southern Illinois University*. Carbondale: Southern Illinois University Press, 1957.

Pollard, James E. *The History of The Ohio State University, The Bevis Administration, 1940–1956: The Postwar Years and the Emergence of the Greater University, 1945–1956*. Columbus: Ohio State University Press, 1960.

Preston, Donna J. "Newspaper Influence on the Broyles' Bill in the 1951 Illinois Legislature." Master's thesis, University of Illinois, 1952.

Ranney, Austin. *Illinois Politics*. New York: New York University Press, 1960.

"Reporter's Notes." *The Reporter*, October 6, 1955, pp. 4–5.

Richards, James A., Jr. "The Disintegration of a Christian College." *Progressive*, March 1949, pp. 19–21.

Rorty, James. "The Attack on our Liberties." In *The First Freedom*, pp. 303–310. Edited by Robert B. Downs. Chicago: American Library Association, 1960.

Sarasohn, Stephen B., and Sarasohn, Vera H. *Political Party Patterns in Michigan*. Detroit: Wayne State University Press, 1957.

Sawyer, Robert B. *The Democratic State Central Committee in Michigan, 1949–1959*. Ann Arbor: Institute of Public Administration, University of Michigan, 1960.

Smith, Carl O., and Sarasohn, Stephen B. "Hate Propaganda in Detroit." *Public Opinion Quarterly* 10 (Spring 1946):24–52.

Sorenson, Dale. "The Anti-Communist Impulse in Indiana, 1945–1957." Ph.D. dissertation, Indiana University, 1980.

Straetz, Ralph A. *PR Politics in Cincinnati: Thirty-two Years of City Government Through Proportional Representation*. Washington Square, N.Y.: New York University Press, 1958.

Strickland, Arvah E. *The History of the Chicago Urban League*. Urbana: University of Illinois Press, 1966.

Thayer, Frederick C., Jr. "The Ohio Un-American Activities Commission." Master's thesis, Ohio State University Press, 1954.

Thelen, David P., and Thelen, Esther S. "Joe Must Go: The Movement to Recall Senator Joseph McCarthy." *Wisconsin Magazine of History* 49 (Spring 1966):185–209.

Weissman, David L. "Heresy and the Illinois Bar." *Lawyers Guild Review* 9 (Winter 1959): 126–64.

Williamson, Harold F., and Wild, Payson S. *Northwestern University, A History, 1850–1975.* Evanston: Northwestern University Press, 1976.

Wilson, James Q. *The Amateur Democrat: Club Politics in Three Cities.* Chicago: University of Chicago Press, 1962.

Woodford, Frank B. *Alex J. Groesbeck: Portrait of a Public Man.* Detroit: Wayne State University Press, 1962.

Zeidenstein, Harvey. "The A.C.L.U. and the Broyles Bills, 1949–1955." Master's thesis, University of Chicago, 1957.

Ziegler, Ruth. "The Chicago Civil Liberties Committee, 1929–1938." Master's thesis, University of Chicago, 1938.

B. General Works

Altbach, Philip, and Peterson, Patti. "Before Berkeley." In *The New Pilgrims: Youth Protest in Transition,* pp. 13–31. Edited by Philip Altbach and Robert Laufer. New York: McKay Co., 1972.

Altbach, Philip. *Student Politics in America: A Historical Analysis.* New York: McGraw-Hill Co., 1974.

American Municipal Association. *Loyalty Oaths for Municipal Employees.* Chicago: American Municipal Assoc., 1954.

"Anti-Intellectualism in the U.S." *Journal of Social Issues* 9, no. 3 (1955).

Auerbach, Jerold S. *Unequal Justice: Lawyers and Social Change in Modern America.* New York: Oxford University Press, 1976.

Barth, Alan. *Government by Investigation.* New York: Viking Press, 1955.

———. *The Loyalty of Free Men.* New York: Archon Books, 1965.

Beale, Howard K. *Are American Teachers Free?* New York: Scribners, 1936.

———. *A History of Freedom of Teaching in American Schools.* New York: Scribners, 1941.

Bean, Louis H. *Influences in the 1954 Mid-term Elections: War, Jobs, Parity, McCarthy.* Washington: Public Affairs Institute, 1954.

Beck, Carl. *Contempt of Congress: A Study of the Prosecutions Initiated by the Committee on Un-American Activities, 1945–1957.* New Orleans: Houser Press, 1959.

Beck, Hubert. *Men Who Control Our Universities.* New York: King's Crown Press, 1947.

Belknap, Michael. *Cold War Political Justice: The Smith Act, the Communist Party, and American Civil Liberties.* Westport, Conn.: Greenwood Press, 1977.

———. "Joe Must Go." *Reviews in American History* 7 (June 1979):256–61.

Bell, Daniel. "Interpretations of American Politics." In *The New American Right,* pp. 3–32. Edited by Daniel Bell. New York: Criterion Books, 1955.

———. ed. *The Radical Right.* Garden City, N.Y.: Doubleday, 1964.

Berman, William C. "Civil Rights and Civil Liberties." In *The Truman Period as a Research Field,* p. 187–212. Edited by Richard Kirkendall. Columbia: University of Missouri Press, 1967.

———. *The Politics of Civil Rights in the Truman Administration.* Columbus: Ohio State University Press, 1970.

Bernstein, Barton J. "Commentary." In *The Truman Period as a Research Field: A Reapprais al, 1972*, pp. 161–190. Edited by Richard Kirkendall. Columbia: University of Missouri Press, 1974.

———. "Hindsight on McCarthyism." *The Progressive*, June 1971, pp. 43–45.

———. "America in War and Peace: The Test of Liberalism." In *Towards a New Past: Dissenting Essays in American History*, pp. 289–321. Edited by Barton J. Bernstein. New York: Vintage Books, 1967.

———. "Truman, the 80th Congress, and the Transformation of Political Culture." *Capitol Studies* 2 (Spring 1973):65–75.

Biberman, Herbert. *Salt of the Earth: The Story of a Film*. Boston: Beacon Press, 1965.

Bigman, Stanley. "The 'New Internationalism' Under Attack." *Public Opinion Quarterly* 14 (Summer 1950):235–61.

Blanshard, Paul. *The Right to Read: The Battle Against Censorship*. Boston: Beacon Press, 1955.

Bontecou, Eleanor. *The Federal Loyalty-Security Program*. Ithaca: Cornell University Press.

Borah, Donald. "Free Expression in Four State Supreme Courts." Master's thesis, University of Illinois, 1966.

Breslow, Paul. "Students for America: Campus McCarthyism." *Nation* 178 (March 20, 1954):240–41.

Brock, Clifton. *Americans for Democratic Action*. Washington: Public Affairs Press, 1965.

Brown, Ralph S., Jr. *Loyalty and Security: Employment Tests in the United States*. New Haven: Yale University Press, 1958.

Brubacher, John S., and Rudy, Willis. *Higher Education in Transition: A History of American Colleges and Universities*. New York: Harper and Row Publ., 1976.

Bryson, Joseph E. *Legality of Loyalty Oath and Non-oath Requirements for Public School Teachers*. Boone, N.C.: Miller Printing Co., 1963.

Buckley, William F. *God and Man at Yale*. Chicago: Regnery, 1951.

———, and Bozell, L. Brent. *McCarthy and His Enemies*. Chicago: Regnery, 1954.

Butts, R. Freeman. "Public Education and Political Community." In *History, Education, and Public Policy*, pp. 90–116. Edited by Donald Warren. Berkeley: McCutchan Publ. Corp., 1978.

Calkins, Fay. *The CIO and the Democratic Party*. Chicago: University of Chicago Press, 1952.

Carleton, Don E. "A Crisis of Rapid Change: The Red Scare in Houston, 1945–1955." Ph.D. dissertation, University of Houston, 1978.

Carr, Robert K. *The House Committee on Un-American Activities, 1945–1950*. Ithaca: Cornell University Press, 1952.

Casper, Jonathan D. "Lawyers and Loyalty-Security Litigation." *Law and Society Review* 3 (May 1969):575–96.

———. *The Politics of Civil Liberties*. New York: Harper and Row, 1972.

Caughey, John W. "McCarthyism Rampant." In *The Pulse of Freedom: American Liberties, 1920–1970s*, pp. 154–210. Edited by Alan Reitman. New York: Norton, 1975.

Caute, David. *The Great Fear: The Anti-Communist Purges Under Truman and Eisenhower*. New York: Simon and Schuster, 1978.

Chafee, Zechariah, Jr. *Free Speech in the United States*. Cambridge: Harvard University Press, 1941.

Cochran, Bert. *Labor and Communism: The Conflict that Shaped American Unions*. Princeton: Princeton University Press, 1977.

Cohen, Sol. "History of Education as a Field of Study: An Essay on the Recent History of American Education." In *History, Education, and Public Policy*, pp. 35–55. Edited by Donald Warren. Berkeley: McCutchan Publ. Corp., 1978.

Crampton, John A. *The National Farmers Union: Ideology of a Pressure Group*. Lincoln: University of Nebraska Press, 1965.

Cramton, Roger C. "The Supreme Court and State Power to Deal with Subversion and Loyalty." *Minnesota Law Review* 43 (May 1959):1025-82.

Cremin, Lawrence A. "Public Education and the Education of the Public." In *History, Education, and Public Policy*, pp. 22-34. Edited by Donald Warren. Berkeley: McCutchan Publ. Corp., 1978.

_____. *The Transformation of the School: Progressivism in American Education, 1876-1957.* New York: Knopf, 1961.

Crosby, Donald F. *God, Church, and Flag: Senator Joseph R. McCarthy and the Catholic Church, 1950-1957.* Chapel Hill: University of North Carolina Press, 1978.

Dahl, Robert A. "A Critique of the Ruling Elite Model." *American Political Science Review* 52 (June 1958):463-69.

Dalfiume, Richard M. "The 'Forgotten Years' of the Negro Revolution." *Journal of American History* 55 (June 1968):90-106.

"The Danger Signals." *Time*, April 13, 1953, pp. 85-88.

David, Paul T., et al., eds. *Presidential Nominating Politics in 1952: The Middle West.* vol. 4. Baltimore: Johns Hopkins Press, 1954.

Davis, David Brion, ed. *The Fear of Conspiracy: Images of Un-American Subversion from the Revolution to the Present.* Ithaca: Cornell University Press, 1971.

Davis, H. Chandler. "From an Exile." In *The New Professors*, pp. 182-201. Edited by Robert O. Bowen. New York: Harcourt, Brace, and World, 1960.

Dennis, Peggy. *The Autobiography of an American Communist: A Personal View of a Political Life.* Westport: Lawrence Hill and Co., 1977.

Dickstein, Morris. *Gates of Eden: American Culture in the 60s.* New York: Basic Books, 1977.

Donner, Frank J. *The Age of Surveillance: The Aims and Methods of America's Political Intelligence System.* New York: A. A. Knopf, 1980.

_____. *The Un-Americans.* New York: Ballantine Books, 1961.

Dreyfus, Benjamin, and Walker, Doris B. "Grounds and Procedures for Discipline of Attorneys." *Lawyers Guild Review* 18 (Summer 1958):67-78.

Dunaway, David King. *How Can I Keep from Singing: Pete Seeger.* New York: McGraw-Hill, 1981.

Dyson, Lowell K. *Red Harvest: The Communist Party and American Farmers.* Lincoln: University of Nebraska Press, 1982.

Edelman, Murray. *The Symbolic Uses of Politics.* Urbana: University of Illinois Press, 1967.

"Effectiveness of State Anti-Subversive Legislation." *Indiana Law Journal* 28 (Summer 1953):492-520.

Elazar, Daniel. *American Federalism: A View from the States.* New York: Thomas Y. Crowell, 1972.

_____. *Cities of the Prairie: The Metropolitan Frontier and American Politics.* New York: Basic Books, 1970.

Fiske, Marjorie. *Book Selection and Censorship: A Study of School and Public Libraries in California.* Berkeley: University of California Press, 1959.

FitzGerald, Frances. *America Revised: History Schoolbooks in the Twentieth Century.* Boston: Little, Brown, and Co., 1979.

Foster, James C. *The Union Politic: The CIO-Political Action Committee.* Columbia: University of Missouri Press, 1975.

Freeland, Richard. *The Truman Doctrine and the Origins of McCarthyism: Foreign Policy, Domestic Policy, and Internal Security, 1946-1948.* New York: Knopf, 1973.

Fried, Richard M. *Men Against McCarthy.* New York: Columbia University Press, 1976.

Fund for the Republic. *Digest of the Public Record of Communism in the United States.* New York: Fund for the Republic, 1955.

Gaddis, John Lewis. *The United States and the Origins of the Cold War, 1941-1947.* New York: Columbia University Press, 1972.

Gallup, George H. *The Gallup Poll: Public Opinion, 1935-1951.* New York: Random House, 1972.

Gardner, David P. *The California Oath Controversy.* Berkeley: University of California Press, 1967.

Gellhorn, Walter, ed. *The States and Subversion.* Ithaca: Cornell University Press, 1952.

Gellhorn, Walter. *Security, Loyalty, and Science.* Ithaca: Cornell University Press, 1950.

Glazer, Nathan, and Lipset, Seymour M. "The Polls on Communism and Conformity." In *The New American Right,* pp. 141-65. Edited by Daniel Bell. New York: Criterion Books, 1955.

Glazer, Nathan. *The Social Basis of American Communism.* New York: Harcourt, Brace, 1961.

Goldman, Eric. *The Crucial Decade—And After, 1945-1960.* New York: Vintage Books, 1960.

————. *Rendezvous with Destiny.* New York: Vintage Books, 1955.

Goldstein, Robert J. *Political Repression in Modern America.* Cambridge: Schenkman Publ. Co., 1978.

Goodman, Walter. *The Committee: The Extraordinary Career of the House Committee on Un-American Activities.* New York: Farrar, Strauss and Giroux, 1964.

Gornick, Vivian. *The Romance of American Communism.* New York: Basic Books, 1977.

Griffith, Robert. "American Politics and the Origins of 'McCarthyism.'" In *The Specter: Original Essays on the Cold War and the Origins of McCarthyism,* pp. 2-17. Edited by Athan Theoharis and Robert Griffith. New York: Franklin Watts, 1974.

————. "The Political Context of McCarthyism." *Review of Politics* 33 (January 1971):24-35.

————. "The Politics of Anti-Communism." *Wisconsin Magazine of History* 54 (Summer 1971):299-308.

————. *Politics of Fear: Joseph R. McCarthy and the Senate.* Lexington: University of Kentucky Press, 1970.

Grissom, Thomas. "Education and the Cold War: The Role of James B. Conat." In *Roots of Crisis: American Education in the Twentieth Century,* pp. 177-97. Edited by Clarence J. Karier, et al. Chicago: Rand McNally College Publ. Co., 1973.

Gruber, Carol S. *Mars and Minerva: World War One and the Uses of Higher Learning In America.* Baton Rouge: Louisiana University Press, 1975.

Gunther, John. *Inside the U.S.A.* New York: Harper and Brothers, 1947.

Hamby, Alonzo L. *Beyond the New Deal: Harry S. Truman and American Liberalism.* New York: Columbia University Press, 1973.

————. "The Clash of Perspectives and the Need for New Syntheses." In *The Truman Period as a Research Field: A Reappraisal, 1972,* pp. 113-48. Edited by Richard Kirkendall. Columbia: University of Missouri Press, 1974.

————. "The Liberals: Truman and FDR as Symbol and Myth." *Journal of American History* 56 (March 1970), 859-967.

Harper, Alan. *The Politics of Loyalty: White House and the Communist Issue, 1946-1952.* Westport, Conn.: Greenwood Publ. Corp., 1969.

Harrington, Michael. *Fragments of the Century: A Personal and Social Retrospective of the 50's and 60's.* New York: Simon and Schuster, 1972.

Hartz, Louis. *The Liberal Tradition in America.* New York: Harcourt, Brace, and World, 1955.

Hawley, Willis D., and Wirt, Frederick M., eds. *The Search for Community Power.* Englewood Cliffs, N.J.: Prentice-Hall, 1968.

Heath, Jim F. "Domestic America during World War Two: Research Opportunities for Historians." *Journal of American History* 58 (September 1971):384-414.

Henry, David Dodds. *Challenges Past, Challenges Present: American Higher Education since 1930.* San Francisco: Jossey-Bass Publ., 1975.

"Higher Education: The Fortune Survey." *Fortune* 40 (September 1949): supplement, pp. 1-16.

Hofstadter, Richard. *Academic Freedom in the Age of the College.* New York: Columbia University Press, 1961.

————. *Anti-Intellectualism in American Life.* New York: Vintage Books, 1962.

————. *The Paranoid Style in American Politics, and Other Essays*. New York: Knopf, 1965.

————. *The Progressive Historians: Turner, Beard, Parrington*. New York: Knopf, 1968.

Holmes, Thomas. "The Specter of Communism in Hawaii." Ph.D. dissertation, University of Hawaii, 1975.

Hunt, Alan Reeve. "Federal Supremacy and State Anti-Subversive Legislation." *Michigan Law Review* 53 (January 1955):407–38.

Hyman, Herbert H., and Sheatsley, Paul B. "Trends in Public Opinion on Civil Liberties." *Journal of Social Issues* 9, no. 3 (1953):6–16.

"The Independence of the Bar." *Lawyers Guild Review* 13 (Winter 1953):158–73.

International Encyclopedia of the Social Sciences, s.v. "Elites," by Suzanne Keller.

International Encyclopedia of the Social Sciences, s.v. "Social Movements: The Study of Social Movements," by Joseph R. Gusfield.

International Encyclopedia of the Social Sciences, s.v. "Social Movements: Types and Functions of Social Movements," by Rudolf Heberle.

Iverson, Robert W. *The Communists and the Schools*. New York: Harcourt Brace, 1959.

Johnson, Ronald. "The Communist Issue in Missouri, 1946–1956." Ph.D. dissertation, University of Missouri, 1973.

Karier, Clarence. *Shaping the American Educational State, 1900 to the Present*. New York: Free Press, 1975.

Keller, Suzanne. *Beyond the Ruling Class: Strategic Elites in Modern Society*. New York: Random House, 1963.

Key, V. O., Jr. *American State Politics: An Introduction*. New York: Knopf, 1965.

————. *Politics, Parties, and Pressure Groups*. New York: Thomas Y. Crowell, 1958.

————. *Public Opinion and American Democracy*. New York: A. A. Knopf, 1964.

Kirkendall, Richard S., ed. *The Truman Period as a Research Field: A Reappraisal, 1972*. Columbia: University of Missouri Press, 1974.

Ladd, Everett C., and Lipset, Seymour, M. *The Divided Academy: Professors and Politics*. New York: McGraw-Hill, 1975.

Laslett, John H. M., and Lipset, Seymour, eds. *Failure of a Dream? Essays in the History of American Socialism*. Garden City, N.Y.: Doubleday, 1974.

Latham, Earl. *The Communist Conspiracy in Washington: From the New Deal to McCarthy*. Cambridge: Harvard University Press, 1960.

Lazarsfeld, Paul, and Thielens, Wagner, Jr. *The Academic Mind: Social Scientists in a Time of Crisis*. Glencoe, Ill.: Free Press, 1958.

Lerner, Charles. "Students for America: McCarthy's Class of '54." *New Foundations* 7 (Spring 1954):13–18.

Levering, Ralph B. *American Opinion and the Russian Alliance, 1939–1945*. Chapel Hill: University of North Carolina Press, 1976.

Lipset, Seymour M., and Riseman, David. *Education and Politics at Harvard*. New York: McGraw-Hill, 1975.

Lipset, Seymour M. *Passion and Politics: Student Activism in America*. Boston: Little, Brown, and Co., 1971.

Lipset, Seymour M., and Raab, Earl. *The Politics of Unreason: Right-wing Extremism in America, 1790–1970*. New York: Harper and Row, 1970.

Lloyd, R. Grann. "Loyalty Oaths and Communist Influences in Negro Colleges and Universities." *School and Society* 75 (January 5, 1952):8–9.

Lubell, Samuel. *The Revolt of the Moderates*. New York: Harper and Brothers, 1956.

Lynd, Robert S., and Lynd, Helen M. *Middletown: A Study in Modern American Culture*. New York: Harcourt, Brace, and World, 1929.

McAuliffe, Mary S. *Crisis on the Left: Cold War Politics and American Liberals, 1947–1954*. Amherst: University of Massachusetts Press, 1978.

McCoy, Donald R., ed. *Conference of Scholars on the Truman Administration and Civil

Rights. Independence: The Harry S. Truman Institute for National and International Affairs, 1968.

McCoy, Donald, and Ruetten, Richard T. *Quest and Response: Minority Rights and the Truman Administration*. Lawrence: University Press of Kansas, 1973.

MacDougall, Curtis D. *Gideon's Army*. New York: Marzani and Munsell, 1965.

MacIver, Robert. *Academic Freedom in Our Time*. New York: Columbia University Press, 1955.

McLeod, Jack M. "A Thematic Analysis of the American Legion Magazine, 1919–1951." Master's thesis, University of Wisconsin, 1953.

McWilliams, Carey. *The Education of Carey McWilliams*. New York: Simon and Schuster, 1978.

Maddux, Thomas R. *Years of Estrangement: American Relations with the Soviet Union, 1934–1941*. Tallahassee: Florida State University, University Presses of Florida, 1980.

Markowitz, Norman. *The Rise and Fall of the People's Century: Henry A. Wallace and American Liberalism, 1941–1948*. New York: Free Press, 1973.

Matthews, J.B. "Communism and the Colleges." *American Mercury* 76 (May 1953):111–44.

Meier, August, and Rudwick, Elliott. *CORE: A Study in the Civil Rights Movement, 1942–1968*. New York: Oxford University Press, 1973.

Metzger, Walter. *Academic Freedom in the Age of the University*. New York: Columbia University Press, 1961.

Miller, Douglas T., and Nowak, Marion. *The Fifties: The Way We Really Were*. Garden City, N.Y.: Doubleday, 1977.

Minott, Rodney. *Peerless Patriots: Organized Veterans and the Spirit of Americanism*. Washington, D.C.: Public Affairs Press, 1962.

Mitchell, Morris, et al. "The Battle for Free Schools." *Nation*, October 27, 1951, pp. 344–47.

Mitford, Jessica. *A Fine Old Conflict*. New York: Knopf, 1977.

Mommer, Anthony W. "State Loyalty Programs and the Supreme Court." *Indiana Law Journal* 43 (Winter 1968):462–85.

Morris, Arval A. "Academic Freedom and Loyalty Oaths." *Law and Contemporary Problems* 28 (Summer 1963):487–514.

Morris, Robert C. "Era of Anxiety: An Historical Account of the Effects and Reactions to Right-Wing Forces Affecting Education during the Years 1949 to 1954." Ph.D. dissertation, Indiana State University, 1976.

Mowry, George. *The Urban Nation, 1920–1960*. New York: Hill and Wang, 1965.

Murphy, Paul L. *The Constitution in Crisis, 1918–1969*. New York: Harper and Row, 1972.

_____. *The Meaning of Freedom of Speech: First Amendment Freedoms from Wilson to FDR*. Westport, Conn.: Greenwood Publ. Co., 1972.

Murray, Robert K. *Red Scare: A Study in National Hysteria, 1919–1920*. New York: McGraw-Hill, 1955.

Nash, George H. *The Conservative Intellectual Movement in America Since 1945*. New York: Basic Books, 1976.

Nelson, Jack, and Roberts, Gene, Jr. *The Censors and the Schools*. Boston: Little, Brown, 1963.

Nisbet, Robert. *The Degradation of Academic Dogma: The University in America, 1945–1970*. New York: Basic Books, 1971.

Nye, Russel B. *Midwestern Progressive Politics, 1870–1958*. East Lansing: Michigan State University Press, 1959.

O'Brien, F. S. "The Communist-Dominated Unions in the U.S. since 1950." *Labor History* 9 (Spring 1968):184–209.

Parmet, Herbert S. *The Democrats: The Years After FDR*. New York: Macmillan, 1976.

Paterson, Thomas G. *On Every Front: The Making of the Cold War*. New York: W.W. Norton, 1979.

Patterson, James T. *The New Deal and the States: Federalism in Transition.* Princeton: Princeton University Press, 1969.

Patterson, Samuel C. "The Political Cultures of the American State." *Journal of Politics* 30 (February 1968):187–209.

Polenberg, Richard. *War and Society: The United States, 1941–1945.* Philadelphia: Lippincott, 1972.

Polsby, Nelson W. *Community Power and Political Theory: A Further Look at Problems of Evidence and Inference.* 2nd enlarged edition. New Haven: Yale University Press, 1980.

———. "Towards an Explanation of McCarthyism." *Political Studies* 8 (October 1960): 250–71.

Prendergast, William. "State Legislatures and Communism: The Current Scene." *American Political Science Review* 44 (September 1950):556–74.

Preston, William Jr. "Shadows of War and Fear." In *The Pulse of Freedom: American Liberties, 1920–1970s,* pp. 105–153. Edited by Alan Reitman. New York: Norton, 1975.

Prickett, James. "Communism and Factionalism in the United Auto Workers, 1939–1947." *Science and Society* 32 (Summer 1968):272–77.

———. "Some Aspects of the Communist Controversy in the CIO." *Science and Society* 33 (Summer 1969):299–321.

Ravitch, Diane. "The Revisionists Revised: Studies in the Historiography of American Education." *Proceedings of the National Academy of Education* 4, part 1 (1977).

Record, Wilson. *Race and Radicalism: The NAACP and the Communist Party in Conflict.* Ithaca: Cornell University Press, 1964.

Reeves, Thomas C. *Freedom and the Foundation: The Fund for the Republic in the Era of McCarthyism.* New York: Knopf, 1969.

———. *The Life and Times of Joe McCarthy.* New York: Stein and Day, 1982.

———. "McCarthyism: Interpretations since Hofstadter." *Wisconsin Magazine of History* 60 (Autumn 1976):42–54.

Reichley, James. *States in Crisis: Politics in Ten American States, 1950–1962.* Chapel Hill: University of North Carolina Press, 1964.

Reutter, E. Edmund, Jr. *The School Administrator and Subversive Activities: A Study of the Administration of Restraints on Alleged Subversive Activities of Public School Personnel.* New York: Bureau of Publication, Teachers College, 1951.

Riesman, David. "The Found Generation." *American Scholar* 25 (Autumn 1956):421–36.

———. "Orbits of Tolerance, Interviewers, and Elites." *Public Opinion Quarterly* 20 (Spring 1955):49–73.

Robinson, James A. *Anti-Sedition Legislation and Loyalty Investigations in Oklahoma.* Norman: Bureau of Government Research, University of Oklahoma, 1956.

Roche, John P. *The Quest for the Dream: The Development of Civil Rights and Human Relations in Modern America.* New York: Macmillan, 1963.

Rogin, Michael Paul. *The Intellectuals and McCarthy: The Radical Specter.* Cambridge: Massachusetts Institute of Technology Press, 1967.

Rogow, Arnold A. "The Loyalty Issue in Iowa, 1951." *American Political Science Review* 55 (December 1961):861–69.

Root, E. Merrill. *Brainwashing in the High Schools* New York: Devin-Adair, 1958.

———. *Collectivism on the Campus.* New York: Devin-Adair, 1955.

Rovere, Richard H. *Senator Joe McCarthy.* Cleveland: World Publ. Co., 1959.

Roy, Ralph S. *Communism and the Churches.* New York: Harcourt, Brace, and Co., 1960.

Sanders, Jane. *Cold War on the Campus: Academic Freedom at the University of Washington, 1946–1964.* Seattle: University of Washington Press, 1979.

Schriffrin, Andre. "The Student Movement in the 1950s: A Reminiscence." *Radical America* 2 (May-June 1968):26–40.

Schlesinger, Arthur M., Jr. Review of *The Great Fear*, by David Caute. *New York Times Book Review*, 19 March 1978, pp. 1, 44–45.

Schmidt, Karl M. *Henry Wallace: Quixotic Crusade*. Syracuse: Syracuse University Press, 1960.

Shannon, David A. *The Decline of American Communism: A History of the CPUSA since 1945*. New York: Harcourt, Brace, and Co., 1959.

Sharkansky, Ira. *Regionalism in American Politics*. Indianapolis: Bobbs-Merrill Co., 1970.

Shils, Edward. *The Torment of Secrecy: The Background and Consequences of American Security Policies*. Glencoe, Ill.: Free Press, 1956.

Sitkoff, Harvard. "Years of the Locust: Interpretations of Truman's Presidency since 1965." In *The Truman Period as a Research Field: A Reappraisal, 1972*, pp. 75–112. Edited by Richard Kirkendall. Columbia: University of Missouri Press, 1974.

Sklar, Robert. *Movie-Made America: A Cultural History of American Movies*. New York: Random House, 1975.

Small, Melvin. "How We Learned to Love the Russians: American Media and the Soviet Union during World War II." *The Historian* 36 (1974):455–78.

Smith, Geoffrey S. *To Save a Nation: American Countersubversives, the New Deal, and the Coming of World War II*. New York: Basic Books, 1973.

———."'Harry, We Hardly Know You': Revisionism, Politics and Diplomacy, 1945–1954." *American Political Science Review* 70 (June 1976):560–82.

Spinrad, William. *Civil Liberties*. Chicago: Quadrangle Books, 1970.

Starobin, Joseph R. *American Communism in Crisis, 1943–1957*. Cambridge: Harvard University Press, 1972.

Stouffer, Samuel. *Communism, Conformity, and Civil Liberties: A Cross-Section of the Nation Speaks Its Mind*. Garden City, N.Y.: Doubleday 1955.

Theoharis, Athan. "The Escalation of the Loyalty Program." In *Politics and Policies of the Truman Administration*, pp. 242–268. Edited by Barton J. Bernstein. Chicago: Quadrangle Books, 1972.

———. "The Rhetoric of Politics: Foreign Policy, Internal Security and Domestic Politics in the Truman Era, 1945–1950." In *Politics and Policies of the Truman Administration*, pp. 196–241. Edited by Barton J. Bernstein, Chicago: Quadrangle Books, 1972.

———. *Seeds of Repression: Harry S. Truman and the Origins of McCarthyism*. Chicago: Quadrangle Books, 1971.

———. *Yalta Myths*. Columbia: University of Missouri Press, 1970.

Thompson, Francis H. *The Frustration of Politics: Truman, Congress, and the Loyalty Issue, 1945–1953*. Rutherford: Fairleigh Dickinson Press, 1979.

Thompson, Mindy. *The National Negro Labor Council*. New York: American Institute for Marxist Studies, 1978.

Touraine, Alain. *The Academic System in American Society*. New York: McGraw-Hill, 1974.

Tyack, David B. *The One Best System: A History of American Urban Education*. Cambridge: Harvard University Press, 1974.

Unger, Irwin. *The Movement: A History of the American New Left, 1959–1972*. New York: Dodd, Mead, and Co., 1974.

Urban, Wayne J. "Some Historiographical Problems in Revisionist Education History." *American Education Research Journal* 12 (Summer 1975):337–50.

"U.S. Campus Kids of 1953: Unkiddable and Unbeatable." *Newsweek*, November 2, 1953, pp. 52–55.

Verba, Sidney. "Comparative Political Culture." In *Political Culture and Political Development*, pp. 512–60. Edited by Lucian W. Pye and Sidney Verba. Princeton: Princeton University Press, 1965.

Violas, Paul C. "Academic Freedom and the Public School Teacher, 1930–1960." In *Roots of Crisis: American Education in the Twentieth Century*, pp. 163–76. Edited by Clarence J.

Karier, et al. Chicago: Rand McNally College Publ., 1973.

Warren, Donald R. "A Past for the Present." In *History, Education, and Public Policy*, pp. 1–20. Edited by Donald R. Warren. Berkeley: McCutchan Publ. Corp., 1978.

Whyte, William. "The Class of '49." *Fortune*, June 1949, pp. 84–87.

Wilner, Daniel, and Fearing, Franklin. "The Structure of Opinion: A 'Loyalty Oath' Poll." *Public Opinion Quarterly* 14 (Winter 1950–51):729–43.

Wittner, Lawrence S. *Rebels Against the War: The American Peace Movement, 1941–1960*. New York: Columbia University Press, 1969.

Wolfskill, George. *The Revolt of the Conservatives: A History of the American Liberty League, 1934–1940*. Boston: Houghton Mifflin, 1962.

Yarnell, Allen. *Democrats and Progressives: The 1948 Presidential Election as a Test of Postwar Liberalism*. Berkeley: University of California Press, 1974.

Young, Roland. *American Law and Politics: The Creation of Public Order*. New York: Harper and Row, 1967.

Index